Global Queer Politics

Series editors
Jordi Diez
University of Guelph
Guelph, Canada

Sonia Corrêa
Brazilian Interdisciplinary Association
for AIDS (ABIA)
Rio de Janeiro, Rio de Janeiro, Brazil

David Paternotte
Univerté Libre de Bruxelles Brussels
Brussels, Belgium

Matthew Waites
University of Glasgow
Glasgow, United Kingdom

D1545856

The Global Queer Politics book series is a new outlet for research on political and social processes that contest dominant heteronormative orders in both legal and policy frames and cultural formations. It presents studies encompassing all aspects of queer politics, understood in the expansive terms of much activism as addressing the politics of sexual orientation, gender identity and expression and intersex status, as well as non-heteronormative sexualities and genders more widely – including emerging identities such as asexual, pansexual, or non-binary. As struggles over violence, human rights and inequalities have become more prominent in world politics, this series provides a forum to challenge retrenchments of inequalities, and new forms of contestation, criminalization and persecution, situated in wider geopolitics. Particularly welcome are works attentive to multiple inequalities, such as related to class and caste, race and ethnicity, nationalism, religion, disability and age, imperialism and colonialism. Global, regional, transnational, comparative and national studies are welcome, but that speak to international processes.

The Global Queer Politics book series welcomes:

All academic disciplines and approaches that can contribute to the study of politics, including, but not limited to, international relations, political theory, sociology, socio-legal studies, contemporary history, social policy, development, public policy, cultural studies, media studies and gender and sexuality studies.

Methodologies which may include comparative works and case studies with relevant transnational dimensions, and analyses of global processes.

Research from authors who have activist, governmental and international experience, as well as work that can contribute to the global debate over LGBTIQ rights with perspectives from the Global South.

More information about this series at
http://www.springer.com/series/15246

Lukasz Szulc

Transnational Homosexuals in Communist Poland

Cross-Border Flows in Gay and Lesbian Magazines

Lukasz Szulc
London School of Economics and Political Science
United Kingdom

Global Queer Politics
ISBN 978-3-319-86505-8   ISBN 978-3-319-58901-5   (eBook)
DOI 10.1007/978-3-319-58901-5

Cover illustration: helovi / iStock / Getty Images Plus

Printed on acid-free paper

This Palgrave Macmillan imprint is published by Springer Nature
The registered company is Springer International Publishing AG
The registered company address is: Gewerbestrasse 11, 6330 Cham, Switzerland

PREFACE

It is a pleasure to introduce this book, *Transnational Homosexuals in Communist Poland: Cross-Border Flows in Gay and Lesbian Magazines*, authored by Lukasz Szulc. This is the first volume in the new *Global Queer Politics* series, co-edited by Jordi Díez, Sonia Corrêa, David Paternotte and Matthew Waites, and hence the editors are particularly proud to present it. We believe this work is valuable in fulfilling a central objective of the series, to contribute new perspectives to the global debate over lesbian, gay, bisexual, trans, intersex and queer (LGBTIQ) rights—particularly by de-centring Western understandings.

Szulc's Introduction and opening chapters provide a very helpful way in to the *Global Queer Politics* series, offering a strong and sharply focused review of contemporary international literature on globalization in relation to LGBT identities and politics. This highlights how movements in the United States and Western Europe have become the measure against which others are judged. The book demonstrates the limits of Western knowledge of Central and Eastern Europe, before proceeding to challenge problematic discourses. In Central and Eastern Europe generally Szulc shows a wide diversity among states with respect to legal and social circumstances, demonstrating the idea of a homogenous and essentialist attitude to homosexuality in the Eastern Bloc to be a myth. Proceeding to take Poland as a specific case study to explore this in the major part of the book, he then emphasizes the early decriminalization of same-sex sexual behaviour in 1932 as a key historical context.

The primary focus is on social changes during the 1980s—ahead of the fall of the Berlin Wall in 1989—including the emergence of gay and lesbian magazines as sites of homosexual self-identification and self-organization.

The book illustrates how careful empirical research can form the basis of a strong argument for re-orienting analytical perspectives. In this case Szulc provides an original analysis focused particularly on two Polish magazines, *Biuletyn/Etap* and *Filo,* which were produced in the 1980s—highlighting the formative role of the (then) International Lesbian and Gay Association (ILGA) in the emergence of the former. It is through combining careful scrutiny of the magazines' contents with interviews of those who authored these periodicals, and with careful scrutiny of their transnational conditions of production (as critical media studies endorse) that the author generates insights. What emerges from the methodological deployment of transnationalism is a distinctive sense that these new discursive sites were transnational from the outset, with travelling cultural signifiers from *Cabaret* to Tom of Finland and Stonewall described as constituting a 'queer cosmopolitanism'. Yet, the magazines simultaneously offered glimpses of previously unrepresented spaces and worlds, especially the Polish *pikiety*—public spaces from nude beaches to toilets used for cruising and having sex. Moreover, the emerging political strategies only drew selectively on Western discourses, in a manner considerably shaped by Polish contextual circumstances such as Operation Hyacinth, involving mass arrests of homosexuals in the mid-1980s. Such analysis has the potential to assist contemporary movements worldwide to critically grasp dynamics involved when transnational activist elites forge a queer cosmopolitan imaginary for movement identification which is beyond realization for most participants.

Szulc concludes by proposing a challenge to those who seek to emphasize polarization in contemporary geopolitics, whereby support for LGBT human rights or political homophobia are mobilized in competing nationalisms—as recently analysed by Dennis Altman and Jonathan Symons in their book *Queer Wars* (2016). Szulc proposes instead a greater attention to transnational flows of various kinds across national and regional boundaries, and greater attention to contexts which do not fit into the dichotomies of prevailing political discourses. Hence, if a national context is analysed together with cross-border flows, as here, then such a case study can yield much wider insights into social and cultural processes, inequalities and power relations.

Guelph, Canada	Jordi Díez
Rio de Janeiro, Brazil	Sonia Corrêa
Brussels, Belgium	David Paternotte
Glasgow, UK	Matthew Waites

ACKNOWLEDGEMENTS

This book started as a side project. The first time I heard about gay and lesbian magazines published in communist Poland was right before I defended my doctoral dissertation in February 2015, when I looked through the 'Before '89' issue of *DIK Fagazine*, released by artist Karol Radziszewski in 2011. It was quite a revelation to me to learn that homosexuals on that side of the Iron Curtain created their own cultural products and organized themselves already before 1989. Another revelation came when I managed to locate nearly all issues of the two most successful magazines, *Biuletyn/Etap* and *Filo*, and realized that they both abounded in information about Western gay, and to a lesser extent lesbian, cultures and movements. Thanks to the postdoctoral fellowship of the Research Foundation Flanders and with the support of my wonderful mentors, Alexander Dhoest and Bart Eeckhout, I was able to fully dedicate my work in the Department of Communication Studies at the University of Antwerp to delve into the lives of transnational homosexuals in communist Poland. What was supposed to be just a side project—resulting in one, maybe two, academic articles—morphed into a two-year intense research, culminating in this very book. I finished the book after joining the Department of Media and Communications at the London School of Economics and Political Science at the beginning of 2017.

While I take sole responsibility for the content of this book, I would have never finished it without the help of many informers, colleagues and friends. My deepest gratitude goes to Polish activists who started organizing themselves in the 1980s and were kind enough to share with me their time, knowledge and memories, particularly Ryszard Kisiel, Paulina

Pilch and Andrzej Selerowicz as well as Waldemar Zboralski and Ryszard Ziobro. I also want to thank many people for helping me to access primary or secondary sources which proved to be invaluable for this project, including Phillip Ayoub, Catherine Baker, Briand Bedford-Eichler, Agnès Chetaille, Agata Fiedotow, Johann Kirchknopf, Jerzy Krzyszpień, Mariusz Kurc, Paweł Leszkowicz, Rasa Navickaitė, James Omolo, Monika Płatek, Andrew DJ Shield, Krzysztof Tomasik, Wojciech Szot, Judit Takács, Tim Veith, Lien Verpoest, Błażej Warkocki and Agnieszka Weseli. Some other materials I could access only thanks to the courtesy of a number of institutions: Lambda Warszawa, Schwules Museum in Berlin, International Gay/Lesbian Information Centre and Archive (IHLIA) in Amsterdam, Institute of National Remembrance (IPN) in Warsaw, Polish Public Opinion Research Centre (CBOS), *Polityka* weekly and Homikoteka online project (http://homiki.pl/index.php/homikoteka/), for which I am also very grateful. In addition, my thanks go to my friends who hosted me during my research trips: Anna Dobrowolska in Warsaw, Rafał Morusiewicz in Vienna and Tim Savenije in Amsterdam, and also to my mum, Halina Szulc, who was regularly sending to my office in Antwerp all the materials I had ordered to my home address in Poland.

Before being published, each chapter of this book had been read and reviewed by at least one of my big-hearted colleagues. I want to thank Jordi Díez, Bart Eeckhout, AJ Haider, Magdalena Mikulak, Megan Milota, David Paternotte, Anna Safuta, Nella van den Brandt and anonymous reviewers for helping me not only to improve my language and style but also to advance my argument. I was also able to refine the content of this book thanks to the valuable feedback I received when presenting the first drafts of some chapters at a number of academic conferences, including 'Sex and Sexuality in East-Central Europe, Past and Present' in Budapest in October 2015, 'Communist Homosexuality 1945–1989' in Paris in February 2017, the International Communication Association (ICA) conference (LGBTQ Interest Group) in Fukuoka in June 2016 and the conference of the European Communication Research and Education Association (ECREA) in Prague in November 2016. Some bits and pieces of this project—along with my early thoughts on the topic of this book— have been published on the popular-science blog *Notches: (Re)marks on the History of Sexuality*, benefiting from the expertise of its editors, in particular Justin Bengry and Katya Motyl. Additionally, my thanks go to the editors at the New York's office of Palgrave Macmillan, Chris Robinson and John Stegner, as well as the series editors, Jordi Díez, Sonia Corrêa,

David Paternotte and Matthew Waites, for their patience, advice and trust in this project. I am also indebted to the Palgrave's design team for creating such a beautiful cover and to Cathy Hannabach from 'Ideas on Fire' for compiling an excellent index for this book.

Finally, I want to express my gratitude to my closest friends, particularly Szymon Brzóska, Magdalena Mikulak and Marion Wasserbauer, who for the last two years have always been there for me when I needed a consolation, motivation, love, hug or drink. Big thank you!

CONTENTS

LIST OF ABBREVIATIONS

ACT UP   AIDS Coalition to Unleash Power
AIDS   Acquired Immune Deficiency Syndrome
CBOS   Centrum Badania Opinii Społecznej (Public Opinion Research
            Centre)
CEE   Central and Eastern Europe
COC   Cultuur- en Ontspanningscentrum (Cultural and Recreational
            Centre)
CoE   Council of Europe
EEIP   Eastern Europe Information Pool
EU   European Union
FHAR   Front Homosexuel d'Action Révolutionnaire (Homosexual Front
            for Revolutionary Action)
GAA   Gay Activist Alliance
GLF   Gay Liberation Front
GMHC   Gay Men's Health Crisis
GUKPPiW   Główny Urząd Kontroli Prasy, Publikacji i Widowisk (Main Office
            for the Control of the Press, Publications and Public
            Performances)
GUS   Główny Urząd Statystyczny (Central Statistical Office of Poland)
HIB   Homosexuelle Interessengemeinschaft Berlin (Homosexual
            Interest Group Berlin)
HIV   Human Immunodeficiency Virus
HOSI   Homosexuelle Initiative Wien (Homosexual Initiative Vienna)
ICSE   International Committee for Sexual Equality
IGA/ILGA   International Gay Association (now International Lesbian, Gay,
            Bisexual, Trans and Intersex Association)
IHLIA   International Gay/Lesbian Information Centre and Archive

ILIS	International Lesbian Information Service
IPN	Instytut Pamięci Narodowej (Institute of National Remembrance)
KOR	Komitet Obrony Robotników (Workers' Defence Committee)
KPH	Kampania Przeciw Homofobii (Campaign Against Homophobia)
LGBT	Lesbian, Gay, Bisexual and Transgender
MOPS	Męskie Ochotnicze Pogotowie Seksualne (Male Volunteer Sexual Service)
PEPFAR	President's Emergency Plan for AIDS Relief
PRL	Polska Republika Ludowa (People's Republic of Poland)
PZPR	Polska Zjednoczona Partia Robotnicza (Polish United Workers' Party)
ROPCiO	Ruch Obrony Praw Człowieka i Obywatela (Movement for Defense of Human and Civic Rights)
ŠKUC	Študentski Kulturno-Umetniški Center (Student Cultural Centre)
THT	Terrence Higgins Trust
UN	United Nations
UNAIDS	Joint United Nations Programme on HIV/AIDS
WhK	Wissenschaftlich-humanitäres Komitee (Scientific Humanitarian Committee)
WLSR	World League for Sexual Reform
WRH	Warszawski Ruch Homoseksualny (Warsaw Homosexual Movement)
WRON	Wojskowa Rada Ocalenia Narodowego (Military Council of National Salvation)

List of Figures

LIST OF TABLES

CHAPTER 1

Introduction: A Sexual Cold War and Its Myths

We live in an age of 'queer wars', Dennis Altman and Jonathan Symons (2016) argue in their recent book entitled, indeed, *Queer Wars*. This is an age of cultural battles around gender and sexuality in general, and LGBT rights in particular (where LGBT stands for lesbian, gay, bisexual and transgender people). Altman and Symons (2016, p. 7) elaborate their thesis by explaining that contemporary international debates tend to focus more often on LGBT issues, which 'come to stand for broader debates about culture, tradition and human rights'. They do not specify when exactly those queer wars broke out, though they do connect the outbreak to the growing visibility of LGBTs and the considerable progress in LGBT rights in the West, beginning in the late 1960s. Those advancements, the authors go on, have provoked a conservative backlash against LGBTs, both within and against Western countries, and have resulted in new forms of polarization in world politics between 'gay-friendly' and 'homophobic' or, alternatively, 'decadent' and 'decent' countries, cultures, regions or even entire 'civilizations' (Inglehart and Norris 2003). At the international level, the dividing line seems to be rather clear in the discourse and runs between 'the West' and 'the Rest', where the former category usually implies, in this context, North America, Western Europe, Australia and Israel, and the latter, in Altman and Symons's words (2016, p. 3), 'countries struggling with colonial legacies or other forms of social disorder'.

© The Author(s) 2018   1
L. Szulc, *Transnational Homosexuals in Communist Poland*,
Global Queer Politics, DOI 10.1007/978-3-319-58901-5_1

Other authors (e.g. Engeli et al. 2012; Picq and Thiel 2015; Weber 2016) and mainstream media (e.g. *Economist* 2014; *Washington Post* 2015) too point to the increasing importance of gender and sexuality, including LGBT-related issues, in world politics in recent decades. Ronald Inglehart and Pippa Norris (2003, p. 63) refer to the controversial thesis of Samuel Huntington (1993) about a clash of civilizations to argue that the 'true' clash of civilizations 'is not about democracy but sex'. Drawing on two waves of World Value Survey (1995–1996 and 2000–2002), the authors assert that it is attitudes towards such topics as abortion, divorce and homosexuality that truly divide what they lump together as 'Muslim' and 'non-Muslim' societies. Jasbir Puar (2007, 2013) takes a more critical look at world politics and, instead of searching for a 'true' dividing line between civilizations, argues that the *rhetoric* of a sexual clash of civilizations is used to render the West essentially gay-friendly and the Rest (especially the Middle East, Arabs and Islam) essentially homophobic. She has coined the term 'homonationalism' to mark the practice of incorporating (some) LGBT rights into national identities of Western countries in order to justify, for example, the US invasions of Afghanistan or Iraq (Puar 2007), or the Israeli occupation of Palestine (Kuntsman 2008; Puar 2011), in terms of saving or protecting LGBTs. Other authors describe similar tendencies in Western European countries, especially in the Netherlands (Bracke 2012; El-Tayeb 2012; Mepschen and Duyvendak 2012) and also in France (Fassin 2010), Germany (Haritaworn and Petzen 2011) and the United Kingdom (Raboin 2013), where LGBT rights have been used primarily against immigrants, once again mostly Arabs and Muslims.

Central and Eastern Europe (CEE) for some time stayed outside of the discourse of queer wars, in which the Rest has normally referred to the Middle East and North Africa as well as other regions of the world formerly colonized by the West. CEE has tended to be perceived as not that radically different from the West, placed somewhere in between the two 'extremes' of the 'First' and 'Third' Worlds (Chari and Verdery 2009), of the 'West' and the 'Orient' (Wolff 1994); united with the West through the common denominator of whiteness and Christianity (El-Tayeb 2011, p. xx). Or, as Jill Owczarzak (2009, p. 6) puts it, CEE as 'the West's intermediary "Other," neither fully civilized nor fully savage'. This is not to say that CEE and the West have been considered as equal or homologous. The key difference between the two, however, has been understood in temporal rather than spatial (or cultural) terms: haunted by its communist past—where communism is imagined as a backward force, putting on hold economic, political and social advancements—CEE is frequently considered as simply lagging behind the West (Todorova 2005). After the fall of communism in Europe, the narrative goes on, CEE could finally start catching up with the West, transitioning from communism to capitalism and democracy (Kubik 2013) as well as to the Western ideals of norms, values and rights (Kulpa 2014; Kulpa and Mizielińska 2011), under the careful guidance of Western institutions, especially the European Union (EU) (Slootmaeckers et al. 2016). Accordingly, CEE is also conceived as lagging behind the West in terms of LGBT-related issues, 'probably with a delay of some two or three decades', as Aleksandar Štulhofer and Theo Sandfort (2005, p. 16) claim, and is expected to gradually adopt LGBT-related legal provisions, the demands growing in importance in the EU accession process since the 1990s (Slootmaeckers and Touquet 2016).

CEE, however, has not straightforwardly followed the trajectory of 'Westernization', or 'Europeanization', and, consequently, it too has recently joined the discourse of queer wars. The strongest divergence from the trajectory can be observed of course in the politics of Russia. After the fall of the Soviet Union in 1991, the country aspired to move towards the West and began to change its conservative stance towards homosexuality accordingly: in 1993, Russia decriminalized male same-sex acts in order to join the Council of Europe (CoE), and in 1999, it depathologized homosexuality by adopting the World Health Organization's classification of diseases, which recognizes homosexuality and bisexuality as normal variations in sexual orientation (Kon 2009, p. 45). This politics shifted again at the beginning of the millennium, when Vladimir Putin rose to power and revived the idea of Russian self-sufficiency as well as its political supremacy in the region and moral superiority over the West. Already in the spring of 2002, a draft law recriminalizing same-sex acts was brought before the State Duma, even though it was quickly turned down (Kon 2009, p. 46). Andrey Makarychev and Sergei Medvedev (2015) demonstrate that the last couple of years have brought even more intensified politics of 'sexual sovereignty' in Russia; they speak of a 'biopolitical turn', starting with Putin's third term as president and marked by the introduction of such infamous laws as those preventing the organization of gay parades in Moscow for the next 100 years (adopted in 2012) and forbidding so-called 'homosexual propaganda' (adopted in 2013) (see also Romanets 2017, Stella 2013). Not surprisingly, therefore, Altman and Symons (2016) start their book on *Queer Wars* by referring to the Russian case, more specifically to the negative reactions of Russian politicians to the bearded drag queen

Conchita Wurst winning the 2014 Eurovision Song Contest (p. 1), and argue that after the re-election of Putin in Russia and Barack Obama in the United States, 'homosexuality emerged as a possible theme of a cultural Cold War' (p. 11).

Other CEE countries, although usually still devoted to the Western model of organizing their economies and politics, have also begun to question more overtly the Western ethics, typified (at least in very recent history) by a more liberal, if selective, stance on gender- and sexuality-related issues, including LGBT rights. Lien Verpoest (forthcoming) discusses a new wave of opposition against LGBT rights in the countries of the EU's Eastern Partnership, particularly Ukraine, which signed the Association Agreement with the EU in 2014, after Euromaidan anti-government protests starting at the end of 2013. Despite its *Vybor za Evropu* (European Choice), Ukraine seems to draw the line of its compliance with the EU at LGBT rights and use the rights instrumentally for what Verpoest names 'geopolitical othering'. Similar tendencies can be observed in the CEE countries which have already been members of the EU for more than ten years. As the authors of a collection on *Anti-Gender Campaigns in Europe* (Kuhar and Paternotte 2017) observe, the very recent years have seen new right-wing mobilizations in CEE, as well as in some Western European countries, against the so-called gender ideology, usually encompassing a very wide range of topics such as abortion, sex education, reproductive technologies, marriage equality and transgender rights (see also Campoy 2016; Graff and Korolczuk 2017a; Korolczuk 2014).

In this context, some prominent Western media have begun to ponder: Quo Vadis, CEE? *The Washington Post* appears to be among the optimists, reporting, for example, that 'Gay rights in eastern Europe just took a big step forward' (2014) with reference to the coming out of the Latvian Foreign Minister and that 'Eastern Europe, long a stronghold of virulent homophobia, is reexamining attitudes toward gays and lesbians' (2015). *The Huffington Post*, meanwhile, seems to be more sceptical, asking in a headline, 'Eastern Europe's Gay Rights Battle: Is LGBT Equality Out of Reach?' (2013). Such narratives are surely grounded in certain facts and do reflect certain real changes in CEE with respect to LGBT rights, which I described in previous paragraphs. At the same time, however, they tend to blend facts with fictions and thus, individually and collectively, perpetuate recurrent myths of a homogenized CEE as historically and essentially homophobic ('long a stronghold of virulent homophobia', 'Is LGBT Equality Out of Reach?'), which in turn needs to be educated by the allegedly more progressive West (Kulpa 2014) so it can finally catch up with it (in the best-case scenario) in terms of norms, values and rights, especially those related to gender and sexuality (Mizielińska and Kulpa 2011). The general aim of this book is to challenge these recurrent myths, which I will now discuss in more detail, arguing that the key factor enabling and sustaining them is the dehistoricization of homosexuality in CEE.

1.1   MYTHS AND NO HISTORY

The three most persistent myths about CEE .with respect to LGBT issues are related to (1) the homogeneity and (2) the essence of the region, as well as (3) the teleological narrative of the CEE's 'transition' after 1989 from communism to Western ideals of capitalism, democracy and ethics. They are all based on yet another myth of (4) the near total isolation of CEE during the Cold War, and stem from the dehistoricization of homosexuality in the region.

Regarding the myth of homogeneity, both CEE and the West are all too frequently created as relatively uniform geopolitical entities adopting relatively uniform approaches to gender- and sexuality-related issues. An important effect of this myth is the very production as well as maintenance of a clear-cut *difference* between CEE and the West: CEE is understood as distinctly different from the West (Bakić-Hayden 1995; Kuus 2006). To create and sustain the idea of a homogenous CEE and an equally homogenous West, differences *within* the two geopolitical entities are downplayed, if not simply ignored, and differences *between* them exaggerated. This way, it is possible to make grandiose statements about 'the cross-continental divide' between Eastern and Western Europe over homosexuality (Pew Research Center 2013) or, indeed, about a 'cultural Cold War' (Altman and Symons 2016). Yet, CEE and the West are not only homogenized but also habitually essentialized; that is, as relatively uniform geopolitical entities, each of them is thought to possess a unique essence regarding LGBT issues. From the current Western perspective, the West is imagined as essentially progressive, that is, post-racial, post-feminist and post-gay, and CEE as essentially backward, that is, racist, sexist and homophobic, which is evident, for example, in discourses of the so-called Soviet mindset or Balkan mentality (Stella 2015, p. 7; see also Renkin 2016). Rasa Navickaitė (2014, 2016) shows how the two myths of homogeneity and essence are also reproduced in some recent academic publications on gender and sexuality in post-communist Europe, where ideas of the progressive West and the backward CEE are either maintained (CEE as backward) or reversed (CEE as queer) but not challenged: at the very core, these publications assume 'the essential and unchanging distinction between "East" and "West"' (Bakić-Hayden 1995, p. 950). The difference is also reproduced in the recent campaigns against a 'gender ideology' in CEE, although, of course, in the inverted logic in which the West is imagined as decadent and CEE as decent and morally superior to the West (Kuhar and Paternotte 2017).

Unlike the first two myths of homogeneity and essence, which are spatial (or cultural) in scope, the third myth of teleology is of a temporal nature. It assumes that after the fall of communism in Europe in 1989, CEE began its process of transition so it could catch up with the West not only economically and politically but also ethically, adopting more liberal stances towards gender- and sexuality-related issues. The myth has also been internalized by CEE, for example in the discourse of a 'return to Europe' (Sztompka 1993), as a part of what Anikó Imre (2007) calls 'voluntary colonisation'. Within this myth, the time before 1989 is perceived as wasted, a kind of no-time of no economic, political and social advancements, including the absence of any adoption of LGBT rights and any development of LGBT activism. LGBT activism in CEE, as we may learn from the recent *Wiley Blackwell Encyclopedia of Gender and Sexuality Studies,* 'began in earnest with the collapse of state-socialist regime beginning in 1989' (Pearce and Cooper 2016). Joanna Mizielińska and Robert Kulpa (2011) provide a potent critique of the teleological narrative, which they name a 'Western progress narrative', arguing that it fixes CEE as a region of a never-ending transition, perpetually catching up with the West, constantly one step behind the ever-developing developed world. Additionally, they note that the evolution of LGBT activism in CEE after 1989 has not followed what they call the 'Western time of sequence', that is, the trajectory from homophile movement to gay liberation to queer activism, but its own 'Eastern time of coincidence', characterized by the adoption of different models of activism at different times or, indeed, of 'everything at once' (Mizielińska and Kulpa 2011, p. 15). Navickaitė (2016, p. 128) supplements this critique by pointing out that such a teleological narrative denies CEE the possibility of political innovation and condemns the respective countries to a state of perpetual belatedness: 'everything that will ever happen in postsocialist societies is going to be just an imitation of what has already happened in the West.'

The three myths just described are primarily rooted in yet another myth of the CEE's near total isolation during the Cold War, even though they can be traced as far back as the Enlightenment (Wolff 1994). It was during the Cold War when two new distinct entities, the Eastern and Western Blocs, were brought to life and separated from each other by such powerful metaphors as the 'Iron Curtain' and the 'Berlin Wall' (Underhill 1976). It is true that the separation was not only symbolic but also material. The travelling of people and cultural products, and thus the exchange of ideas, between the two blocs was indeed restrained during the Cold War. It was, however, by no means impossible. Still, the idea of the near total isolation of the Eastern Bloc, 'of being locked behind "the Iron Curtain"', as Judit Takács and Roman Kuhar (2007, p. 11) put it in the introduction to their collection *Beyond the Pink Curtain*, continues to haunt discussions on gender and sexuality in CEE. It is the idea of the near total isolation of the Eastern Bloc that enables, and reinforces, the myth of a homogenous CEE, essentially different from the West, at least in terms of gender- and sexuality-related issues. And it is the idea of the near total isolation of the Eastern Bloc, combined with the notion of communist stagnation (communist no-time), that perpetuates the teleological narrative of CEE's transition from no LGBT rights and activism to a Western ethics of gender and sexuality. The year 1989, which witnessed the collapse of the Iron Curtain and the fall of the Berlin Wall, then marks the end of the isolation and, thus, is established as the beginning of time for CEE: the beginning of the process of catching up with the West as well as the beginning of the introduction of LGBT rights and the emergence of LGBT activism.

As already mentioned, these myths are not entirely untrue. Indeed, their power lies precisely in blending facts with fictions, in simplifying, obscuring and distorting history. Yet, even though the myths rest on historical facts and events, such as the formation of Eastern and Western Blocs during the Cold War and the end of communism in Europe in 1989, they are best characterized by historical amnesia. Only by dehistoricizing homosexuality in CEE is it possible to view the region as homogenous, essentially homophobic and in need of transition after 1989. When we take a closer look at the actual history of homosexuality in particular cultural environments within the Eastern Bloc, which is the ambition of this book, a strikingly different image emerges. To begin with, state laws and practices regarding homosexuality, the coverage of homosexuality in mainstream media as well as the development of homosexual activism all differed radically across the Eastern Bloc. With regard to the former, for example, while the Soviet Union criminalized male same-sex acts in 1933–1934 and continued to do so until 1993 (Baer 2011; Healey 1993, 2002), Poland decriminalized same-sex acts as early as 1932 and has not recriminalized them ever since (Płatek 2009). Moreover, Poland decriminalized same-sex acts before many countries of the allegedly more progressive West did, including Denmark (1933), Sweden (1944), England (1967), Canada (1969), West Germany (1969), Austria (1971), Finland (1971), Norway (1972) and the United States (fully only in 2003) (Hildebrandt 2014). It seems relevant to ask: Who was lagging behind whom, at least as far as the legal status of homosexuality is concerned?

The dehistoricization of homosexuality in CEE also surfaces in some more critical works on the topic. In one of the previous paragraphs, I mentioned an important critique of the 'Western progress narrative' offered by Mizielińska and Kulpa (2011) in *De-Centring Western Sexualities*. While the authors set out to challenge the teleological narrative of the step-by-step transition of CEE after 1989, they nevertheless reproduce the myths of homogeneity, essence and near total isolation of the region during the Cold War. In her review of the book, Navickaitė (2014, p. 173) notes that Mizielińska and Kulpa's concepts of a 'Western time of sequence' and an 'Eastern time of coincidence', as well as what they call a 'temporal disjunction' between the two, mark 'the schism between the West and the East, as well as the homogeneity of these two imagined entities both before and after 1989'. Besides, she shows that the authors conceive the region as 'the victim of Western orientalisation' and, therefore, try to redeem it by presenting CEE as essentially queer, that is, unpredictable and fluid, coincidently mixing different models of LGBT activism, in contrast to the 'straight', that is, sequential development of LGBT activism in the West (Navickaitė 2014, p. 176). Finally, Navickaitė (2014, p. 173) points out that Mizielińska and Kulpa (2011) separate the Eastern Bloc from its Western counterpart, as if the two blocs did not influence each other and there was no communication between homosexuals on opposite sides of the Iron Curtain. My argument is that the problems Navickaitė (2014) identifies lie, again, in the widespread dehistoricization of homosexuality in CEE. Mizielińska and Kulpa (2011, p. 15) recognize the year 1989 as the beginning of all the 'knotting' and 'looping' of an Eastern time of coincidence and, thus, like many other academic and media discourses, as the beginning of the introduction of LGBT rights and the emergence of LGBT activism in CEE.

1.2 UNDE VENIS, CEE?

The dehistoricization of homosexuality in CEE lies at the core of the myths of homogeneity and essence of the region, as well as the myths of its teleological transition after 1989 and near total isolation during the Cold War. Therefore, to counter these myths, but also to better understand why CEE is where it is right now in regard to LGBT issues, I propose to shift the question from Quo Vadis? to Unde Venis, CEE? The chief aim of this book is thus to historicize homosexuality in CEE. Some key questions I am going to interrogate include: What were the similarities and differences in governing and discussing homosexuality in Eastern Bloc countries? When did homosexuals in the region make their first attempts at more systematic forms of activism? How did they organize themselves? What were they inspired by? Also, and most crucially for this book project, what were the transnational connections between homosexuals, especially homosexual activists, on opposite sides of the Iron Curtain? What were the cross-border flows of cultural products, identity paradigms and activism models related to homosexuality? Can we in fact trace some aspects of the globalization of homosexuality, or LGBT identities and politics, in CEE already before 1989?

To provide a comprehensive and detailed history of homosexuality in the entire Eastern Bloc is an impossible task. Nobody has the linguistic skills and cultural knowledge to cover this vast terrain single-handedly. Therefore, I find it both necessary and desirable to centre my analysis around particular case studies in a particular country. This, however, does not mean I am willing to surrender to methodological nationalism. My intention is to follow a transnational approach to the study of sexuality (e.g. Bacchetta 2002; Canaday 2009; Grewal and Kaplan 2001; Kim-Puri 2005; McLellan 2017; Povinelli and Chauncey 1999), which is multiscalar, that is, it stresses the interconnections between different spatial scales of analysis such as the local, the national, the regional and the global. Unlike some studies of globalization, the transnational approach does not simply disregard countries as units of analysis—as if we could buy into the illusion of a post-national world—but rather requires to supplement the national with the non-national and it 'shifts analyses to linkages across cultural contexts rather than reproduces analyses of scale' (Kim-Puri 2005, p. 143). During the period under investigation, national boundaries did clearly matter for homosexuals in the Eastern Bloc, for example in terms of state laws and practices regarding homosexuality. But so did other scales, including the subnational, such as the city (e.g. in terms of number of homosexuals and level of anonymity), and the supranational, such as the political bloc (e.g. easier travelling within one bloc than between blocs) and continent (e.g. stronger connections with activists in Western Europe than beyond). Importantly, it is not those different scales separately but their combination and imbrication that created unique conditions, with unique opportunities and challenges, for lives and activisms of homosexuals in the Eastern Bloc. Therefore, while this book will be primarily based on an archival analysis of gay and lesbian magazines in late communist Poland, it will not be confined to Polish borders but will move back and forth between the subnational, the national and the supranational.

Why Poland? The country has a somewhat special status in the region. Often considered as the leader of the bloodless overthrow of communism in Europe, it is currently the biggest CEE member state of the EU. After 1989, it underwent drastic economic, political and social transformations that included the introduction of some new harsh laws regarding gender and sexuality, most strikingly the 1993 abortion law, still in power, according to which abortion is illegal unless (1) the mother's life or health is endangered, (2) she became pregnant as a result of a criminal act or (3) the foetus is seriously malformed (Kulczycki 1995; Zielińska 1993, 2000). Issues of gender and sexuality, including LGBT rights, regularly become hot topics in the new Poland, in particular when the national identity is considered to be in danger, as was the case before the 2003 referendum on Polish EU accession, when Eurosceptics warned that accession would automatically lead to 'gay marriage' (Szczerbiak 2005; Szulc 2014). Most recently, Poland has observed a new wave of right-wing activism against the so-called gender ideology, initiated by a pastoral letter by the Polish Bishops' Conference at the end of 2013 and soon reinforced by conservative politicians (who established a parliamentary group, 'Stop the Gender Ideology!') and grassroots activists (who proposed a bill criminalizing nearly all forms of abortion) (Duda 2016; Graff 2014; Graff and Korolczuk 2017b). The change in power from October 2015, which has put the conservative Law and Justice party in charge, has only energized the crusade against the 'gender ideology', both in the country (Detwiler and Snitow 2016; Mikulak 2016; Szulc 2016) and beyond: the respective Polish and Hungarian leaders, Jarosław Kaczyński and Viktor Orbán, have recently pledged to wage a 'cultural counter-revolution' in Europe (Foy and Buckley 2016). No doubt, then, Poland is an interesting case study. But I would fall into the trap of exceptionalism if I argued that the country is somehow more interesting than any of its close or distant neighbours. A transnational approach to the study of the history of homosexuality in CEE could, and someday hopefully will, be adopted to the study of any CEE country (or other geographical scales). In the end, my choice of Poland is primarily motivated by my own academic expertise, personal interest, cultural background and language skills.

Why does it make sense, finally, to turn to gay and lesbian magazines? This is, in fact, how this book project started: with the discovery of the existence of gay and lesbian magazines in communist Poland, which I first heard of thanks to the artist Karol Radziszewski and the 'Before '89' issue of his *DIK Fagazine*, published in 2011. After digging into archives, I managed to locate the two earliest and most successful (in the sense of having been published relatively regularly for about four years) Polish gay and lesbian magazines: the majority of issues of *Biuletyn*, later renamed *Etap*, published by Andrzej Selerowicz in Vienna between 1983 and 1987, and all issues of *Filo*, published by Ryszard Kisiel in Gdańsk between 1986 and 1990 (see Chap. 5). Additionally, I managed to get in touch with three of the magazines' authors: Selerowicz, Kisiel and Paulina Pilch, the only regular female contributor to *Filo*; and I conducted in-depth face-to-face interviews with them. I consider the magazines as principal historical sources in written form, which provide first-hand accounts of homosexual self-identification and self-organization as well as bearing the traces of the transnational construction of homosexuality in Poland before 1989. What is more, it was these two magazines within and around which two of the three main activist groups were formed in Poland, the Wrocław-based Etap and the Gdańsk-based Filo, which makes the history of the magazines inseparable from the history of homosexual activism in the country. Their analysis offers compelling evidence for the fact that Polish homosexuals created their own cultural products and organized themselves already before 1989 and that they were in touch with activists in other countries of the Eastern as well as Western Bloc during the twilight years of the Cold War.

Apart from the gay and lesbian magazines and the interviews with their makers, this book will rely on a number of additional primary and secondary sources. Most importantly, it will provide a detailed analysis of all Eastern Europe Information Pool (EEIP) reports published annually between 1982 and 1989 and commissioned by the International Gay Organization (IGA, later ILGA). These reports contain a lot of background information about homosexuality in CEE in the 1980s, highlight the complexity of the region in this regard and document transnational connections between the authors of the reports—homosexual activists based in the Western Bloc—and their counterparts in the Eastern Bloc. All reports are available in English at the International Gay/Lesbian Information Centre and Archive (IHLIA) in Amsterdam. Other primary sources will include documents from the Polish Institute of National Remembrance (IPN) regarding Operation Hyacinth (launched in Poland in 1985 by the police forces in order to create a kind of state 'homosexual inventory', see Szulc 2011 and Chap. 4), articles on homosexuality published in popular and alternative media in Poland in the 1980s, as well as a 1988 survey on Poles' attitudes towards homosexuality. Furthermore, the book will draw on a number of secondary sources, especially relevant academic literature in English and Polish, but also related publications in Polish mainstream and alternative media such as the already mentioned 'Before '89' issue of *DIK Fagazine* (2011) but also the magazine's special issue on 'Communist Homosexuality 1945–1989' (2017) as well as the 'Homosexuality in the PRL' series in the *Replika* magazine (2008–2009), where PRL stands for the People's Republic of Poland.

Before I start to describe the structure of this book, a short note on terminology is in order. First, some readers might have noticed my frequent use of the outdated word 'homosexual', and its different variants, even in the title of the book. Although the word has been criticized for its medical connotations both in English (e.g. Weeks 2011) and in Polish (e.g. Krzyszpień 2010; Szulc 2012), I decided to use it here for the purpose of historical precision: it was the most common word employed for self-description in the magazines I analysed. Although the words 'gay' and 'lesbian' were also quite common in the magazines, they were used more often as adjectives rather than nouns, for example in the subtitle of *Biuletyn/Etap*, 'Gay News-Sheet', and various subtitles of *Filo* such as 'Gay Cultural Bulletin', 'Gay Magazine' but also 'Magazine of Gays and Lesbians'. For that reason, I also prefer to speak of 'gay and lesbian' rather than 'homosexual' magazines in late communist Poland, but I refer to *Biuletyn/Etap* simply as a 'gay magazine' because it had no content relevant to lesbians whatsoever. At the same time, I use the more inclusive abbreviation LGBT with reference to more general and recent discussions on the topic. Second, there is still disagreement over what to call Soviet-like political and economic systems during the Cold War. The most popular options include 'communist', 'socialist' and 'state-socialist'. Following the recommendations of Andrew Roberts (2004) in his extensive discussion of these terms, I will use the word 'communist', as well as the phrase 'Eastern Bloc', as a general label for CEE countries during the Cold War, encompassing the Soviet Union and its satellite countries (Bulgaria, Czechoslovakia, East Germany, Hungry, Poland and Romania) as well as non-aligned communist states of Albania and Yugoslavia. Finally, I prefer the term 'transnationalism' to 'globalization' in reference to my own research because, as I explained earlier, I adopt in this book a transnational approach to the study of sexuality. At the same time, I use the word 'globalization' to discuss broader literature on this topic (see Chap. 2).

1.3   BOOK STRUCTURE

The book is divided into two main parts. The first one, *Global, Eastern and Polish Homosexuals*, will focus on debunking the already mentioned myths about CEE in regard to LGBT issues: the region's homogeneity, essence, teleological 'transition' after 1989 and near total isolation during the Cold War. It will provide a theoretical framework and contextual background for the book as well as discuss some original research results, based mainly on my analysis of the EEIP reports but also some other historical materials such as Polish official state documents and mainstream media articles from the 1980s. I analysed these historical materials employing a qualitative content analysis and adopting an inductive research approach so to allow the most prevalent themes to emerge from the data itself (Silverman 2009), though of course the results of such a bottom-up analysis also reflect my own interests, experience and knowledge. On the one hand, I treated the materials as principal information sources, which provide unique information about homosexuality in CEE in the 1980s. On the other hand, I critically reflected on their production process and carefully examined some of their biases to put into perspective the stories and histories they tell. To arrive at a more accurate image of the region at that time, I will juxtapose the information found in the materials with academic accounts of homosexuality in the Eastern Bloc.

In Chap. 2, I will outline the emergence of dominant modern LGBT identities and politics, and discuss the processes of their globalization, drawing on some seminal works on this topic, particularly those employing postcolonial and transnational perspectives. In the last section of that chapter, I will additionally examine the place of CEE in this body of literature, arguing that the globalization of homosexuality in the region has been recognized virtually only after the fall of communism in Europe.

Therefore, in Chap. 3, I will look into homosexuality in CEE before 1989. Drawing primarily on the EEIP reports, I will zoom in on a number of issues most commonly addressed in the reports such as state laws and practices regarding homosexuals, public discourses on homosexuality as well as homosexual self-organizing. My prime aim there will be to emphasize the complexity of the Eastern Bloc in relation to homosexuality and highlight the transnational dimensions of early homosexual activism in the region. Chapter 4 will further narrow down the geographical scope of this book by providing a detailed account of the emergence of a more systematically organized homosexual activism in late communist Poland. After presenting the broader political and social context of Poland under communism and introducing some homosexuality-related issues in the country before 1980, I will devote the rest of the chapter to discuss early Polish homosexual groups established during the last decade of the Cold War: their transnational origins, greater mobilizations after the police's intensified harassment of homosexuals as well as first demands for official recognition, framed within the discourses of HIV and AIDS.

The second part, *Transnationalism in Gay and Lesbian Magazines*, will principally focus on transnational dimensions of *Biuletyn/Etap* and *Filo*. It will offer critical insights into cross-border flows of cultural products, identity paradigms and activism models from the perspective of late communist Poland and provide abundant evidence for the active participation of Polish homosexual activists in the globalization of homosexuality already before 1989. This part will be based on my qualitative and inductive analysis of the magazines' content (altogether 310 pages) and in-depth face-to-face interviews with three key people behind them (altogether 215 minutes). *Filo* will receive more space than *Biuletyn/Etap* in that part for a number of reasons. First, it was much bigger in size, comprising 265 pages compared to 45 pages of *Biuletyn/Etap* (although I failed to locate three early issues of *Biuletyn/Etap*, it is highly unlikely that any of them had more than two pages). Second, *Filo* was more diverse in scope: the last issues of the magazine included more information about, for and by lesbians as well as some sporadic mentions of transsexualism, while *Biuletyn/Etap* remained exclusively devoted to gay men. Finally, *Biuletyn/Etap* was authored exclusively by Selerowicz, while *Filo* was more of a collaborative project, authored for the most time of its existence by the core team of five or six people, which made its content more diverse and complex than the content of *Biuletyn/Etap*.

In Chap. 5, I will first draw on the theories of alternative media to consider the media's role for social movements and discuss the importance of the transnational network of gay and lesbian press for shaping homosexual identities and politics in the West. Next, I will present the Polish publishing context in the 1980s and describe the history, production and general content of *Biuletyn/Etap* and *Filo*. In the two following chapters, I will take a closer look at the content of the two magazines, focusing on the ways they were '(Re)constructing Identities' (Chap. 6) and '(Re)building Politics' (Chap. 7). I put the prefix 're' in parentheses in the titles of both chapters to indicate the dialectical aspects of the two processes. On the one hand, homosexual identities and politics coming to the existence in the magazines were reconstructed and rebuilt because they were much influenced by Western ideas about what it means to be a homosexual and what it entails to do homosexual activism. On the other hand, the Western ideas were not simply copied but rather selectively adopted as well as strategically and creatively adapted in the magazines, which requires to recognize the agency of the magazines' authors in constructing their own unique identities and building their own original politics. Chapter 6 will show how *Biuletyn/Etap* and *Filo* put forward the concept of homosexuality as natural, promoted self-acceptance and coming out among homosexuals as well as affirmed particular notions of romantic, sexual and collective selves. Chapter 7, in turn, will explain how the magazines encouraged their readers to self-organize, told the histories of homosexual activism, developed their own vision for the Polish homosexual movement as well as preoccupied themselves with visibility politics and information activism.

In Conclusion (Chap. 8), I will bring together the key insights from this book to once again dispel the recurrent myths about CEE in respect to LGBT issues. In particular, I will challenge the idea of a wholesale rupture in 1989 in the region, problematize the narrative of the region's teleological transition after the collapse of the Iron Curtain and reflect on the concept of CEE as a 'region'. Furthermore, I will urge to recognize that the processes of the globalization of homosexuality, or LGBT identities and politics, have taken place in CEE already during the Cold War, emphasizing that homosexual activists in the Eastern Bloc were active participants in that process. I will also propose to refine the theoretical framework about the globalization of homosexuality, or more broadly sexuality, by developing a model of networked sexual globalization. Informed by the research results presented in this book, I will point out that such model needs to combine both spatial and temporal aspects of globalization as

well as to recognize that geopolitical structures and local agencies inter-
twine in specific cultural and historical contexts in a myriad of ways. At
the end of Chap. 8, I will come back to the idea of queer wars proposed
by Altman and Symons (2016), arguing that those queer wars are a hoax,
that is, they stem from regional othering rather than 'essential' differences
between particular regions.

Finally, I would like to encourage readers to consult the timeline of
key events related to the emergence of homosexual activism in late communist Poland, which is available at the end of this book, as well as to
visit the book's website, www.transnationalhomosexuals.pl, where I offer
more information about this project and provide additional resources such
as digital copies of the analysed magazines and video excerpts from the
interviews with their makers. The website also allows everybody interested
in the topic of the book to share their thoughts, comments and questions
in order to continue the discussion about the transnational construction
of homosexuality, or LGBT identities and politics, in communist Poland,
CEE and beyond.

BIBLIOGRAPHY

Altman, D., & Symons, J. (2016). *Queer wars*. Cambridge: Polity.
Bacchetta, P. (2002). Rescaling transnational "queerdom": Lesbian and "lesbian"
identitary-positionalities in Delhi in the 1980s. *Antipode, 34*(5), 947–973.
Baer, B. J. (2011). Queer in Russia: Othering the other of the West. In L. Downing
& R. Gillett (Eds.), *Queer in Europe: Contemporary case studies* (pp. 173–188).
Farnham: Ashgate.
Bakić-Hayden, M. (1995). Nesting orientalisms: The case of former Yugoslavia.
Slavic Review, 54(4), 917–931.
Bracke, S. (2012). From "saving women" to "saving gays": Rescue narratives and
their dis/continuities. *European Journal of Women's Studies, 19*(2), 237–252.
Campoy, A. (2016). A conspiracy theory about sex and gender is being peddled
around the world by the far right. *Quartz*. Retrieved January 6, 2017, from
https://qz.com/807743/conservatives-have-created-a-fake-ideology-to-combat-
the-global-movement-for-lgbti-rights/
Canaday, M. (2009). Thinking sex in the transnational turn: An introduction. *The
American Historical Review, 114*(5), 1250–1257.
Chari, S., & Verdery, K. (2009). Thinking between the posts: Postcolonialism,
postsocialism, and the ethnography after the Cold War. *Comparative Studies in
Society and History, 51*(1), 6–34.
Detwiler, K., & Snitow, A. (2016). Gender trouble in Poland. *Dissent, 63*(4),
57–66.

Duda, M. (2016). *Dogmat płci: Polska wojna z gender*. Gdańsk: Katedra.

Economist. (2014, October 9). The gay divide. Retrieved March 8, 2017, from http://www.economist.com/news/leaders/21623668-victories-gay-rights-some-parts-world-have-provoked-backlash-elsewhere-gay

El-Tayeb, F. (2011). *European others: Queering ethnicity in postnational Europe*. Minneapolis: University of Minnesota Press.

El-Tayeb, F. (2012). "Gays who cannot properly be gay": Queer Muslims in the neoliberal European city. *European Journal of Women's Studies, 19*(1), 79–95.

Engeli, I., Green-Pedersen, C., & Larsen, L. T. (Eds.). (2012). *Morality politics in Western Europe: Parties, agendas and policy choices*. Basingstoke: Palgrave Macmillan.

Fassin, É. (2010). National identities and transnational intimacies: Sexual democracy and the politics of immigration in Europe. *Public Culture, 22*(3), 507–529.

Foy, H., & Buckley, N. (2016). Orban and Kaczynski vow "cultural counter-revolution" to reform EU. *Financial Times*. Retrieved March 8, 2017, from https://www.ft.com/content/e825f7f4-74a3-11e6-bf48-b372cdb1043a

Graff, A. (2014). Report from the gender trenches: War against "genderism" in Poland. *European Journal of Women's Studies, 21*(4), 431–435.

Graff, A., & Korolczuk, E. (2017a). Towards an illiberal future: Anti-genderism and anti-globalization. *Global Dialogue, 7*(1), 27–29.

Graff, A., & Korolczuk, E. (2017b). "Worse than communism and Nazism put together": War on gender in Poland. In R. Kuhar & D. Paternotte (Eds.), *Anti-gender campaigns in Europe: Mobilizing against equality*. Lanham: Rowman & Littlefield.

Grewal, I., & Kaplan, C. (2001). Global identities: Theorizing transnational studies of sexuality. *GLQ: A Journal of Lesbian and Gay Studies, 7*(4), 663–679.

Haritaworn, J., & Petzen, J. (2011). Invented traditions, new intimate publics: Tracing the German "Muslim homophobia" discourse. In C. Flood, S. Hutching, G. Miazhevich, & H. Nickels (Eds.), *Islam in its international context: Comparative perspectives* (pp. 48–64). Cambridge: Cambridge Scholars.

Healey, D. (1993). The Russian revolution and the decriminalisation of homosexuality. *Revolutionary Russia, 6*(1), 26–54.

Healey, D. (2002). Homosexual existence and existing socialism. New light on the repression of male homosexuality in Stalin's Russia. *GLQ: A Journal of Lesbian and Gay Studies, 8*(3), 349–378.

Hildebrandt, A. (2014). Routes to decriminalization: A comparative analysis of the legalization of same-sex sexual acts. *Sexualities, 17*(1/2), 230–253.

Huffington Post. (2013). Eastern Europe's gay rights battle: Is LGBT equality out of reach? Retrieved March 8, 2017, from http://www.huffingtonpost.com/2013/02/11/gay-rights-eastern-central-europe-concerns_n_2659829.html

Huntington, S. P. (1993). The clash of civilizations? *Foreign Affairs, 72*, 22–49.

Imre, A. (2007). "Affective nationalism" and transnational postcommunist lesbian visual activism. In K. Marciniak, A. Imre, & Á. O'Healy (Eds.), *Transnational feminism in film and media* (pp. 147–162). New York: Palgrave Macmillan.

Inglehart, R., & Norris, P. (2003). The true clash of civilizations. *Foreign Policy, 135*, 62–70.

Kim-Puri, H. J. (2005). Conceptualizing gender-sexuality-state-nation: An introduction. *Gender and Society, 19*(2), 137–159.

Kon, I. (2009). Homophobia as a litmus test of Russian democracy. *Sociological Research, 48*(2), 43–64.

Korolczuk, E. (2014). "The war on gender" from a transnational perspective— Lessons for feminist strategising. In Heinrich Böll Foundation (Ed.), *Anti-gender movements on the rise? Strategising for gender equality in Central and Eastern Europe* (pp. 43–53). Berlin: Heinrich Böll Foundation.

Krzyszpień, J. (2010). Język i emancypacja LGBT: Uwagi praktyczne. In J. Kochanowski, M. Abramowicz, & R. Biedroń (Eds.), *Queer studies: Podręcznik kursu* (pp. 139–146). Warszawa: KPH.

Kubik, J. (2013). From transitology to contextual holism: A theoretical trajectory of postcommunist studies. In J. Kubik & A. Linch (Eds.), *Postcommunism from within: Social justice, mobilization, and hegemony* (pp. 27–94). New York: NYU Press.

Kuhar, R., & Paternotte, D. (2017). *Anti-gender campaigns in Europe: Mobilizing against equality*. Lanham: Rowman & Littlefield.

Kulczycki, A. (1995). Abortion policy in postcommunist Europe: The conflict in Poland. *Population and Development Review, 21*(3), 471–505.

Kulpa, R. (2014). Western leveraged pedagogy of Central and Eastern Europe: Discourses of homophobia, tolerance, and nationhood. *Gender, Place & Culture: A Journal of Feminist Geography, 21*(4), 431–448.

Kulpa, R., & Mizielińska, J. (Eds.). (2011). *De-centring Western sexualities: Central and Eastern European perspectives*. Farnham: Ashgate.

Kuntsman, A. (2008). The soldier and the terrorist: Sexy nationalism, queer violence. *Sexualities, 11*(1/2), 142–170.

Kuus, M. (2006). The double enlargement and the remapping of the East. In S. Engel-Di Mauro (Ed.), *The European's burden: Global imperialism in EU expansion* (pp. 225–242). New York: Peter Lang.

Makarychev, A., & Medvedev, S. (2015). Biopolitics and power in Putin's Russia. *Problems of Post-Communism, 62*(1), 45–54.

McLellan, J. (2017). Lesbians, gay men and the production of scale in East Germany. *Cultural and Social History, 14*(1), 89–105.

Mepschen, P., & Duyvendak, J. W. (2012). European sexual nationalisms: The culturalization of citizenship and the sexual politics of belonging and exclusion. *Perspectives on Europe, 42*(1), 70–76.

Mikulak, M. (2016). Poland: A change so good, it makes you want to cry. *EUROPP: European Politics and Policy.* Retrieved March 8, 2017, from http://blogs.lse.ac.uk/europpblog/2016/03/29/poland-a-change-so-good-it-makes-you-want-to-cry/

Mizielińska, J., & Kulpa, R. (2011). "Contemporary peripheries": Queer studies, circulation of knowledge and East/West divide. In R. Kulpa & J. Mizielińska (Eds.), *De-centring Western sexualities: Central and Eastern European perspectives* (pp. 11–26). Farnham: Ashgate.

Navickaitė, R. (2014). Postcolonial queer critique in post-communist Europe: Stuck in the Western progress narrative? *Tijdschrift voor Genderstudies, 17*(2), 167–185.

Navickaitė, R. (2016). Under the Western gaze: Sexuality and postsocialist "transition" in East Europe. In S. Ponzanesi & G. Colpani (Eds.), *Postcolonial transitions in Europe: Contexts, practices and politics* (pp. 119–132). London: Rowman & Littlefield.

Owczarzak, J. (2009). Introduction: Postcolonial studies and postsocialism in Eastern Europe. *Focaal—European Journal of Anthropology, 53,* 3–19.

Pearce, S. C., & Cooper, A. (2016). LGBT activism in Eastern and Central Europe. In N. Naples (Ed.), *The Wiley Blackwell encyclopedia of gender and sexuality studies.* Retrieved September 8, 2016, from http://onlinelibrary.wiley.com/doi/10.1002/9781118663219.wbegss707/abstract

Pew Research Center. (2013). Eastern and Western Europe divided over gay marriage, homosexuality. Retrieved September 7, 2016, from http://www.pewresearch.org/fact-tank/2013/12/12/eastern-and-western-europe-divided-over-gay-marriage-homosexuality/

Picq, M. L., & Thiel, M. (Eds.). (2015). *Sexualities in world politics: How LGBTQ claims shape international relations.* Abingdon: Routledge.

Płatek, M. (2009). Sytuacja osób homoseksualnych w prawie karnym. In R. Wieruszewski & M. Wyrzykowski (Eds.), *Orientacja seksualna i tożsamość płciowa* (pp. 49–81). Warszawa: Instytut Wydawniczy EuroPrawo.

Povinelli, E. A., & Chauncey, G. (1999). Thinking sexuality transnationally: An introduction. *GLQ: A Journal of Lesbian and Gay Studies, 5*(4), 439–450.

Puar, J. (2007). *Terrorist assemblages: Homonationalism in queer times.* Durham: Duke University Press.

Puar, J. (2011). Citation and censorship: The politics of talking about the sexual politics of Israel. *Feminist Legal Studies, 19,* 133–142.

Puar, J. (2013). Rethinking homonationalism. *International Journal of Middle East Studies, 45*(2), 336–339.

Raboin, T. (2013). Constructing a queer haven: Sexuality and nationhood in discourses on LGBT asylum in the UK. Doctoral dissertation. University College London.

Renkin, H. Z. (2016). Biopolitical mythologies: Róheim, Freud, (homo)phobia, and the sexual science of Eastern European otherness. *Sexualities, 19*(1/2), 168–189.

Roberts, A. (2004). The state of socialism: A note on terminology. *Slavic Review, 63*(2), 349–366.

Romanets, M. (2017). Virtual warfare: Masculinity, sexuality, and propaganda in the Russo-Ukrainian war. *East/West: Journal of Ukrainian Studies, IV*(1), 159–177.

Silverman, D. (2009). *Interpreting qualitative data: Methods for analyzing, talk, text and interaction.* Los Angeles: Sage.

Slootmaeckers, K., & Touquet, H. (2016). The co-evolution of EU's Eastern enlargement and LGBT politics: An ever gayer union? In K. Slootmaeckers, H. Touquet, & P. Vermeersch (Eds.), *The EU enlargement and gay politics: The impact of Eastern enlargement on rights, activism and prejudice* (pp. 19–44). London: Palgrave Macmillan.

Slootmaeckers, K., Touquet, H., & Vermeersch, P. (Eds.). (2016). *The EU enlargement and gay politics: The impact of Eastern enlargement on rights, activism and prejudice.* London: Palgrave Macmillan.

Stella, F. (2013). Queer space, pride, and shame in Moscow. *Slavic Review, 72*(3), 458–480.

Stella, F. (2015). *Lesbian lives in Soviet and post-Soviet Russia: Post/socialism and gendered sexualities.* Basingstoke: Palgrave Macmillan.

Štulhofer, A., & Sandfort, T. (2005). Introduction: Sexuality and gender in times of transition. In A. Štulhofer & T. Sandfort (Eds.), *Sexuality and gender in postcommunist Eastern Europe and Russia* (pp. 1–25). Binghamton: Haworth Press.

Szczerbiak, A. (2005). History trumps government unpopularity: The June 2003 Polish EU referendum. In A. Szczerbiak & P. Taggart (Eds.), *EU enlargement and referendums* (pp. 115–134). Abington: Routledge.

Sztompka, P. (1993). Civilizational incompetence. The trap of postcommunist societies. *Zeitschrift für Soziologie, 22*(2), 85–95.

Szulc, L. (2011). Queer in Poland: Under construction. In L. Downing & R. Gillett (Eds.), *Queer in Europe: Contemporary case studies* (pp. 159–172). Farnham: Ashgate.

Szulc, L. (2012). From queer to gay to Queer.pl: The names we dare to speak in Poland. *Lambda Nordica, 17*(4), 65–98.

Szulc, L. (2014). Conchita's Europe: Eurovision, homonationalism and the politics of sexuality. *Notches: (Re)marks on the History of Sexuality.* Retrieved September 13, 2016, from http://notchesblog.com/2014/05/19/conchitas-europe-eurovision-homonationalism-and-the-politics-of-sexuality/

Szulc, L. (2016). The new Polish government and "gender ideology". *Notches: (Re)marks on the History of Sexuality.* Retrieved September 13, 2016, from http://notchesblog.com/2016/04/28/the-new-polish-government-and-gender-ideology/

Takács, J., & Kuhar, R. (2007). Introduction: What is beyond the Pink Curtain? In R. Kuhar & J. Takács (Eds.), *Beyond the Pink Curtain: Everyday life of LGBT people in Eastern Europe* (pp. 11–12). Ljubljana: Peace Institute.

Todorova, M. (2005). The trap of backwardness: Modernity, temporality, and the study of Eastern European nationalism. *Slavic Review, 64*(1), 140–164.

Underhill, W. R. (1976). Semantics of the "Iron Curtain" metaphor. *ETC: A Review of General Semantics, 33*(3), 293–300.

Verpoest, L. (forthcoming). *State violence and geopolitical othering: LGBT policies in Russia and Ukraine.*

Washington Post. (2014, November 6). Gay rights in Eastern Europe just took a big step forward. Retrieved March 8, 2017, from https://www.washington-post.com/news/worldviews/wp/2014/11/06/gay-rights-in-eastern-europe-just-took-a-big-step-forward/

Washington Post. (2015, July 25). Gay rights in Eastern Europe: A new battle-ground for Russia and the West. Retrieved March 8, 2017, from https://www.washingtonpost.com/world/europe/gay-rights-in-eastern-europe-a-new-battleground-for-russia-and-the-west/2015/07/24/8ad04d4e-2ff2-11e5-a879-213078d03dd3_story.html

Weber, C. (2016). *Queer international relations: Sovereignty, sexuality and the will to knowledge.* Oxford: Oxford University Press.

Weeks, J. (2011). *The languages of sexuality.* London: Routledge.

Wolff, L. (1994). *Inventing Eastern Europe: The map of civilization on the mind of the enlightenment.* Stanford: Stanford University Press.

Zielińska, E. (1993). Recent trends in abortion legislation in Eastern Europe, with particular reference to Poland. *Criminal Law Forum, 4*(1), 47–93.

Zielińska, E. (2000). Between ideology, politics and common sense: The discourse of reproductive rights in Poland. In S. Gal & G. Kligman (Eds.), *Reproducing gender: Politics, publics, and everyday life after socialism* (pp. 23–57). Princeton: Princeton University Press.

PART I

Global, Eastern and Polish Homosexuals

CHAPTER 2

Globalization of LGBT Identities
and Politics

As contested as it is, the term 'globalization' has been steadily gaining in
popularity in social sciences, at least since the 1990s (Turner 2010). Sexuality
studies are no exception, which is reflected in the titles of some key books in
the field, including *The Global Emergence of Gay and Lesbian Politics* (Adam
et al. 1999c), *Global Sex* (Altman 2001), *Queer Globalizations* (Cruz-
Malavé and Manalansan 2002a), *The Globalization of Sexuality* (Binnie
2004), *Speaking in Queer Tongues: Globalization and Gay Language* (Leap
and Boellstorff 2004), *Understanding Global Sexualities* (Aggleton et al.
2012), *Love and Globalization* (Padilla et al. 2012), *Global Homophobia*
(Weiss and Bosia 2013) and *A Global History of Sexuality* (Buffington et al.
2014). In his book organized around keywords in sexuality studies, Jeffrey
Weeks (2011, p. 71) too recognizes the importance of globalization, which
he interprets as a stretching of social, political, cultural and economic relations, intensification of global interconnectedness, and speeding up of
global interactions. He points out that works on the globalization of sexuality cover a wide range of diverse topics such as flows of people escaping from
persecution due to their sexualities, flows of sexual tourism, flows of sexually
transmitted infections, flows of media that make sexual news and representations, flows of science that try to interpret the sexual world, flows of
discourse around human sexual rights, flows of drugs with erotic connotations, flows of cybersex, flows of love as well as flows of lesbian, gay, bisexual
and transgender (LGBT) identities and politics (Weeks 2011, pp. 72–73).

© The Author(s) 2018
L. Szulc, *Transnational Homosexuals in Communist Poland*,
Global Queer Politics, DOI 10.1007/978-3-319-58901-5_2

The globalization of sexuality also lies at the heart of the thesis of queer wars (Altman and Symons 2016), or the growing importance of gender and sexuality, particularly LGBT-related issues, in world politics. As discussed in Chap. 1, Dennis Altman and Jonathan Symons (2016) connect the emergence of the wars with the increasing social, cultural and political recognition of LGBTs in the West since the late 1960s. That this recognition has been Western rather than national in scope, and that it has provoked a backlash not only in the West but also in the 'Rest', attests to its global resonance. The queer wars have been heavily concentrated on the issue of LGBT rights, which entered the discourse of universal human rights and were put on the agenda of such international institutions as the Council of Europe (CoE), European Union (EU) and United Nations (UN) in the early 1990s (Corrêa 1997; Kollman and Waites 2009; Paternotte and Seckinelgin 2015; Petchesky 2000). But the wars have also been the (unintended) effects of the globalization of LGBT identities, which has made LGBT rights thinkable, as well as the globalization of LGBT politics, which has helped the rights to gain prominence at the international level. It is important to recognize geopolitical structures here: just as the concept of human rights originates from the Western political philosophy (Parker et al. 2014), so too dominant modern LGBT identities and politics have their roots in the West, which has provoked their contestation as one of the facets of Western neoimperialism.

The aim of this chapter is to provide a theoretical framework for the discussion of the globalization of LGBT identities and politics, zooming in on the selected aspects of that process relevant to this book. In the first two sections, I will briefly discuss the origin and spread of modern Western LGBT identities and politics, and point to the hegemony of the West in the processes of sexual globalization. In the third section, I will look into the role of the HIV/AIDS epidemic in the processes, focusing primarily on the development of HIV/AIDS activism, often closely intertwined with LGBT activism. Next, I will delve into the relationship between the West and the Rest. Drawing on some postcolonial and transnational works, I will problematize the thesis of 'Westernization', according to which global flows simply go from the West to the Rest, and consider other conceptualizations of the globalization processes. Finally, I will analyse the place of Central and Eastern Europe (CEE), with a particular focus on Poland, in the discussions of the globalization of LGBT identities and politics, showing that the region enters the discussions virtually exclusively after the fall of communism in Europe in 1989, which confirms my argument from Chap. 1 that the Eastern Bloc tends to be perceived as a nearly totally isolated place of no-time.

2.1   GLOBAL LGBT IDENTITIES

The discussion of the origin and spread of LGBT identities rests on the assumption that sexuality is not (purely) a natural phenomenon but also, and primarily, a cultural and historical construction. As Weeks (2000, p. 12) puts it, 'The physical acts may seem broadly the same across all cultures, all historic periods, but their meanings change all the time'. Mary McIntosh (1968) was one of the first authors who asked to recognize such a social constructivist character of homosexuality, a 'homosexual role' rather than just a 'homosexual behaviour', as she calls it, where the former encompasses social expectations about who homosexuals are and what they do. Focusing mainly on England, she traces the emergence of homosexual role back to the late seventeenth century, though she also points out that the conception of homosexuality at that time does not entirely overlap with the modern conception (McIntosh 1968, p. 187). The emergence of the modern homosexual (Plummer 1981), that is, homosexuality understood as an identity—an interior of the soul rather than a temporary aberration, crime or sin—is usually located at the end of the nineteenth century and the beginning of the twentieth century in the West, a result of the Industrial Revolution marked by the processes of urbanization, secularization and individualization (D'Emilio 1992) and the rise of what Michel Foucault (1978) names *scientia sexualis* (science of sexuality), that is, scientific discourses on sexuality, including homosexuality. Modern homosexuals can be characterized by, as summarized by Altman (1997, p. 425), their wish to express their sexual identity openly, have long-term primary relationships with other homosexuals and mix with other homosexuals (for postmodern critiques of such social constructivist accounts, see e.g. Bravmann 1997, pp. 3–14 and Sedgwick 1990, pp. 44–48).

Homosexuals might have been discovered as a distinct species more than a century ago, but it was only in the 1970s when they fully embraced the idea of sexual identity themselves (Weeks 2011, p. 186). In the aftermath of the Stonewall Riots—protests in the summer of 1969 against a police raid on the gay bar Stonewall Inn in New York—activists established the gay liberation movement, which asserted a new affirmative sexual identity. Old self-descriptions, such as offensive 'queer', 'poofter' or 'faggot' but also medicalized 'homosexual', were rejected in favour of the new term 'gay', an indicator of agency, self-confidence and sexual and political revolution: 'gay is good', 'gay pride', 'gay power' (Weeks 2011, pp. 63–68). Accused of marginalizing the experiences of anyone but gay men, the activists subsequently embraced additional self-descriptions, especially 'lesbian' but also 'bisexual' and 'transgender', to arrive at a currently popular acronym 'LGBT' or 'LGBTQ', adding 'queers' and/or 'questioning'. The emergence of the term 'queer' in the 1990s, first in the United States and later also elsewhere, decentred (or rather dismantled) the core of dissident sexual identities. In its current use, the word originates in a new form of politics against the mishandling of HIV/AIDS crisis by conservative administrations in the United States as well as against binary oppositions such as heterosexual versus homosexual or male versus female. As Annamarie Jagose (1996, p. 98) explains, 'queer marks a suspension of identity as something fixed, coherent and natural', in a much postmodern fashion; it rejects the minoritizing logic of stable LGBT identities in favour of a more situational positioning against 'regimes of the normal' (Warner 1993, p. xxvi). Importantly, those different models of dissident sexual identities, including anti-identities, do not simply supersede one another but coexist with each other: different people embrace different sexual identities or simply refuse to identify themselves through their sexuality.

'In modernity, identities become global', Inderpal Grewal and Caren Kaplan (2001, p. 663) begin their essay on global identities and sexuality. They explain that the works on the emergence of LGBT identities tend to focus on the United States and Europe, and on white middle-class life in particular, and ask for adopting a more transnational approach to the studies of sexualities. Such an attempt has been made by Altman (1996, 1997, 2001) in his early works on the globalization of sexuality, including LGBT identities. He came up with the concept of the 'global gay', most often a man rather than a woman, who is 'young, upwardly mobile, sexually adventurous, with an in-your-face attitude toward traditional restrictions and an interest in both activism and fashion' (Altman 1996, p. 77). Weeks (2011, p. 36) supplements the description by explaining that the global gay 'can potentially feel at home in all parts of the worlds where a similar repertoire of cafés, bars, clubs, saunas, cruising areas, local neighbourhoods, styles of dress, modes of behaviour and values systems provide the material base for a "queer cosmopolitanism"'. In these accounts, the globalization of LGBT (mainly gay) identities is strongly connected with the idea of a commercialized gay lifestyle: it is about what gay men wear, where they go to and what they are interested in;—ultimately, what they spend their money for. Besides, globalization is understood as a homogenizing force and a form of cultural imperialism, commercially driven Westernization, if not simply Americanization. I will discuss some critiques of such conceptualizations of globalization further in this chapter.

The globalization of commercialized LGBT identities is, of course, very limited since relatively few around the world can afford such an expensive gay lifestyle. It seems, however, that—at a somewhat deeper level—the modern idea of homosexuality as identity, tied to a set of particular expectations about, for example, distinct gender roles and romantic monogamous relationships, has indeed been quickly proliferating worldwide, if still coexisting with more local understandings of same-sex desires and practices. One important aspect of such a deeper globalization of LGBT identities is a global dissemination of English self-descriptions, especially the word 'gay', which 'seemed to be on the road to being a global signifier of same-sex activities, appearing in a variety of different languages' (Weeks 2011, p. 64). As many authors have shown, the self-descriptions travelling from the West to the Rest most often are not simply adopted but rather adapted by non-Western subjects: sometimes the words take on subtly different meanings, other times, they are decontextualized and recontextualized, acquiring more radically different connotations (see e.g. Boellstorff 2003; Enteen 2010; Jackson 2001; Phillips 2000). Nevertheless, the fact that the sexual self-descriptions originate in English rather than any other language does point to the global hegemony of the West, particularly of Anglo-American culture, in relation to LGBT identities. It also provokes the question of the mechanisms through which the hegemony has been established, to which I will turn to in the rest of this section.

Most fundamentally, current geopolitical structures stem from the era of colonialism. While conquering and exploiting the 'Third World', the 'First World' most often also enforced its own medieval laws against so-called sodomy or unnatural fornication, which included (mainly male) same-sex acts, considered at that time as offences against God (e.g. Kirby 2013; Nesvig 2001). The most notable exception was France (at least during the Second French Empire), which decriminalized same-sex acts already in 1791, a result of the secularization of the country after the French Revolution (Hildebrandt 2014). Right after decolonization, many of the anti-sodomy laws remained in power, both in the colonizing and the formerly colonized countries, though some newly independent countries (especially in Central and South America) voluntarily adopted the French model soon after regaining independence in the nineteenth century. With a handful of exceptions, the West started to gradually repeal the anti-sodomy laws only after the Second World War, largely due to new medical and legal discourses around sexuality as well as the work of early homosexual movements. In the early 1990s, when most Western European countries had repealed anti-sodomy laws, sexual rights officially entered the discourse of universal human rights, actively promoted by the West. A major turning point came in 1993, when sexual rights were included in the declaration of the World Conference on Human Rights in Vienna (Petchesky 2000) and the International Lesbian, Gay, Bisexual, Trans and Intersex Association (ILGA) acquired official consultative status at the UN Economic and Social Council (Sanders 1996). In the 2000s, the idea of LGBT rights as human rights became so strong that the protection of the rights started to be discussed as aid conditions (e.g. by Barrack Obama's or David Cameron's administrations, see Chávez 2013) and accession requirements (e.g. by the CoE and EU, see Slootmaeckers et al. 2016).

While the idea of LGBT rights is anchored in and, thus, naturalizes essentialist LGBT identities, it is the more informal, cultural imperialism that has arguably played the crucial role in the globalization of the identities. In the introduction to *Queer Globalizations*, Arnoldo Cruz-Malavé and Martin Manalansan (2002a, p. 1) specifically point to the importance of global circulation of media representations: 'Whether in advertising, film, performance art, the Internet, or the political discourses of human rights in emerging democracies, images of queer sexualities and cultures now circulate around the globe'. Considered as *the* medium of globalization, the internet is most often credited with the popularization of LGBT representations (e.g. Heinz et al. 2002; Martin 2009). Altman and Symons (2016, p. 31) write that '[t]he Web has created new sites for sexual encounters, but even more so for the global dissemination of a language that cultivates sexuality-based identities'. Though, some authors argue that because the production of internet content is more diversified than the production of traditional media content, the internet actually promotes a greater diversity of sexual identity models (Alexander 2002, p. 81; Plummer 2015, p. 80). The representations of LGBTs in global film and cinema have been more tightly controlled by a limited group of people in the US film industry; so film and cinema could play a more substantial role in promoting Western LGBT identities. Indeed, research points to the importance of Western media products for identifications of LGBT people around the world, for example, in the case of such cult films and TV series as *Philadelphia* (1993) (e.g. in Turkey, Görkemli 2010) and *Dynasty* (1981–1989) (e.g. in South Africa, Donham 1998), particularly in the context of the growing worldwide popularity of LGBT film festivals (Rhyne 2006; Schoonover and Galt 2016). In the second part of this book, I will demonstrate that the early gay and lesbian press, both Western and non-Western, also played a crucial role in the globalization of LGBT, or at least homosexual, identities.

2.2 GLOBAL LGBT POLITICS

The origin and spread of LGBT identities is related to the emergence of LGBT activism, which, as Barry Adam, Jan Willem Duyvendak and André Krouwel (1999a, p. 350) point out, 'becomes imaginable only if people have sexual identities'. The Scientific Humanitarian Committee (WhK) was the first homosexual rights organization in the world, established in Berlin in 1897 by a sexologist Magnus Hirschfeld (Beachy 2014; Hekma 2015). Hirschfeld was also the key person behind the Institute for Sexual Science, created in 1919, and the World League for Sexual Reform (WLSR), founded in 1928, both organizations devoted to the fight for the recognition of diverse sexual rights, including reproductive and homosexual rights. As the name of the last organization suggests, these early activist initiatives were already transnational in scope. The congresses of the WLSR were held in different European cities, including Berlin (1921), Copenhagen (1928), London (1929), Vienna (1930) and Brno (1932) (Dose 2003, p. 1). The WLSR also had its chapters in CEE, for example in Czechoslovakia, founded in 1931 (Huebner 2010), and Poland, founded in 1933 (Gawin and Crozier 2006; Kościańska 2016), while Soviet sexologists rose to prominence at the League's congresses thanks to the Soviets' decriminalization of same-sex acts in 1922 (recriminalized in 1933–1934) (Healey 1993, 2002). The WhK too had its chapters in different European countries, most notably in the Netherlands (called simply the Dutch WhK), which existed since 1912 until the Nazi invasion in 1940 (Hekma 2015, p. 24). In the United States, in turn, a Bavaria-born Henry Gerber established the Society for Human Rights in Chicago in 1924, modelled on a German homosexual group, which held the same name—Bund für Menschenrecht—and had been organized by Friedrich Radszuweit in the 1920s (Baim 2012, p. 81). The German-led movement was suppressed by the Nazis in 1933, who, among other things, publically burnt the archive of the Institute for Sexual Science (Marhoefer 2015).

The pre-war activists provided inspiration for the 1950s and the early 1960s homophile movement, again a transnational project characteristic of Western Europe and the United States (Churchill 2008; Rupp 2011, 2014). The word 'homophile' was coined by a German physician and activist in 1924, and was later adopted by many groups and magazines in the West (Jackson 2015, p. 31). It was created in a direct opposition to the word 'homosexual', emphasizing love rather than sex and a person rather than a behaviour. The movement adopted a cautious and assimi-lationist strategy for a gradual change, firmly anchored in the discourses of liberal democracy, human rights and respectability. The idea was to present homosexuality as a natural and universal phenomenon and homo-sexuals as respectable citizens. Therefore, homophile activists usually dis-approved of pornography and prostitution as well as gender transgression, for which John D'Emilio (1983) labels the movement as 'the retreat to respectability'. The homophile movement was dominated by white men in their thirties and, in a transnational context, by the Dutch organization Cultural and Recreational Centre (COC), founded already in 1946. But there were also some lesbian groups such as the Daughters of Bilitis in the United States (Schultz 2001) and Alle for Een Klubben (All for One Club) in Denmark (Rupp 2011, p. 1021), both founded in 1954. Under the leadership of COC and with the involvement of organizations from Denmark, Italy, Switzerland, the United Kingdom and West Germany, homophile activists established in 1951 the International Committee for Sexual Equality (ICSE), which soon also attracted groups from other countries, including the United States, and existed for about a decade (Rupp 2011, 2014). The strong transnational character of the homophile movement was also facilitated by the emergence of the popular gay and lesbian press, which I will discuss in more detail in Chap. 5.

The late 1960s and the early 1970s witnessed a radical change in the strategies of homosexual activism and a major shift of its symbolic head-quarters from Western Europe to the United States. The Stonewall Riots of 1969 in New York gave birth to gay liberation, a movement which included many organizations in the United States, particularly the Gay Liberation Front (GLF 1969) and Gay Activist Alliance (GAA 1969), but also in other countries, for example, Canada (Vancouver GLF, 1970), the United Kingdom (London GLF, 1970), Australia (Campaign Against Moral Persecution, 1970), France (Homosexual Front for Revolutionary Action, FHAR, 1971) or Spain (Spanish Movement for Homosexual Liberation 1972) (Adam 1999; Llamas and Vila 1999; Weeks 2015). Part of a broader movement of the New Left and the 1968 sexual revolution (Adam et al. 1999b), gay liberation was established in opposition to the homophile movement: it adopted a much more confrontational style of activism (which included demonstrations, occupations, marches, kiss-ins, sit-ins and zaps) and embraced the idea of sexual liberation (which included the explosion of public sex in backrooms, saunas and parties) (Weeks 2015). Yet, similarly to the homophile movement, gay liberation promoted the idea of homosexuality as natural and universal, and practised the identity politics, even though the identity was no longer about respectability but rather about being out and proud, publically affirming and celebrating one's homosexuality.

The history of gay liberation, and the Stonewall Riots in particular, has achieved a near mythical status in the contemporary LGBT movement, both in the United States and abroad. Many authors point to a number of problems such a mythologization of Stonewall entails. First, Thomas Piontek (2006) argues that Stonewall tends to be dehistoricized, as if the homophile movement never happened, and universalized, as if the riots constitute an unquestionable historic moment for everyone, everywhere. He draws on Edward Said's (1975) work on *Beginnings* to explain that the narrative of Stonewall as the beginning of LGBT activism 'risks creating a misleading before-and-after historiography through its overemphasis on discontinuity' (Piontek 2006, p. 10). Second, the history of Stonewall tends to be whitewashed, gaywashed and manwashed, that is, it privileges the representations of white gay men, while erasing the involvement of, for example, black people, lesbians, Filipinos or Puerto Rican drag queens (Bravmann 1997; Manalansan 1995; Piontek 2006). Finally, authors point to the use of Stonewall for producing and reproducing geopolitical structures through what Sharif Mowlabocus (2017) calls the proliferation of the 'Stonewall benchmark', or what Paola Bacchetta (2002) terms the 'from-Stonewall-diffusion-fantasy', which

> forgets the historicity and forms of queer resistance elsewhere, reproduces the dominant US notion of the US as everything universally desirable, reiterates the oppressive US notion of itself as 'the world' (as in 'We are the world...'), and again posits Western notions of identity and activism as the pinnacle. (Bacchetta 2002, p. 952)

The GLF-like organizations were fading away in the mid-1970s (Weeks 2011, p. 67), which James Darsey (1991, p. 48) connects with a number of considerable achievements of the movement and its turn towards a more quiet lobbying, at least in the United States. The new impetus for organizing came in the early 1980s with the outbreak of the HIV/AIDS epidemic. Because at first the epidemic affected mainly gay men in the United States, and because the Ronald Reagan's administration failed to respond to the epidemic appropriately (Brier 2015), it was again the US activists that took a lead. The first groups were formed already in the early 1980s, for example the Gay Men's Health Crisis (GMHC) in 1982 and the AIDS Network in 1983 (Broqua 2015), but it was only in the late 1980s and early 1990s when more militant organizations were established, most famously the AIDS Coalition To Unleash Power (ACT UP) in 1987 and Queer Nation in 1990 (Berlant and Freeman 1992). Following the US example, similar groups were formed in other Western countries, which I will elaborate on in the next section. ACT UP and Queer Nation also gave birth to the transnational queer movement, which developed hand in hand with the postmodern turn in humanities and social sciences, particularly with the emergence of queer theory. Gavin Brown (2015) argues that by the early 2000s, when HIV and AIDS became a somewhat less pressing issue in the West thanks to the introduction of the antiretroviral therapy in 1996, the second incarnation of queer movement emerged, characterized by forming new coalitions with anarchists, anti-capitalists and alter-globalists.

While transnational connections between LGBT activists, at least those located in the West, have existed since the very beginning of their movement, the most powerful manifestation of the global LGBT politics has been the establishment of professional organizations focused on lobbying international institutions through a human rights discourse. The turning point was the foundation of the International Gay Association (IGA, now ILGA) in 1978 in the United Kingdom, the origins of which could be tracked back to the ICSE (Rupp 2011, p. 1036). ILGA was established by a number of exclusively Western organizations but soon extended its reach to all parts of the world and became a truly global organization, now encompassing six regional sub-organizations focused on Africa, Asia, Europe, Latin America and the Caribbean, North America, and Oceania. It has also achieved a considerable success in lobbying many international institutions, including the CoE, EU and UN (LaViolette and Whitworth 1994; Paternotte 2016). Other important organizations focused on international lobbying through human rights discourse include Outright: Action International, established in 1990 as the International Gay and Lesbian Human Rights Commission (LaViolette and Whitworth 1994,

p. 570), and Transgender Europe, founded in 2005 and currently count-ing 105 member organizations in 42 different countries in Europe and Central Asia (September, 2016) (Balzer and Hutta 2014). Importantly, as David Paternotte and Hakan Seckinelgin (2015) note, more recently LGBT rights have expanded beyond LGBT organizations and entered the agenda of an increasing number of civil society and political actors, con-firming the fact that LGBT-related issues have become one of the most prominent issues in world politics.

2.3   THE IMPACT OF HIV/AIDS

The HIV/AIDS epidemic marked a turning point in the globalization of LGBT identities and politics as well as queer wars. According to Altman and Symons (2016, pp. 32–33), 'Without the high-level attention that AIDS generated, much of the subsequent focus on gay rights would have been far less likely'. HIV/AIDS probably originated in central Africa but it was first identified in the United States (McGough and Bliss 2014). In the summer of 1981, the US Centers for Disease Control and Prevention informed about the appearance of an unusual disease among otherwise healthy gay men in New York and San Francisco. Quickly labelled as a 'gay cancer', 'gay plague' or, more professionally, GRID (gay related immune deficiency), HIV/AIDS became strongly associated with gay men as well as some other stigmatized groups such as drug users, sex workers and immi-grants. In the context of virtual ignorance of the epidemic by Reagan's administration, especially during his first term (1981–1985), AIDS service organizations were established in the United States in the first half of the 1980s, including the already-mentioned GHMC in New York but also AIDS Action Committee in Boston, STOP AIDS in Los Angeles and the San Francisco AIDS Foundation (Brier 2015; Patton 2002). As Weeks (2000, p. 153) notes, the early activism drew much on identity politics: 'Individuals were confirming their sense of common identity through involvement in the fight against HIV and AIDS' as well as creating new identity positions such as 'People with AIDS'. Yet, some within the US gay and lesbian community at first downplayed the epidemic, afraid of losing the achievements of the unfinished sexual revolution as well as of remedicalization, or even recriminalization, of homosexuality (Streitmatter 1995; Weeks 2000).

The first tentative steps taken by Reagan against HIV/AIDS during his second term (1985–1989), much provoked by his close friend and famous actor Rock Hudson becoming ill and dying of AIDS in October 1985, favoured conservative solutions (e.g. calls for sexual abstinence and compulsory testing) over the more liberal ones (e.g. promotion of condom use and sex education) (Brier 2015). Disappointed with this late and minimalistic— as well as homophobic and sex-negative—reaction of the administration, some activists established more militant groups such as ACT UP and Queer Nation. ACT UP was formed in New York in March 1987 after a conference at the Lesbian and Gay Community Services Center, where Larry Kramer (ironically, himself rather conservative in sexual matters) gave a passionate speech against the government's sluggishness and community's resignation to the epidemic and made a new call to action. Two weeks later, motivated activists organized a protest on the Wall Street against the immoral practices of pharmaceutical companies and established the first chapter of ACT UP, with other chapters soon popping up in different cities across the United States (Broqua 2015). Queer Nation, in turn, was founded at the ACT UP meeting in New York in April 1990, aiming to expand the scope of the organization by going beyond the narrow focus on HIV/AIDS and including broader public discourses around sexuality (Berlant and Freeman 1992; Brown 2015). These new organizations drew on the repertoire of actions of gay liberation, though instead of kiss-ins they organized die-ins, and shouted out such slogans as 'AIDS Is Not Over', 'Women Die Faster', 'I Am a Fag' and 'Silence Equals Death' (Geltmaker 1992).

US activists had a strong influence on their UK counterparts, who were embedded in a comparable political context of the rise of the New Right (Margaret Thatcher as a prime minister between 1979 and 1990) with its neoliberal devotion to deregulation and individualism as well as moralism. Just as in the United States, so too in the United Kingdom the first HIV/AIDS organizations were formed in the early 1980s and they were community-based groups engaged in identity politics, such as the most famous Terrence Higgins Trust (THT), created in 1983 (Weeks 2000). Five years into the crisis, the Thatcher's government started to implement a more progressive AIDS policy, for example by promoting sex education. Though, it also took some more restrictive and regressive measures such as, most infamously, the 1988 implementation of Section 28 of the Local Government Act, which prohibited the use of public funds for the 'intentional promotion' of homosexuality, but also Thatcher's personal veto on the governmental support for research of sexual behaviour related to HIV/AIDS (Brown 2015; Weeks 2000). Partially responding to these homophobic measures and partially echoing activist developments in the

United States, a direct action group ACT UP London was established in 1989. Soon, other organizations emerged in the United Kingdom, modelled more on Queer Nation rather than ACT UP, such as OutRage!, formed in 1990 out of ACT UP London, and Homocult in Manchester.

Activists in other Western countries too got inspired by the US movement. Most notably, new chapters of ACT UP were formed in other Anglophone countries such as Australia (Power 2011) and Canada (Brown 1997). But the 'diffusion of the ACT UP "brand"', as Gavin Brown (2015, p. 77) calls it, reached far beyond the Anglophone world. Christophe Broqua (2006, 2015) argues that outside the United States, ACT UP achieved the greatest success in France, which was one of the most affected by HIV/AIDS countries in Europe. Here too the early HIV/AIDS activism consisted primarily of community-based groups such as Vaincre le sida (Defeat AIDS), established in 1983, and AIDES (Support), founded in 1994. AIDES was created in response to the death of Foucault, by his partner Daniel Defert, who was inspired by the London THT, which itself was inspired by the New York GMHC (Broqua 2015, p. 64). ACT UP Paris, in turn, was formed in 1989 by Didier Lestrade, a journalist of the popular French gay magazine *Gai Pied* (Gay Foot), and two of his colleagues, who appropriated some of the US actions (e.g. die-ins) and slogans (e.g. 'Silence Equals Death') (Broqua 2006). Chapters of ACT UP were also created in other Western European cities, for example in Barcelona, Berlin and Stockholm, as well as outside the West, for example in Moscow, Tokyo and Warsaw. Abigail Halcli (1999, p. 141) lists more than a hundred of ACT UP chapters existing in 1991, which included groups both within and outside the United States.

The HIV/AIDS epidemic has also worked as a catalyst for the emergence of gay and lesbian identities and politics in 'developing' countries. In one of the early articles on this topic, Matthew Roberts (1995) argues that in many developing countries (in his work mainly those in Asia, the Caribbean, Latin America and sub-Saharan Africa) AIDS prevention work greatly facilitated what he calls 'gay identity migration', for example, through enabling the establishment of the first gay and lesbian organizations (often with the support of foreign and domestic institutions) and strengthening the interaction between Western and non-Western activists. More recent works support the Roberts' argument as well as update it by pointing to the emergence and growing involvement of international institutions and organizations in global HIV/AIDS programmes at the end of the 1990s and the beginning of the 2000s (Altman 1998, 2008;

Broqua 2015; Epprecht 2012; McGough and Bliss 2014). They mention, for example, the Joint United Nations Programme on HIV/AIDS (UNAIDS) launched in 1996, Global HIV/AIDS Program by the World Bank launched in 2000, Global Fund to Fight AIDS, Tuberculosis and Malaria established in 2002, and the United States President's Emergency Plan for AIDS Relief (PEPFAR) created in 2003. Such programmes not only provide an aid for HIV/AIDS prevention work in developing countries, but also influence local sexual norms and practices, for example by sparking the discussion on men who have sex with men (as in the case of UNAIDS) or promoting conservative sexual values (as in the case of PEPFAR) (Broqua 2015). Yet, as Broqua (2015, p. 69) concludes, 'AIDS, as a grassroots cause, seems to be a double-edged sword: it allows some to legitimize new or intensified gay activism in this context, but in some cases it is also used to stigmatize homosexuals as spreading HIV'.

The key impact of the HIV/AIDS epidemic on the globalization of LGBT identities and politics seems to be that the epidemic opened up a new space for discussions on sex in general and homosexuality in particular. And this proves to be true for both Western and non-Western countries. Altman (2001, pp. 76–77), for instance, notes that 'it was the threat of HIV which ended taboos on advertising condoms on TV in countries such as Australia and France' and 'led to more open discussion of masturbation not only in the west but also as part of HIV prevention in countries such as Uganda'. Weeks (2000, p. 157), in turn, emphasizes the impact of the HIV/AIDS epidemic on increasing the visibility of homosexuality in public discourse as well as legitimizing gay and lesbian community—'legitimization through disaster'—who has gradually become an important participant in national and international HIV/AIDS politics. The fears of some members of the community at the dawn of the epidemic that it would squander the gains of the unfinished sexual revolution did not materialize. Quite to the contrary, as Dagmar Herzog (2011, p. 183) argues in her book *Sexuality in Europe: A Twentieth-Century History*, 'Far from marking an end to the sexual revolution, [...] the emergence of the disease and the fight to contain it were accompanied by ongoing sexual liberalization'.

2.4   Postcolonial and Transnational Responses

Largely due to geopolitical structures, the West in general and the United States in particular have played a crucial role in the globalization of dominant modern LGBT identities and politics. This is why some authors, most prominently Altman (1996, 1997, 2001), while somewhat stretching the point, speak of the Westernization, or Americanization, of LGBT identities and politics. In his article on 'Re-orienting Desire' (2002) and a subsequent book *Desiring Arabs* (2007), Joseph Massad puts forward a similar argument in relation to Arab and/or Muslim sexualities. As a student of Said, the famous author of *Orientalism* (1978) and one of the founding fathers of postcolonial theory, Massad primarily focuses on how Arab and/or Muslim sexualities are imagined and acted upon in the West. In particular, he discusses global human rights discourse and international LGBT organizations, which he dubs 'the gay international', to argue that their prime goal is to 'liberate Arab and Muslim "gays and lesbians" from the oppression under which they allegedly live' (Massad 2002, p. 362). The author uses the inverted commas in the phrase 'Arab and Muslim "gays and lesbians"' because he argues that gays and lesbians have never existed in the Arab world. Of course, he does not deny that same-sex contacts between Arabs and/or Muslims have ever existed, but he argues that to view them through the perspective of gay and lesbian identity is to impose on them a Western sexual epistemology. Moreover, Massad refers to Foucault's (1978) concept of 'incitement to discourse' to explain that the gay international, together with a 'small minority' of Arab activists whom he perceives as Westernized, provokes a discourse of LGBT rights and identities where such a discourse has not existed before. This, according to him, results in 'heterosexualizing a world that is being forced to be fixed by a Western binary' and the worsening of the everyday lives of Arab and/or Muslim same-sex practitioners by drawing unwanted attention to them (Massad 2002, p. 383).

Similar rhetoric has also been used in homophobic discourses of some leaders in postcolonial Africa (Aarmo 1999; Msibi 2011), but also in the postcolonial world more broadly (İlkkaracan 2008; Puri 2004), to altogether deny the existence of same-sex desires and practices in the non-West. Margaret Aarmo (1999) gives an example of a speech given in 1995 by the Zimbabwean president Robert Mugabe during which he claimed that homosexuality does not exist in African cultures and has been imposed on them by colonial forces. In a similar vein, a Foreign Minister of Singapore opposed to discuss 'homosexual rights' at the 1994 Human Rights Conference considering homosexuality as a specifically Western issue (Altman 1997, p. 433) and the Saudi Telecom Company protested in 2013 against the introduction of the .gay domain into internet structure, arguing that the internet governance institution should not 'enforce western culture and values into other societies' (Szulc 2015, p. 1531). Other authors (e.g. Hawley 2001; Stychin 1998) additionally point to similar arguments surfacing in early postcolonial studies. Carl Stychin, for example, looks at Frantz Fanon's (1967) famous *Black Skin, White Masks* and notes that

> Fanon (1967, p. 180) asserts that male homosexuality is not indigenous to Martinique, the focus of his attention, which is explainable by 'the absence of the Oedipus complex in the Antilles'. Rather, Martinican men are susceptible to (passive) male homosexual acts only because of economic necessity in Europe. In this way, homosexuality is further constructed as a colonial exploitation and a metaphorical castration of the colonized. (Stychin 1998, p. 62)

Not denying the existence of same-sex practices in the non-West, authors like Altman and Massad argue for the recognition of local conceptualizations of such practices. Similarly, Huseyin Tapinc (1992) identifies four models of 'Turkish male homosexuality', which are related to different sexual practices (penetrating or being penetrated) and assumed gender roles (feminine or masculine), where the 'masculine gay' is the most recent model imported from the West. Natalie Oswin (2006, p. 782), however, challenges the dichotomies of global versus local, Western versus non-Western, and modern versus traditional embedded in such works: 'Altman's Americanization thesis allows only one modern (read: Western) gay identity that can do nothing other than either trump or exist alongside a set of pre-existing traditional (read: non-Western) same-sex practices'. She points out that some in the non-West choose not to adopt Western sexual identities. Instead, they embrace the identities which cannot be understood in relationship to the West but, just as the Western identities, should be considered as modern rather than traditional, in the sense that they too are products of the processes of modernization. Examples include such identities as *bakla* in the Philippines (Manalansan 2003), *kathoey* in Thailand (Jackson 2003), *lesbi* and *waria* in Indonesia (Blackwood 2005; Boellstorff 2007) and *tongzhi* in China (Wah-Shan 2001). To recognize the coexistence of (equally modern) Western and non-Western models of sexual identities in the non-West, and the choice which same-sex practitioners have between them, is one way to acknowledge the agency of non-Western subjects.

Another way to acknowledge the agency is to problematize the process of adoption of Western sexual identities. As I already mentioned in my remark on self-descriptions travelling from the West to the Rest, identities are most often adapted rather than adopted in new cultural contexts. Authors write about such processes as hybridization (Martin 2009; Özbay 2010), creolization (Enteen 2010) or dubbing (Boellstorff 2003), which involve active appropriations of Western sexual identities; as Peter Jackson (2001, p. 5) puts it in his work on Thailand, 'a selective and strategic use of foreign forms to create new ways of being Asian *and* homosexual'. Similarly, responding to Massad's (2002, 2007) work on same-sex practices among Arabs and/or Muslims, Sara Ahmed (2011, p. 131) warns us that '[j]ust as we should not make Muslim "foreign" to queer, we also should not make queer "foreign" to Muslim: either strategy makes Muslims who identify as queer into foreigners'. The so-called global gay lifestyle—as supposedly manifested in generic gay bars, cafés and discos around the world—too is not the same in different places; Jillana Enteen (2010, p. 125) argues writing about Bangkok: 'These commercial venues are not merely replications—they have been altered to reflect the "contact zone" created by their simultaneous international and local circumstances'. Therefore, authors working on the concept of 'gay imperialism' (e.g. Ahmed 2011; Haritaworn et al. 2008) insist on recognizing both Western cultural imperialism *and* non-Western creative agency: Western models of LGBT identities and politics are hegemonic, but they are not simply imposed on the Rest and they are not by default extraneous, irrelevant and harmful imports.

Still, the concept of hybridization and the likes often imply the existence of two essentialized entities, which merge into a new (often treacherously static and fixed) hybrid, as if there ever existed homogenous and isolated Western or non-Western sexual identities. Such conceptualizations tend to create and maintain the difference between the West and the Rest and perpetuate 'the myth that there is knowable, coherent, and decidedly not fluid Western gayness' (Oswin 2006, p. 783), ignoring the differences within the West, for example, between different Western countries. Moreover, in the prototype of the West, the United States, LGBT identities and politics are neither homogenous nor essentialist but heterogeneous and hybridized. For one thing, as many authors show, they have been co-constituted by first- and second-generation immigrants from, for example, Cuba (Peña 2004), the Philippines (Manalansan 2000, 2003), Puerto Rico (Negrón-Muntaner 1999) and Europe (Povinelli and Chauncey 1999, p. 440; see also Binnie's [2016] discussion of the region as assemblage). Therefore, Grewal and Kaplan (2001) as well as Oswin (2006) ask to challenge the dichotomy of global equals Western equals modern versus local equals non-Western equals traditional. The global and the local do not constitute discrete spheres but infiltrate and co-create each other. The global, as Oswin (2006, p. 785) explains, 'is not conceived as a synonym for the West and presumed to exist somewhere in abstract space constantly threatening to impose itself on the local. Rather, it is territorialized as potentially always and everywhere already present'.

Oswin (2006, p. 785) continues by proposing to *de*centre rather than *multi*centre or *re*centre what she calls 'queer globalization'. She suggests to do so by adopting a multiscalar approach, which is at the heart of this book project, as I explained in Chap. 1. Still, I would not use the word 'decentre' here since, in my view, it fails to acknowledge geopolitical structures: after all, there are cities, countries or regions in the world which are more influential in world politics and culture than others in many different respects, which Oswin (2006, p. 788) also recognizes. I think it is more useful to conceive of a globalized world in terms of a network (Crane 2008; Radhakrishnan 2010), with many (more or less influential) nodes and many (more or less heavy) flows in different directions: from centres to margins but also from margins to centres as well as between centres and between margins. A comprehensive multiscalar analysis of such a network seems impossible to me. Still, as Bacchetta (2002, p. 953) proposes, it is possible to address different geographical scales, while pinpointing only one of them, and argues that '[p]erhaps transnational queerdom could be reimagined in terms of a thickly historicized, contextualized, rescaled transversality'. In such an approach, which I also aim to adopt in this book, the focus is on a specific case study, which is analysed within its historical and geographical (or cultural) context, the latter encompassing different scales such as city, country, region and the world. Drawing on my research results presented in this book, I will propose in Chap. 8 to further refine the theoretical framework about the globalization of homosexuality using the metaphor of a network.

2.5   THE FORGOTTEN SECOND WORLD

The brief review of the literature on the globalization of LGBT identities and politics just presented clearly indicates that the literature focuses primarily on the relationship between the First and Third Worlds. The Second World enters the discussions virtually only after it ceases to exist, that is, after the fall of communism in Europe in 1989. The year marks the end of what is often considered as the near total isolation of the Eastern Bloc and the beginning of the process of the Westernization, or Europeanization (Radaelli 2003), of CEE: 'Once the Iron Curtain was gone, "the West" and all it stood for quickly flooded into "the East"', as Herzog (2011, p. 184) puts it writing about the recent history of sexuality in Europe (see also Baer 2009, p. 22). She continues by pointing to far-reaching economic and political changes in the region after 1989; the former related to adopting capitalism (including e.g. the rapid spread of contraceptives, pornography and sex toys) and the latter to establishing democracy (including e.g. the emergence of more free talk about sex in the public). Additionally, Herzog (2011) emphasizes the impact of the opening of the borders between the Western and Eastern Blocs, which has resulted in increased sex tourism and more binational marriages as well as greater mobility of LGBT activists (Binnie and Klesse 2010, 2013). To be sure, all those changes in relation to sexuality did not always meant a shift towards a more substantial progress in issues related to gender and sexuality: for example, Tomasz Kitlinski, Pawel Leszkowicz and Joe Lockard (2005) note that 'the radical expansion of the sex business in Poland [after 1989] reflects not sexual freedom but rampant heterosexism and exploitation of women'.

The process of the Europeanization of CEE, however, did bring some fundamental, if limited, advancements in LGBT-related legislation in the region, which has been linked to the ambition of post-communist countries to join European institutions, especially the EU but also CoE (Baker 2017b; Long 1999; O'Dwyer 2010; Torra 1998). To explain this process, it is necessary to understand that Europe has recently become a 'Rainbow Europe', in the words of Phillip Ayoub and David Paternotte (2014); that is, the concept of Europe has been closely tied to LGBT-friendliness at both political level (e.g. through the EU's accession conditions, see O'Dwyer 2012, 2013; Slootmaeckers and Touquet 2016) and cultural level (e.g. through the Eurovision Song Contest, see Baker 2017a; Gluhovic 2013). Francesca Ammaturo (2015) criticizes this merging of Europe and LGBT, which she dubs 'European homonationalism', arguing that it creates a dichotomy between tolerant and intolerant countries within Europe. Assuming the self-proclaimed position of LGBT tolerance, the EU has begun to formally monitor LGBT issues in candidate countries, particularly through the European Commission Progress Reports (Bilić 2016a, p. 5), and require from the future members to recognize basic LGBT rights such as decriminalization of same-sex acts, equal age of consent for same-sex and opposite-sex acts, no discrimination in employment as well as, more recently, asylum based on sexual orientation (Ayoub 2016, p. 9). Thus, these basic rights have been usually introduced in the post-communist EU countries where they had not been guaranteed before in a top-down fashion, often without the existence of a strong LGBT movement or firm public support for the legal changes (Herzog 2011, p. 184; Torra 1998, p. 73).

When the candidate countries guaranteed the basic LGBT rights and became EU members, it was expected that they would soon introduce further, more far-reaching, LGBT rights. Here, however, the trajectories of different CEE countries have differed substantially. Poland, for example, changed its labour code in 2002 to forbid discrimination based on sexual orientation in employment—one of the conditions of EU accession—and joined the EU in 2004, but has not introduced any other major LGBT rights since then (Szulc 2011). Croatia, in turn, adopted much wider spectrum of LGBT rights, including registered partnership for same-sex couples as well as broad anti-discrimination, hate speech and hate crime provisions based on both sexual orientation and gender identity (Butterfield 2016), which could be partially related to the fact that Croatia joined the EU only in 2013 and was therefore subjected to stricter LGBT-related accession conditions than Poland (Bilić 2016a, p. 13). The differences among CEE countries are additionally explained by different levels of societal homophobia and religious nationalism—be it Catholic as in Hungary and Poland or Orthodox as in Romania and Ukraine (Ayoub 2016; Herzog 2011; O'Dwyer 2013)—but also by different levels of visibility of LGBT-related issues as well as the countries' openness to international organizations and information flows (Ayoub 2016). Authors also point out that the EU's pressure on candidate countries to adopt LGBT rights has provoked some backlashes, particularly in those countries where the rights have been considered as incompatible with national identities, though Ayoub (2016), Jon Binnie and Christian Klesse (2011) and Conor O'Dwyer (2012, 2013) argue that such backlashes nevertheless tend to be short-lived and help to raise the visibility of LGBT issues in public sphere as well as strengthen LGBT movements, which in this context integrate around a clear goal and common enemy, and form new coalitions.

Another key aspect of the globalization of LGBT identities and politics in CEE, as discussed in the literature, relates to the development of professional LGBT activism in the region after 1989. While the first LGBT groups were established in CEE already before 1989, as I will demonstrate in the following chapter, they have managed to obtain an official recognition only after the fall of the Iron Curtain, with the exception of Hungarian Homeros Lambda, registered already in March 1988 (Kurimay and Takács 2016; Takács 2014). Besides, many new LGBT organizations popped up in CEE in the early 1990s (Herzog 2011, p. 186) and, from the very beginning of their existence, closely cooperated with and relied on the support of Western organizations, particularly ILGA but also the Dutch COC and Danish National Association for Gays and Lesbians (Ayoub 2013; Dioli 2011; Torra 1998; Woodcock 2004). Over time, some of the organizations in CEE got professionalized and institutionalized, adopting more ILGA-like modes of activism with the major focus on political lobbying. In Poland, the first officially registered organizations, mainly members of the Association of Lambda Groups registered in 1990 (Adamska 1998, pp. 129–135; Gruszczyńska 2009), dedicated their work to community service and considered themselves as apolitical, while those created at the beginning of the 2000s, particularly the Campaign Against Homophobia (KPH 2001), concentrated on political lobbying and visibility raising, and managed to secure funds from such international institutions as the EU and Open Society Institute (O'Dwyer 2012).

The transnational aspects of the newly established LGBT organizations in CEE have not been limited to importing modes of activism and mobilizing international resources but extended to a deeper, symbolic level. One prominent example is the use of the word 'lambda'—first adopted by GAA in New York in 1970—in the names of some of the new organizations, including Lambda Belarus, created in 1998 (Bortnik 2007); Lambda Warszawa in Poland, created in 1997 (Szulc 2016); and already-mentioned Homeros Lambda in Hungary (Takács 2014). Another example is common references to the 1969 Stonewall Riots in New York: some academics and activists speak of key LGBT developments in CEE countries in terms of 'local Stonewalls' such as 'Polish Stonewall', in reference to the 1985 Operation Hyacinth (Szulc 2011, p. 162) or the KPH's 2003 campaign 'Let's Them See Us' (Leszkowicz and Kitliński 2005, p. 7); 'Romanian Stonewell', in reference to the 2006 pride march in Bucharest (Woodcock 2011, p. 74); or 'Serbian Stonewall', in reference to the 2001 pride march in Belgrade (Bilić 2016b, p. 121). In fact, just organizing pride marches itself can be considered as the Stonewall legacy since the marches were first held in the United States in commemoration of the Stonewall Riots (D'Emilio 2000), though some activists in CEE strategically renamed them 'dignity', 'equality' or 'tolerance' marches

(Baker 2017b, p. 235). In Poland, activists also use Stonewall as a label in the name of the Stonewall Fund, launched by Lambda Warszawa in 2009 (Mizielińska 2011, p. 94), and the Stonewall Group, formed in Poznań in 2015 (http://grupa-stonewall.pl/).

Finally, HIV/AIDS in CEE too is most commonly discussed only after 1989. In the article 'AIDS and the globalization of sexuality', Altman (2008) explains that the region witnessed rapid spread of the epidemic after the fall of the Iron Curtain, which he connects with the greater mobility of people after 1989, the introduction of new market economy and the decline of state services, resulting in increased sex tourism, rapidly growing prostitution and higher rate of needle use. Indeed, while up to the end of 1995 HIV/AIDS did not reach an epidemic level in any of CEE countries, between 1995 and 1997 the number of HIV cases reported in the region increased more than fivefold, reaching about 46,500 cases, with Ukraine, Russia and Belarus accounting for about 90 per cent, and people who inject drugs for more than 50 per cent, of all new cases (Dehne et al. 1999). At the end of 2008, Russia and Ukraine alone had twice as many HIV-infected people as all of the Western and Central Europe combined, with numbers reaching 940,000 and 440,000 cases, respectively (Cohen 2010). Poland has never witnessed such a scale of the epidemic, though the number of officially registered HIV cases has been steadily growing from the mid-1980s to the mid-2010s, with the cumulative number of about 20,000 cases reported at the beginning of 2016, mainly among people who inject drugs and men who have sex with men (Janiszewski 2013; Niedźwiedzka-Stadnik 2016; Rosinska 2006). The emergence of HIV/AIDS activism in CEE is normally dated at the beginning of the 1990s. Authors emphasize that in the context of a widespread political, social and religious opposition to the HIV/AIDS activism in the region in the early 1990s, the activists strongly relied on Western support (Herzog 2011, pp. 185–186; Owczarzak 2010).

2.6 Conclusion

The globalization of LGBT identities and politics has recently become one of the key themes in social and cultural studies of sexuality (Plummer 2008; Weeks 2011). Scholars show how LGBT identities have been constructed, naturalized and universalized as well as adopted, adapted or resisted by many people around the world. Some key factors behind the globalization of LGBT identities include the emergence of human right discourse, global media products and transnational LGBT politics, the latter first centred in Western Europe and later on in the United States. The outbreak of the HIV/AIDS epidemic played a crucial role in the process, especially by increasing visibility of homosexuality in public discourses of many countries and by facilitating the establishment of many new, in some cases first, LGBT organizations, which have been well connected with each other transnationally and actively supported by newly established international institutions and organizations in global HIV/AIDS programmes. As many works in postcolonial and transnational studies point out, the globalization of LGBT identities and politics has never been straightforward, unidirectional or simply anchored in the allegedly homogenous and essentialist West. Nevertheless, it is the West, and the United States in particular, that has occupied the hegemonic position in world politics and culture and therefore it should be recognized as the most powerful and influential agent in the globalization of LGBT identities and politics.

At the same time, the discussions of sexual globalization tend to focus on the relationship between the West and the Rest, where the latter most often stands for the 'developing' or 'postcolonial' world. In CEE, different aspects of the globalization of LGBT identities and politics seem to arrive exclusively after the fall of communism in Europe. Regarding economic and cultural globalization, for example, Joanna Mizielińska and Robert Kulpa (2011, p. 16) write that 'When in 1989 "the communist time" ended and the physical borders began to dismantle, the flow and exchange of material products and ideas really took over', and Véra Sokolová (2014, p. 103) and Scott Long (1999, p. 242) argue that the words 'gay' and 'lesbian' appeared, or became popular, in CEE only in the early 1990s. LGBT activism too is often thought to start to internationalize in CEE after the fall of communism, if only because it was 'severely curtailed' (Torra 1998, p. 74) under communism and 'began in earnest' (Pearce and Cooper 2016) only after 1989. In addition, 'the Iron Curtain was described as the world's largest condom', as Altman (2008, p. 147) reminds us, a statement which is probably not that far from the truth but which often precludes any reflections on how the HIV/AIDS epidemic came into the public discourses of the Eastern Bloc and what role it played in the emergence of LGBT movements in the region. No doubt, just as the Stonewall Riots in New York, so too the fall of communism in Europe did change a lot for LGBTs. I argue, however, that such historical moments are better thought of as 'catalytic events' (Darsey 1991) rather than beginning points of LGBT movement or sexual globalization.

While not denying the special importance of the fall of communism in Europe, such an approach allows us to investigate the continuities of sexual change in CEE and trace the globalization of LGBT identities and politics in the region before 1989. Josie McLellan (2011, p. 9) provides a good example of such an approach when in the introduction to her book *Love in the Time of Communism* she criticizes what she calls 'a false dichotomy between East and West', specifically referring to the discourses about the 1968 sexual revolution. Even though most authors consider the sexual revolution as a primarily Western phenomenon and argue that CEE 'where "real socialism" governed had to wait until the end of dictatorship before a sexual revolution could begin' (Hekma and Giami 2014, p. 10), McLellan (2011) details the profound changes in gender- and sexuality-related issues which happened before 1989 in East Germany, the subject of her book (see also Herzog 2008). Challenging the false dichotomy between the Western and Eastern Blocs, McLellan (2011), but also Berry Adam (2001), lists a number of similar larger socio-economic processes in both blocs—such as industrialization, urbanization and secularization—which fostered some similar changes in gender- and sexuality-related issues. She also points to the important Western influences in East Germany, ranging 'from the ideology of gay liberation to the photography of Helmut Newton' (McLellan 2011, p. 16). Contrary to what the literature on sexual globalization suggests, the Eastern Bloc was not suspended in time—or 'set in aspic', as McLellan (2011, p. 21) puts it—nor was it completely isolated from the outside world. The effects of the globalization of LGBT identities and politics in CEE can be traced much further back before 1989. By following and charting these traces in the rest of this book, focusing primarily on the 1980s in Poland, I hope to open up a space for a broader scholarship on transnationalism and sexuality in the Eastern Bloc.

BIBLIOGRAPHY

Aarmo, M. (1999). How homosexuality became "un-African": The case of Zimbabwe. In E. Blackwood & S. E. Wieringa (Eds.), *Female desires: Same-sex relations and transgender practices across cultures* (pp. 255–280). New York: Columbia University Press.

Adam, B. D. (1999). Moral regulation and the disintegrating Canadian state. In B. D. Adam, J. W. Duyvendak, & A. Krouwel (Eds.), *The global emergence of gay and lesbian politics* (pp. 12–29). Philadelphia: Temple University Press.

Adam, B. D. (2001). Globalization and the mobilization of gay and lesbian communities. In P. Hamel, H. Lustiger-Thaler, J. Nederveen Pieterse, & S. Roseneil (Eds.), *Globalization and social movements* (pp. 166–179). Basingstoke: Palgrave.

Adam, B. D., Duyvendak, J. W., & Krouwel, A. (1999a). Gay and lesbian movements beyond borders? National imprints of a worldwide movement. In B. D. Adam, J. W. Duyvendak, & A. Krouwel (Eds.), *The global emergence of gay and lesbian politics* (pp. 344–371). Philadelphia: Temple University Press.

Adam, B. D., Duyvendak, J. W., & Krouwel, A. (1999b). Introduction. In B. D. Adam, J. W. Duyvendak, & A. Krouwel (Eds.), *The global emergence of gay and lesbian politics* (pp. 1–11). Philadelphia: Temple University Press.

Adam, B. D., Duyvendak, J. W., & Krouwel, A. (Eds.). (1999c). *The global emergence of gay and lesbian politics*. Philadelphia: Temple University Press.

Adamska, K. (1998). *Ludzie obok: Lesbijki i geje w Polsce*. Toruń: Pracownia Duszycki.

Aggleton, P., Boyce, P., Moore, H. L., & Parker, R. (Eds.). (2012). *Understanding global sexualities: New frontiers*. New York: Routledge.

Ahmed, S. (2011). Problematic proximities: Or why critiques of gay imperialism matter. *Feminist Legal Studies, 19*(2), 119–132.

Alexander, J. (2002). Introduction to special issue: Queer webs: Representations of LGBT people and communities on the World Wide Web. *International Journal of Sexuality and Gender Studies, 7*(2/3), 77–84.

Altman, D. (1996). Rupture or continuity? The internationalization of gay identities. *Social Text, 48*(3), 77–94.

Altman, D. (1997). Global gaze/global gays. *GLQ: A Journal of Lesbian and Gay Studies, 3*(4), 417–436.

Altman, D. (1998). Globalization and the "AIDS industry". *Contemporary Politics, 4*(3), 233–245.

Altman, D. (2001). *Global sex*. Chicago: University of Chicago Press.

Altman, D. (2008). AIDS and the globalization of sexuality. *Social Identities, 14*(2), 145–160.

Altman, D., & Symons, J. (2016). *Queer wars*. Cambridge: Polity.

Ammaturo, F. (2015). The "Pink Agenda": Questioning and challenging European homonationalist sexual citizenship. *Sociology, 49*(6), 1151–1166.

Ayoub, P. M. (2013). Cooperative transnationalism in contemporary Europe: Europeanization and political opportunities for LGBT mobilization in the European Union. *European Political Science Review, 5*(2), 279–310.

Ayoub, P. M. (2016). *When states come out: Europe's sexual minorities and the politics of visibility*. New York: Cambridge University Press.

Ayoub, P. M., & Paternotte, D. (2014). Introduction. In P. M. Ayoub & D. Paternotte (Eds.), *LGBT activism and the making of Europe: A rainbow Europe?* (pp. 1–25). Basingstoke: Palgrave Macmillan.

Bacchetta, P. (2002). Rescaling transnational "queerdom": Lesbian and "lesbian" identitary-positionalities in Delhi in the 1980s. *Antipode, 34*(5), 947–973.

Baer, B. J. (2009). *Other Russias: Homosexuality and the crisis of post-Soviet identity.* New York: Palgrave Macmillan.

Baim, T. (2012). Gay news: In the beginning. In T. Baim (Ed.), *Gay press, gay power: The growth of LGBT community newspapers in America* (pp. 79–140). Chicago: Prairie Avenue Productions and Windy City Media Group.

Baker, C. (2017a). The "Gay Olympics"? The Eurovision song contest and the politics of LGBT/European belonging. *European Journal of International Relations, 23*(1), 97–121.

Baker, C. (2017b). Transnational "LGBT" politics after the Cold War and implications for gender history. In C. Baker (Ed.), *Gender in twentieth-century Eastern Europe and the USSR* (pp. 228–251). London: Palgrave Macmillan.

Balzer, C., & Hutta, J. S. (2014). Tran networking in the European vortex: Between advocacy and grassroots politics. In P. M. Ayoub & D. Paternotte (Eds.), *LGBT activism and the making of Europe: A rainbow Europe?* (pp. 171–192). Basingstoke: Palgrave Macmillan.

Beachy, R. (2014). *Gay Berlin: Birth place of a modern identity.* New York: Knopf Doubleday.

Berlant, L., & Freeman, E. (1992). Queer nationality. *Boundary 2, 19*(1), 149–180.

Bilić, B. (2016a). Europeanisation, LGBT activism, and non-heteronormativity in the post-Yugoslav space: An introduction. In B. Bilić (Ed.), *LGBT activism and Europeanisation in the post-Yugoslav space: On the rainbow way to Europe* (pp. 1–22). London: Palgrave Macmillan.

Bilić, B. (2016b). Europe ♥ Gays? Europeanisation and pride parades in Serbia. In B. Bilić (Ed.), *LGBT activism and Europeanisation in the post-Yugoslav space: On the rainbow way to Europe* (pp. 117–153). London: Palgrave Macmillan.

Binnie, J. (2004). *The globalization of sexuality.* London: Sage.

Binnie, J. (2016). Critical queer regionality and LGBTQ politics in Europe. *Gender, Place & Culture: A Journal of Feminist Geography, 23*(11), 1631–1642.

Binnie, J., & Klesse, C. (2010). Transnational geographies of activism around lesbian, gay, bisexual, transgender and queer politics in Poland. *Dialogue and Universalism, 20*(5–6), 41–49.

Binnie, J., & Klesse, C. (2011). Researching transnational activism around LGBTQ politics in Central and Eastern Europe: Activist solidarities and spatial imaginings. In R. Kulpa & J. Mizielińska (Eds.), *De-centring Western sexualities: Central and Eastern European perspectives* (pp. 107–129). Farnham: Ashgate.

Binnie, J., & Klesse, C. (2013). "Like a bomb in the gasoline station": East-West migration and transnational activism around gay, lesbian, bisexual, transgender and queer politics in Poland. *Journal of Ethnic and Migration Studies, 39*(7), 1107–1124.

Blackwood, E. (2005). Transnational sexualities in one place: Indonesian readings. *Gender and Society, 19*(2), 221–242.

Boellstorff, T. (2003). I knew it was me: Mass media, "globalization," and lesbian and gay Indonesians. In C. Berry, F. Martin, & A. Yue (Eds.), *Mobile cultures: New media in queer Asia* (pp. 21–51). Durham: Duke University Press.

Boellstorff, T. (2007). *A coincidence of desires: Anthropology, queer studies, Indonesia.* Durham: Duke University Press.

Bortnik, V. (2007). Hate crimes against lesbian, gay and bisexual people in Belarus. In R. Kuhar & J. Takács (Eds.), *Beyond the pink curtain: Everyday life of LGBT people in Eastern Europe* (pp. 363–375). Ljubljana: Peace Institute.

Bravmann, S. (1997). *Queer fictions of the past: History, culture, and difference.* Cambridge: Cambridge University Press.

Brier, J. (2015). Reagan and AIDS. In A. L. Johns (Ed.), *A companion to Ronald Reagan* (pp. 221–237). Malden: Wiley Blackwell.

Broqua, C. (2006). *Agir pour ne pas mourir! Act Up, les homosexuels et le sida.* Paris: Presses de Sciences Po.

Broqua, C. (2015). AIDS activism from North to global. In D. Paternotte & M. Tremblay (Eds.), *The Ashgate research companion to lesbian and gay activism* (pp. 59–72). Farnham: Ashgate.

Brown, G. (2015). Queer movement. In D. Paternotte & M. Tremblay (Eds.), *The Ashgate research companion to lesbian and gay activism* (pp. 73–86). Farnham: Ashgate.

Brown, M. P. (1997). *RePlacing citizenship: AIDS activism and radical democracy.* New York: Guilford Press.

Buffington, R. M., Luibhéid, E., & Guy, D. J. (Eds.). (2014). *A global history of sexuality: The modern era.* Chichester: Wiley Blackwell.

Butterfield, N. (2016). Discontents of professionalization: Sexual politics and activism in Croatia in the context of EU accession. In B. Bilić (Ed.), *LGBT activism and Europeanisation in the post-Yugoslav space: On the rainbow way to Europe* (pp. 23–58). London: Palgrave Macmillan.

Chávez, K. R. (2013). Pushing boundaries: Queer intercultural communication. *Journal of International and Intercultural Communication, 6*(2), 83–95.

Churchill, D. S. (2008). Transnationalism and homophile political culture in the postwar decades. *GLQ: A Journal of Lesbian and Gay Studies, 15*(1), 31–66.

Cohen, J. (2010). Late for the epidemic: HIV/AIDS in Eastern Europe. *Science, 329*(5988), 160, 162–164.

Corrêa, S. (1997). From reproductive health to sexual rights achievements and future challenges. *Reproductive Health Matters, 5*(10), 107–116.

Crane, D. (2008). Globalization and cultural flows/networks. In T. Bennett & J. Frow (Eds.), *The SAGE handbook of cultural analysis* (pp. 359–381). London: Sage.

Cruz-Malavé, A., & Manalansan, M. F., IV. (2002a). Introduction: Dissident sexualities/alternative globalisms. In A. Cruz-Malavé & M. F. Manalansan, IV (Eds.), *Queer globalizations* (pp. 1–10). New York: NYU Press.

Cruz-Malavé, A., & Manalansan, M. F., IV. (Eds.). (2002b). *Queer globalizations.* New York: NYU Press.

Darsey, J. (1991). From "Gay is Good" to the scourge of AIDS: The evolution of gay liberation rhetoric, 1977–1990. *Communication Studies, 42*(1), 43–66.

Dehne, K. L., Khodakevich, L., Hamers, F. F., & Schwartlander, B. (1999). The HIV/AIDS epidemic in Eastern Europe: Recent patterns and trends and their implications for policy-making. *AIDS, 13*(7), 741–749.

D'Emilio, J. (1983). *Sexual politics, sexual communities: The making of a homosexual minority in the United States, 1940–1970.* Chicago: University of Chicago Press.

D'Emilio, J. (1992). *Making trouble: Essays on gay history, politics, and the university.* New York: Routledge.

D'Emilio, J. (2000). Cycles of change, questions of strategy: The gay and lesbian movement after fifty years. In C. A. Rimmerman, K. D. Wald, & C. Wilcox (Eds.), *The politics of gay rights* (pp. 31–54). Chicago: The University of Chicago Press.

Dioli, I. (2011). From globalization to Europeanization——And then? Transnational influences in lesbian activism of the Western Balkans. *Journal of Lesbian Studies, 15*(3), 311–323.

Donham, D. (1998). Freeing South Africa: The "modernization" of male-male sexuality in Soweto. *Cultural Anthropology, 13*(1), 3–21.

Dose, R. (2003). The World League for Sexual Reform: Some possible approaches. *Journal of the History of Sexuality, 12*(1), 1–15.

Enteen, J. B. (2010). *Virtual English: Queer internets and digital creolization.* New York: Routledge.

Epprecht, M. (2012). Sexual minorities, human rights and public health strategies in Africa. *African Affairs, 111*(443), 223–243.

Fanon, F. (1967). *Black skin, white masks.* New York: Grove.

Foucault, M. (1978). *The history of sexuality, Volume 1: An introduction.* New York: Pantheon Books.

Gawin, M., & Crozier, I. (2006). Światowa Liga Reformy Seksualnej w latach międzywojennych w Anglii i w Polsce. In A. Żarnowska & A. Szwarc (Eds.), *Kobieta i rewolucja obyczajowa. Społeczno-kulturowe aspekty seksualności. Wiek XIX i XX* (pp. 311–334). Warszawa: Wydawnictwo DiG.

Geltmaker, T. (1992). The Queer Nation Acts Up: Health care, politics, and sexual diversity in the County of Angels. *Environment and Planning D: Society and Space, 10*(6), 609–650.

Gluhovic, M. (2013). Sing for democracy: Human rights and sexuality discourse in the Eurovision Song Contest. In K. Fricker & M. Gluhovic (Eds.), *Performing the "New" Europe: Identities, feelings, and politics in the Eurovision song contest* (pp. 194–217). Basingstoke: Palgrave Macmillan.

Görkemli, S. (2010). Legato and practices of "sexual literacy" in Turkey. *Reflections, 9*(2), 21–43.

Grewal, I., & Kaplan, C. (2001). Global identities: Theorizing transnational studies of sexuality. *GLQ: A Journal of Lesbian and Gay Studies, 7*(4), 663–679.

Gruszczyńska, A. (2009). Sowing the seeds of solidarity in public space: Case study of the Poznan March of equality. *Sexualities, 12*(3), 312–333.

Halcli, A. (1999). AIDS, anger and activism: ACT UP as a social movement organization. In J. Freeman & V. Johnson (Eds.), *Waves of protest: Social movements since the sixties* (pp. 135–150). Lanham: Rowman & Littlefield.

Haritaworn, J., Tauqir, T., & Erdem, E. (2008). Gay imperialism: Gender and sexuality discourse in the war on terror. In A. Kuntsman & M. Esperanza (Eds.), *Out of place: Interrogating silences in queerness/raciality* (pp. 71–95). New York: Raw Nerve Books.

Hawley, J. C. (2001). Introduction. In J. C. Hawley (Ed.), *Postcolonial, queer: Theoretical intersections* (pp. 1–18). Albany: SUNY Press.

Healey, D. (1993). The Russian revolution and the decriminalisation of homosexuality. *Revolutionary Russia, 6*(1), 26–54.

Healey, D. (2002). Homosexual existence and existing socialism. New light on the repression of male homosexuality in Stalin's Russia. *GLQ: A Journal of Lesbian and Gay Studies, 8*(3), 349–378.

Heinz, B., Gu, L., Inuzuka, A., & Zender, R. (2002). Under the rainbow flag: Webbing global gay identities. *International Journal of Sexuality and Gender Studies, 7*(2/3), 107–124.

Hekma, G. (2015). Sodomy, effeminacy, identity: Mobilizations for same-sexual loves and practices before the Second World War. In D. Paternotte & M. Tremblay (Eds.), *The Ashgate research companion to lesbian and gay activism* (pp. 1–29). Farnham: Ashgate.

Hekma, G., & Giami, A. (2014). Sexual revolutions: An introduction. In G. Hekma & A. Giami (Eds.), *Sexual revolutions* (pp. 1–24). Basingstoke: Palgrave Macmillan.

Herzog, D. (2008). East Germany's sexual evolution. In K. Pence & P. Betts (Eds.), *Socialist modern: East German everyday culture and politics* (pp. 71–95). Ann Arbor: University of Michigan Press.

Herzog, D. (2011). *Sexuality in Europe: A twentieth-century history*. Cambridge: Cambridge University Press.

Hildebrandt, A. (2014). Routes to decriminalization: A comparative analysis of the legalization of same-sex sexual acts. *Sexualities, 17*(1/2), 230–253.

Huebner, K. (2010). The whole world revolves around it: Sex education and sex reform in First Republic Czech print media. *Aspasia, 4*, 25–48.

İlkkaracan, P. (2008). Introduction: Sexuality as a contested political domain in the Middle East. In P. İlkkaracan (Ed.), *Deconstructing sexuality in the Middle East: Challenges and discourses* (pp. 1–16). Aldershot: Ashgate.

Jackson, J. (2015). The homophile movement. In D. Paternotte & M. Tremblay (Eds.), *The Ashgate research companion to lesbian and gay activism* (pp. 31–44). Farnham: Ashgate.

Jackson, P. A. (2001). Pre-gay, post-queer: Thai perspectives on proliferating gender/sex diversity in Asia. *Journal of Homosexuality, 40*(3–4), 1–25.

Jackson, P. A. (2003). Performative genders, perverse desires: A bio-history of Thailand's same-sex and transgender cultures. *Intersections: Gender, History and Culture in the Asian Context*, 9. Retrieved March 11, 2017, from http://intersections.anu.edu.au/issue9/jackson.html

Jagose, A. (1996). *Queer theory: An introduction*. Victoria: Melbourne University Press.

Janiszewski, J. (2013). *Kto w Polsce ma HIV?* Warszawa: Wydawnictwo Krytyki Politycznej.

Kirby, M. (2013). The sodomy offence: England's least lovely criminal law export? In C. Lennox & M. Waites (Eds.), *Human rights, sexual orientation and gender identity in The Commonwealth: Struggles for decriminalisation and change* (pp. 61–82). London: School of Advanced Study, University of London.

Kitlinski, T., Leszkowicz, P., & Lockard, J. (2005). Poland's transition: From Communism to fundamentalist hetero-sex. *Bad Subjects, 72*. Retrieved March 8, 2017, from http://bad.eserver.org/issues/2005/72/kitlinskileszkowiczlockard.html

Kollman, K., & Waites, M. (2009). The global politics of lesbian, gay, bisexual and transgender human rights: An introduction. *Contemporary Politics, 15*(1), 1–17.

Kościańska, A. (2016). Sex on equal terms? Polish sexology on women's emancipation and "good sex" from the 1970s to the present. *Sexualities, 19*(1/2), 236–256.

Kurimay, A., & Takács, J. (2016). Emergence of the Hungarian homosexual movement in late refrigerator socialism. *Sexualities*. Published online before print. Retrieved February 26, 2017, from http://journals.sagepub.com/doi/abs/10.1177/1363460716665786?journalCode=sexa

LaViolette, N., & Whitworth, S. (1994). No safe haven: Sexuality as a universal human right and gay and lesbian activism in international politics. *Millennium—Journal of International Studies, 23*(3), 563–588.

Leap, W., & Boellstorff, T. (Eds.). (2004). *Speaking in queer tongues: Globalization and gay language*. Urbana: University of Illinois Press.

Leszkowicz, P., & Kitliński, T. (2005). *Miłość i demokracja: Rozważania o kwestii homoseksualnej w Polsce*. Kraków: Aureus.

Llamas, R., & Vila, F. (1999). Passion for life: A history of the lesbian and gay movement in Spain. In B. D. Adam, J. W. Duyvendak, & A. Krouwel (Eds.), *The global emergence of gay and lesbian politics* (pp. 214–241). Philadelphia: Temple University Press.

Long, S. (1999). Gay and lesbian movements in Eastern Europe: Romania, Hungary, and the Czech Republic. In B. D. Adam, J. W. Duyvendak, & A. Krouwel (Eds.), *The global emergence of gay and lesbian politics: National imprints of a worldwide movement* (pp. 242–265). Philadelphia: Temple University Press.

Manalansan, M. F., IV. (1995). In the shadows of Stonewall: Examining gay transnational politics and the diasporic dilemma. *GLQ: A Journal of Lesbian and Gay Studies, 2*(4), 425–438.

Manalansan, M. F., IV. (2000). Diasporic deviants/divas: How Filipino gay transmigrants "play with the world". In C. Patton & B. Sánchez-Eppler (Eds.), *Queer diasporas* (pp. 183–203). Durham: Duke University Press.

Manalansan, M. F., IV. (2003). *Global divas: Filipino gay men in the diaspora.* Durham: Duke University Press.

Marhoefer, L. (2015). *Sex and the Weimar Republic: German homosexual emancipation and the rise of the Nazis.* Toronto: University of Toronto Press.

Martin, F. (2009). That global feeling: Sexual subjectivities and imagined geographies in Chinese-language lesbian cyberspaces. In G. Goggin & M. McLelland (Eds.), *Internationalizing internet studies: Beyond anglophone paradigms* (pp. 285–301). New York: Routledge.

Massad, J. A. (2002). Re-orienting desire: The gay international and the Arab world. *Public Culture, 14*(2), 361–385.

Massad, J. A. (2007). *Desiring Arabs.* Chicago: The University of Chicago Press.

McGough, L. J., & Bliss, K. E. (2014). Sex and disease from syphilis to AIDS. In R. M. Buffington, E. Luibhéid, & D. J. Guy (Eds.), *A global history of sexuality: The modern era* (pp. 89–118). Chichester: Wiley Blackwell.

McIntosh, M. (1968). The homosexual role. *Social Problems, 16*(2), 182–192.

McLellan, J. (2011). *Love in the time of communism: Intimacy and sexuality in the GDR.* Cambridge: Cambridge University Press.

Mizielińska, J. (2011). Travelling ideas, travelling times: On the temporalities of LGBT and queer politics in Poland and the West. In R. Kulpa & J. Mizielińska (Eds.), *De-centring Western sexualities: Central and Eastern European perspectives* (pp. 85–105). Farnham: Ashgate.

Mizielińska, J., & Kulpa, R. (2011). "Contemporary peripheries": Queer studies, circulation of knowledge and East/West divide. In R. Kulpa & J. Mizielińska (Eds.), *De-centring Western sexualities: Central and Eastern European perspectives* (pp. 11–26). Farnham: Ashgate.

Mowlabocus, S. (2017). Afterword: Writing at the precipice. In A. Dhoest, L. Szulc, & B. Eeckhout (Eds.), *LGBTQs, media and culture in Europe* (pp. 277–285). New York: Routledge.

Msibi, T. (2011). The lies we have been told: On (homo) sexuality in Africa. *Africa Today, 58*(1), 54–77.

Negrón-Muntaner, F. (1999). When I was a Puerto Rican lesbian: Meditations on *Brincando el charco: Portrait of a Puerto Rican*. *GLQ: A Journal of Lesbian and Gay Studies, 5*(4), 511–526.

Nesvig, M. (2001). The complicated terrain of Latin American homosexuality. *Hispanic American Historical Review, 81*(3–4), 689–729.

Niedźwiedzka-Stadnik, M. (2016). Ostatnie 10 lat epidemii HIV w Polsce— Kluczowa rola osób starszych w transmisji nowych zakażeń? *Kontra: Biuletyn Krajowego Centrum ds AIDS, 2*(68), 1–3.

O'Dwyer, C. (2010). From conditionality to persuasion? Europeanization and the rights of sexual minorities in post-accession Poland. *European Integration, 32*(3), 229–247.

O'Dwyer, C. (2012). Does the EU help or hinder gay-rights movements in post-communist Europe? The case of Poland. *East European Politics, 28*(4), 332–352.

O'Dwyer, C. (2013). Gay rights and political homophobia in postcommunist Europe: Is there an "EU effect"? In M. L. Weiss & M. J. Bosia (Eds.), *Global homophobia: States, movements and the politics of oppression* (pp. 103–126). Urbana: University of Illinois Press.

Oswin, N. (2006). Decentering queer globalization: Diffusion and the "global gay". *Environment and Planning D: Society and Space, 24*(5), 777–790.

Owczarzak, J. (2010). Activism, NGOs, and HIV prevention in postsocialist Poland: The role of "anti-politics". *Human Organization, 69*(2), 200–211.

Özbay, C. (2010). Nocturnal queers: Rent boys' masculinity in Istanbul. *Sexualities, 13*(5), 645–663.

Padilla, M. B., Hirsch, J. S., Muñoz-Laboy, M., Sember, R. E., & Parker, R. G. (Eds.). (2012). *Love and globalization: Transformations of intimacy in the contemporary world*. Nashville: Vanderbilt University Press.

Parker, R., Garcia, J., & Buffington, R. M. (2014). Sexuality and the contemporary world: Globalization and sexual rights. In R. M. Buffington, E. Luibhéid, & D. J. Guy (Eds.), *A global history of sexuality: The modern era* (pp. 221–260). Wiley Blackwell: Chichester.

Paternotte, D. (2016). The NGOization of LGBT activism: ILGA-Europe and the Treaty of Amsterdam. *Social Movement Studies, 15*(4), 388–402.

Paternotte, D., & Seckinelgin, H. (2015). "Lesbian and gay rights are human rights": Multiple globalizations and LGBTI activism. In D. Paternotte & M. Tremblay (Eds.), *The Ashgate research companion to lesbian and gay activism* (pp. 209–223). Farnham: Ashgate.

Patton, C. (2002). *Globalizing AIDS*. Minneapolis: University of Minnesota Press.

Pearce, S. C., & Cooper, A. (2016). LGBT activism in Eastern and Central Europe. In N. Naples (Ed.), *The Wiley Blackwell encyclopedia of gender and sexuality studies*. Retrieved September 8, 2016, from http://onlinelibrary.wiley.com/doi/10.1002/9781118663219.wbegss707/abstract

Peña, S. (2004). *Pájaration* and transculturation: Language and meaning in Miami's Cuban American gay worlds. In W. Leap & T. Boellstorff (Eds.), *Speaking in queer tongues: Globalization and gay languages* (pp. 231–250). Urbana: University of Illinois Press.

Petchesky, R. (2000). Sexual rights: Inventing a concept, mapping an international practice. In R. Parker, R. Barbosa, & P. Aggleton (Eds.), *Framing the sexual subject: The politics of gender, sexuality and power* (pp. 81–103). Berkeley: University of California Press.

Phillips, O. (2000). Constituting the global gay. In C. Stychin & D. Herman (Eds.), *Sexuality in the legal area* (pp. 17–34). London: The Athlone Press.

Piontek, T. (2006). *Queering gay and lesbian studies.* Urbana: University of Illinois Press.

Plummer, K. (Ed.). (1981). *The making of the modern homosexual.* London: Hutchinson.

Plummer, K. (2008). Studying sexualities for a better world? Ten years of *Sexualities. Sexualities, 11*(1–2), 7–22.

Plummer, K. (2015). *Cosmopolitan sexualities: Hope and the humanist imagination.* Cambridge: Polity.

Povinelli, E. A., & Chauncey, G. (1999). Thinking sexuality transnationally: An introduction. *GLQ: A Journal of Lesbian and Gay Studies, 5*(4), 439–450.

Power, J. (2011). *Movement, knowledge, emotion: Gay activism and HIV/AIDS in Australia.* Canberra: ANU E Press.

Puri, J. K. (2004). *Encountering nationalism.* Malden: Blackwell.

Radaelli, C. (2003). The Europeanization of public policy. In K. Featherstone & C. Radaelli (Eds.), *The politics of Europeanization* (pp. 27–56). Oxford: Oxford University Press.

Radhakrishnan, S. (2010). Limiting theory: Rethinking approaches to cultures of globalization. In B. S. Turner (Ed.), *The Routledge international handbook of globalization studies* (pp. 23–41). London: Routledge.

Rhyne, R. (2006). The global economy of gay and lesbian film festivals. *GLQ: A Journal of Lesbian and Gay Studies, 12*(4), 617–619.

Roberts, M. W. (1995). Emergence of gay identity and gay social movements in developing countries: The AIDS crisis as catalyst. *Alternatives: Global, Local, Political, 20*(2), 243–264.

Rosinska, M. (2006). Current trends in HIV/AIDS epidemiology in Poland, 1999–2004. *Eurosurveillance, 11*(4–6), 94–97.

Rupp, L. J. (2011). The persistence of transnational organizing: The case of the homophile movement. *The American Historical Review, 116*(4), 1014–1039.

Rupp, L. J. (2014). The European origins of transnational organizing: The International Committee for Sexual Equality. In P. M. Ayoub & D. Paternotte (Eds.), *LGBT activism and the making of Europe: A rainbow Europe?* (pp. 29–49). Basingstoke: Palgrave Macmillan.

Said, E. (1975). *Beginnings: Intention and method*. New York: Basic Books.

Said, E. (1978). *Orientalism*. New York: Vintage.

Schoonover, K., & Galt, R. (2016). *Queer cinema in the world*. Durham: Duke University Press.

Schultz, G. (2001). Daughters of Bilitis: Literary genealogy and lesbian authenticity. *GLQ: A Journal of Lesbian and Gay Studies, 7*(3), 377–389.

Sedgwick, E. K. (1990). *Epistemology of the closet*. New York: Harvester Wheatsheaf).

Slootmaeckers, K., & Touquet, H. (2016). The co-evolution of EU's Eastern enlargement and LGBT politics: An ever gayer union. In K. Slootmaeckers, H. Touquet, & P. Vermeersch (Eds.), *The EU enlargement and gay politics: The impact of Eastern enlargement on rights, activism and prejudice* (pp. 19–44). London: Palgrave Macmillan.

Slootmaeckers, K., Touquet, H., & Vermeersch, P. (Eds.). (2016). *The EU enlargement and gay politics: The impact of Eastern enlargement on rights, activism and prejudice*. London: Palgrave Macmillan.

Sokolová, V. (2014). State approaches to homosexuality and non-heterosexual lives in Czechoslovakia during state socialism. In H. Havelková & L. Oates-Indruchová (Eds.), *The politics of gender culture under state socialism: An expropriated voice* (pp. 82–108). London: Routledge.

Streitmatter, R. (1995). *Unspeakable: The rise of the gay and lesbian press in America*. Boston: Faber and Faber.

Stychin, C. F. (1998). *A nation by rights: National cultures, sexual identity politics, and the discourse of rights*. Philadelphia: Temple University Press.

Szulc, L. (2011). Queer in Poland: Under construction. In L. Downing & R. Gillett (Eds.), *Queer in Europe: Contemporary case studies* (pp. 159–172). Farnham: Ashgate.

Szulc, L. (2015). Banal nationalism and queers online: Enforcing and resisting cultural meanings of .tr. *New Media & Society, 17*(9), 1530–1546.

Szulc, L. (2016). Domesticating the nation online: Banal nationalism on LGBTQ websites in Poland and Turkey. *Sexualities, 19*(3), 304–327.

Takács, J. (2014). Queering Budapest. In M. Cook & J. V. Evans (Eds.), *Queer cities, queer cultures: Europe since 1945* (pp. 191–210). London: Bloomsbury.

Tapinc, H. (1992). Masculinity, femininity, and Turkish male homosexuality. In K. Plummer (Ed.), *Modern homosexualities: Fragments of lesbian and gay experience* (pp. 39–49). London: Routledge.

Torra, M. J. (1998). Gay rights after the Iron Curtain. *The Fletcher Forum of World Affairs, 22*(2), 73–87.

Turner, B. S. (2010). Theories of globalization: Issues and origins. In B. S. Turner (Ed.), *The Routledge international handbook of globalization studies* (pp. 3–22). London: Routledge.

Wah-Shan, C. (2001). Homosexuality and the cultural politics of *Tongzhi* in Chinese societies. *Journal of Homosexuality, 40*(3–4), 27–46.

Warner, M. (1993). *Fear of a queer planet: Queer politics and social theory.* Minneapolis: University of Minnesota Press.

Weeks, J. (2000). *Making sexual history.* Cambridge: Polity.

Weeks, J. (2011). *The languages of sexuality.* London: Routledge.

Weeks, J. (2015). Gay liberation and its legacies. In D. Paternotte & M. Tremblay (Eds.), *The Ashgate research companion to lesbian and gay activism* (pp. 45–57). Farnham: Ashgate.

Weiss, M. L., & Bosia, M. J. (Eds.). (2013). *Global homophobia: States, movements, and the politics of oppression.* Urbana: University of Illinois Press.

Woodcock, S. (2004). Globalization of LGBT identities: Containment masquerading as salvation or why lesbians have less fun. In M. Frunză & T. E. Văcărescu (Eds.), *Gender and the (post) East/West divide* (pp. 116–128). Cluj-Napoca: Limes.

Woodcock, S. (2011). A short history of the queer time of "post-socialist" Romania, or are we there yet? Let's ask Madonna! In R. Kulpa & J. Mizielińska (Eds.), *De-centring Western sexualities: Central and Eastern European perspectives* (pp. 63–83). Farnham: Ashgate.

CHAPTER 3

Homosexuality in the Eastern Bloc

In the introduction to their collection *Beyond the Pink Curtain: Everyday Life of LGBT People in Eastern Europe*, Judit Takács and Roman Kuhar (2007, p. 11) point out that 'the most powerful characteristic of "the Iron Curtain" derived from the puzzling fact that no one could really know what was going on behind it.' This lack of information about homosexuality in the Eastern Bloc must have aroused the curiosity of Western activists. Already in its first report, the International Gay Association (IGA, later ILGA) established by Western organizations in 1978, indicated that its committees 'were in charge of investigating the situation in "Socialist (Eastern European) countries"' (Ayoub and Paternotte 2014a, p. 238). Three years later, IGA formalized its efforts and established the Eastern Europe Information Pool (EEIP) programme. The tasks of the programme—to collect information about homosexuality-related issues in the Eastern Bloc, make contacts with local homosexuals and 'encourage the forming of informal interest-groups' (EEIP 1983, p. 2)—were delegated to the Austrian organization Homosexual Initiative Vienna (HOSI), the initiator of the programme. One of the key outputs of HOSI in this regard was annual reports about homosexuality in the Eastern Bloc. The reports were published in English between 1982 and 1989, and constitute an invaluable source of information not only about the homosexuality-related issues in the Eastern Bloc and cross-border flows of information but also about the West-based activists who were producing the reports.

© The Author(s) 2018
L. Szulc, *Transnational Homosexuals in Communist Poland*,
Global Queer Politics, DOI 10.1007/978-3-319-58901-5_3

In this chapter, I will present a comprehensive analysis of all eight EEIP reports published before 1990. My main aim here is twofold. First, I want to highlight the complexity of the Eastern Bloc in relation to homosexuality against the tendency to homogenize and essentialize the region. While it proved to be tempting to lump all communist countries together and make broad claims, for example, that 'prejudice against homosexuality as "a bourgeois degeneracy" became strongly imbued in Communist Parties throughout the world' (Altman 1971, p. 219) or that 'communism left a profoundly destructive legacy in this sphere, bequeathing a history of state repression of gays, lesbians, and bisexuals' (O'Dwyer 2013, p. 103), I will rely on the EEIP reports as well as relevant academic literature to demonstrate the variety of ways in which homosexuality used to be governed and discussed in different Eastern Bloc countries. Second, I intend to emphasize the transnational aspects of the homosexual activism in the region in the 1980s, challenging the myth of the near total isolation of the Eastern Bloc. As explained in the previous chapter, the key role of ILGA and its predecessors (especially the International Committee for Sexual Equality, ICSE) in globalizing homosexual activism has been recognized by many authors in the field (e.g. Ayoub and Paternotte 2014b; Paternotte and Seckinelgin 2015; Rupp 2011), also, though less frequently, in relation to CEE (e.g. Ayoub and Paternotte 2012; Essig 1999, pp. 57–58). Therefore, the EEIP reports, commissioned by ILGA, provide an excellent information source for determining to what extent and how the association managed to penetrate the Iron Curtain and influence the activists in the Eastern Bloc as well as how they perceived the region in relation to homosexuality.

I will start by giving a brief description of the content of the EEIP reports and their production context (authors and sources) drawing on both the reports themselves and my interview with Andrzej Selerowicz, one of the key persons behind the reports. Next, I will discuss their authors' ideological perspective on communism and point to some tensions it produced between activists on opposite sides of the Iron Curtain, especially in the early 1980s. In the following sections, I will present further analysis of the content of the EEIP reports, focusing on three issues commonly raised in the reports: (1) state laws and practices related to homosexuals, (2) public discourses on homosexuality and (3) homosexual self-organizing. As mentioned in Chap. 1, to arrive at a more precise picture of homosexuality in the Eastern Bloc, throughout this chapter, I will complement the information found in the reports by the academic accounts of homosexuality-related issues in the region during the Cold War. Because of my limited knowledge of CEE languages, I will primarily rely on English-language references. Readers who would like to delve into the situation of homosexuals in a particular country are encouraged to consult the bibliographies of the works mentioned in this chapter, which often include entries in CEE languages.

3.1   EEIP Reports

The EEIP reports were produced and published by the ILGA's member organization HOSI. As Phillip Ayoub and David Paternotte (2014a, p. 240) explain, this organization was particularly interested in Eastern Bloc countries 'due to its geographical location in the region—Vienna being further east than Prague, the high number of lesbian and gay refugees in Vienna, and the many informal ties HOSI had to them'. Some of the objectives of the EEIP programme were to collect information about homosexuality in the Eastern Bloc and make contacts with local homosexuals. The key aim, however, was to support the founding of homosexual groups in the region 'according to the Western example' (EEIP 1983, p. 2). As the authors of the reports explained themselves, this proved to be a utopian idea, not only because of the resistance from some communist states but also due to the reluctance on the part of some local homosexuals:

> in those countries with strict anti-homosexual laws (USSR [the Soviet Union], Romania), people are afraid of harassment from the police. This involves not only prison sentences but also imposed resettlement to remote areas. In those countries where a certain amount of liberation prevails, e.g., Hungary and Poland, homosexuals are content with their present freedom and lifestyle, e.g., private parties and nude beaches, and do not want to endanger it by unnecessary manifestos. (EEIP 1983, p. 2)

Therefore, HOSI decided to adopt a more realistic approach of raising 'gay awareness' and consolidating 'the community', for example by distributing a 'mini-newspaper' in Czech, German, Hungarian and Polish (EEIP 1983, p. 2) and organizing sub-regional conferences for homosexual groups in the Eastern Bloc (EEIP 1988, p. 2).

The EEIP reports, prepared for ILGA, were the key outputs of HOSI regarding its task to provide information about homosexuality in the

Eastern Bloc. The first report, published in June 1982, presented an overview of all countries included in the EEIP programme, that is, the Soviet Union and all the aligned countries (Bulgaria, Czechoslovakia, East Germany, Hungary, Poland and Romania) but also Albania and Yugoslavia. The information about the countries was divided into two parts: 'Legal information' and 'General information'. All the subsequent reports were less structured than the first one: instead of presenting a general overview of the entire region, they zoomed in on either particular countries or vital issues emerging at that time in the region, such as the release of the lesbian-themed film *Another Way* (1982) in Hungary (EEIP 1983, pp. 3–5); the organization of the first 'gay culture week' in Ljubljana in 1984 (EEIP 1984, pp. 4–5); or the question of HIV/AIDS arising in the region in the mid-1980s (EEIP 1986, pp. 2–5). As explained in the reports themselves, the strategy behind their structure was to achieve a cumulative effect: the subsequent reports were meant to add new information rather than repeat the already published facts. Partially as a result of this strategy, the reports overrepresented some countries, particularly East Germany and Poland but also Hungary and Yugoslavia, and underrepresented others, particularly Albania, Bulgaria and the Soviet Union (for details see Table 3.1).

Furthermore, the EEIP reports displayed a clear gender bias. Even though the word 'lesbian' was sometimes added to 'gay' in general discussions of homosexuality, the majority of information included in the reports was directly related to men only. Three notable exceptions include a self-introductory letter by the Slovenian lesbian group LILIT, reprinted in the

Table 3.1 Coverage of countries in the EEIP reports (in pages, approximate; 'all total' stands for the overall size of the reports)

Year	1982	1983	1984	1985	1986	1987	1988	1989	Total
All total	13	11	5	22	8	10	13	11	93
Albania	0.5	0.5					0.5		1.5
Bulgaria	1	0.5							1.5
Czechoslovakia	1	0.5		1		0.5		2	5
East Germany	0.5	3.5	1.5	4	0.5	2.5	1	3	16.5
Hungary	1.5	1.5					5		8
Poland	1	3		3.5	2	3	1.5	1.5	15.5
Romania	1.5			3			1		5.5
Soviet Union	1					0.5			1.5
Yugoslavia	1		1.5	3.5	0.5	2	1.5		10

1988 report, as well as two special sections on 'Lesbians in the GDR [East Germany]', submitted by the International Lesbian Information Service (ILIS) (EEIP 1983, pp. 8–9) and a local lesbian activist Birgit Neumann (EEIP 1989, pp. 7–9). The bias was most likely related to the then-existing tensions between women and men within IGA, which added 'lesbian' to its name and transformed into ILGA only in 1986 (Paternotte and Seckinelgin 2015, p. 211). ILIS, originally a secretariat of IGA, was criticizing IGA's leadership for, among other things, the inclusion of misogynist gay male groups. Consequently, as Paola Bacchetta explains, 'many lesbians present at ILGA's 1982 annual meeting in Turin, Italy, myself among them, separated and formed the ILIS' (2002, p. 950) (the conference in Turin actually took place in 1981). The EEIP reports virtually never discussed any issues related to bisexuality, transgenderism or intersexuality.

Central figures behind the reports were members of the HOSI's International Group: Kurt Krickler, who introduced the idea to other HOSI members after the IGA's conference in Turin in 1981; Andrzej Selerowicz, a Polish citizen who immigrated to Austria in the 1970s; and John Clark, a US citizen and partner of Selerowicz. Arguably, Selerowicz was the key person in the team: not only was he the only insider, a native speaker of Polish with great command of German and fair knowledge of English, but also he happened to be employed in an Austrian foreign trade company as a sale representative for CEE, regularly travelling to the Eastern Block: most often to Hungary, quite regularly to Czechoslovakia and Poland, but also to Bulgaria and Yugoslavia. Krickler was mainly responsible for gathering information about East Germany and Clark for translating all the data into English (interview with Selerowicz). Of course, there were also other people involved in EEIP programme, the first report, for example, mentioned additional two forenames: Dieter and Juan (EEIP 1982, p. 13), but the three surely formed the core of the EEIP team. When the format of the reports changed from the general overview of the region to special sections on particular countries and issues, the reports started to additionally include more by-lined articles by guest contributors based in the Eastern Bloc. The examples include a piece on Yugoslavia by Zagreb-based Widmaar Petrovic (EEIP 1987, pp. 5–6) and an already mentioned article on 'Lesbians in the GDR' by Halle-based Birgit Neumann (EEIP 1989, pp. 7–9).

The information sources in the EEIP reports were manifold. For example, to learn about the legal status of homosexuality in Eastern Bloc countries for the first report, Krickler contacted the countries' embassies based in Vienna and, to HOSI's surprise, received a reply from all of them (interview with Selerowicz). However, most of the time the authors of the reports relied on the accounts of local individuals and groups that were involved in some sort of activism or at least were interested in the broader situation of homosexuals in their countries. In limited cases, these sources were clearly identified, as in the examples given in the previous paragraph. Most often, however, they remained anonymous, being labelled simply as 'a gay Hungarian' (EEIP 1982, p. 7) or '"our man" in Bratislava' (EEIP 1983, p. 11). From time to time, the reports also reprinted articles published elsewhere. The 'Introduction' to the first EEIP report itself was an excerpt from the 1977 book *Seminar: Gesellschaft und Homosexualität* (Seminar: Society and Homosexuality) by Rüdiger Lautmann. Other examples include a note on Romania, originally published in the German magazine *Rosa Flieder* (EEIP 1982, pp. 9–10) and an interview with a member of the Hungarian organization Homeros Lambda, reprinted from the Hungarian weekly *KEPES 7* (EEIP 1988, pp. 10–12).

Another source of information was trips of the HOSI members, especially Selerowicz, to Eastern Bloc countries. In the 1983 report, for example, an account on Bulgaria was based on Selerowicz's few-days stay in Sofia and a description of 'Poland under martial law' rested on Selerowicz's two visits to Warsaw. Such trips were especially useful for the countries about which HOSI did not have much information and where it did not have any contact persons. Romania was definitely a case in point. When an anonymous member of HOSI travelled to Bucharest to gather basic information about the situation of homosexuals in the country, his starting points were places listed in the *Spartacus International Gay Guide*, such as the Caru' cu Bere bar on Stavropoleos street and the swimming pool next to the Lido Hotel. While he failed to meet any homosexuals in those places, eventually he did get in touch with a local informer, though under more accidental circumstances:

> I suddenly saw him among the grey masses on a crowded street. His neat appearance, his rather unique sunglasses and the small handbag under his arm made him stand out against the others. For a long time both of us kept looking in the same store window and watching each other. Almost paralyzed with fear—I had been warned about provocateurs—I asked him some stupid question about the time or the street. It turned out that he spoke English and was actually quite nice. He also accepted my invitation to a cup of coffee in a bistro close by. (EEIP 1985, p. 12)

The account continued with a description of an everyday life of a homosexual in Romania from the point of view of the interviewed man.

The majority of information provided in the EEIP reports was accompanied with the disclosure of the information source. Such a transparency increased the reliability of the reports as did a good dose of reflexivity on the part of the reports' authors. An interesting case in point is the description of Albanian legal provisions regarding homosexuality. In the 1982 report, HOSI explained that, at that time, Albania seemed to have the most liberal laws concerning homosexuality in the whole Europe, with no provisions delegalizing same-sex acts and the age of consent set equally for same-sex and opposite-sex acts at 14. At the same time, the authors disclosed that this information was derived from a German translation of the Albanian Penal Code and expressed their doubts about the accuracy of the translation (EEIP 1982, p. 12). In the following report, they returned to that matter and confirmed their previous findings (EEIP 1983, p. 2), which however were not true: Albania did, in theory, decriminalized same-sex acts in 1977 but, in reality, it retained other laws which were used to persecute same-sex acts until 1995 (Hildebrandt 2014; Torra 1998). Nevertheless, the majority of facts presented in the reports, which I checked against the contemporary academic literature in the field, proved to be correct. Apart from occasionally reflecting on their own sources of information, the reports also comprised a rich variety of perspectives, ensured by the inclusion of multiple sources. However, as shown in the previous paragraphs, those sources were quite accidental and their number and quality varied from country to country. Thus, the EEIP reports provided only a scattered, yet substantial, collection of information about homosexuality in the Eastern Bloc.

The EEIP reports were the key but not the only output of HOSI regarding the Eastern Bloc. Most remarkably, in 1984 the organization published a book in German entitled *Rosa Liebe unterm roten Stern: Zur Lage der Lesben und Schwulen in Osteuropa* (Pink Love under the Red Star: The Situation of Lesbians and Gay Men in Eastern Europe, Hauer et al. 1984). The book comprised some information already gathered for the previous EEIP reports but also original contributions about homosexual history and culture in particular countries, for example a chapter on 'Homoerotic themes in Polish 20th-century literature'. *Rosa Liebe unterm roten Stern* was launched at the Frankfurt Book Fair in October 1984 and soon reached the audiences in Western, especially German-language, countries. The authors of the 1985 report declared that the reviews of the book had been published in magazines in Austria, Switzerland and West Germany as well as France, the Netherlands, Norway and Sweden (EEIP 1985, p. 2). Originally, HOSI planned to publish an additional edition of the book in English but, as it explained in the 1986 report, it was unable to find a keen publisher. Apart from the EEIP reports and the book, HOSI was also having a regular column 'Ostreport' (East Report), published in its own magazine in German *Lambda Nachrichten* (Lambda News) (Fig. 3.1).

Fig. 3.1   Cover of the *Rosa Liebe unterm roten Stern* book. Courtesy of IHLIA Amsterdam. Translation: When Friedrich Engels comments: 'I don't find it funny at all...', Karl Marx replies: 'It's outrageous!'

3.2   COMMUNISM AS THEY KNEW IT

Although the work of HOSI on the Eastern Bloc received a lot of acclaim from homosexual activists around Western Europe, it came under criticism from some groups at the other side of the Iron Curtain. A distinctly negative opinion was voiced by Christian Pulz, a member of a working group 'Homosexuals in the Church' organized under the umbrella of the Evangelical Church in East Germany. In his article 'Pink love—not red enough?', published in the West German magazine *Siegessäule* (Victory Column) in 1985 (and reprinted in a EEIP report), Pulz reviewed HOSI's *Rosa Liebe unterm roten Stern*, accusing its authors of 'anti-socialistic sensationalism':

> A distinct anti-communist prejudice stretches through almost all of the articles. Even some of the well-meant articles get caught up in the twilight of a political statement that cannot be accepted by us […] To put it plainly: We lesbians and gay men from the Church working groups of the GDR [East Germany] are basically endeavouring to win sympathy from our society and its socialistic order […] All problems concerning us can only be solved in our context of government or not at all. (EEIP 1985, p. 4)

Pulz continued by calling the book's authors irresponsible and pointing out that their negative attitude towards communism could cause a lot of harm to local activists. By doing so, he articulated the resistance on the part of some Eastern Bloc activists against the 'saving gays' narrative (Bracke 2012), which some Western activists have been accused of in different parts of the world, as discussed in Chap. 1.

HOSI reprinted Pulz's article in the 1985 report together with its official reply, in which the authors rejected the accusation of *Rosa Liebe unterm roten Stern* being 'a slanderous anti-communist piece of garbage' (EEIP 1985, p. 5). On the one hand, they explained that in several places in the book it had been stated that the criticism directed at some Eastern Bloc countries would also apply to some Western Bloc countries and that the legal situation of homosexuals in East Germany was actually more progressive at that time than in Austria or West Germany. On the other hand, the authors maintained that their solidarity with and consideration for homosexuals in the Eastern Bloc cannot be unconditional. They did not see their role as indiscriminately praising all the communist countries but rather as critically reporting on the situation of homosexuals in the region. Their take on communism, as they claimed, had been unprejudiced: 'our attitude towards "true socialism" is a very real one—balanced, pragmatic and non-dogmatic. Our view is clouded neither by blind pro- nor by hateful anti-communism' (EEIP 1985, p. 6).

It would be incorrect to assume that during the Cold War homosexual activists in the West were per se anti-communist. In fact, as Gert Hekma, Harry Oosterhuis and James Steakley (1995, p. 2) note, 'Most gay and lesbian liberation groups that sprang into existence in the wake of the 1969 Stonewall rebellion were radical, leftist, and utopian', which was reflected in their slogans such as the US 'Ho, ho, homosexual—The ruling class is ineffectual' (ca. 1970) or West German 'Brüder und Schwestern, ob warm oder nicht—Kapitalismus bekämpfen ist unsere Pflicht' (Brothers and sisters, whether gay or not—To fight capitalism is our collective job, ca. 1972). This did gradually change as the Cold War progressed due to the communist parties' persistently reluctant attitude towards homosexuality, which often proved to be ambivalent at best and oppressing at worst. Even though, many homosexual activists, both in the East and West, embraced communism and continued to be members of communist parties, including some key ILGA activists such as the Dutch Hein Verkerk and Bram Bol (Ayoub and Paternotte 2014a, p. 238).

In the late EEIP reports, especially those published after HOSI's dispute with East German activists, there were no direct negative statements about communism. However, a clear anti-communist attitude was adopted in the first report. Already on its cover, we find a quote from Dennis Altman (1971) about the prejudice against homosexuality being allegedly characteristic of communist parties 'throughout the world' (EEIP 1982, p. 1). In the introduction to the first report, which was a reprint from a West German book on homosexuality (Brockmann 1977), we read that 'A principle union between Marxist theory and antihomosexuality is not founded. However, the organisational forms and concrete stipulations of the continuing venture at the realization of Marxist socialism have left less room for gay emancipation than in advanced capitalistic societies' (EEIP 1982, p. 3). Besides, authors themselves expressed their unfavourable perception of communism in the description of some countries in the report. For example, when discussing Bulgaria, they commented that 'Anything that does not fit into the framework of communist society (and homosexuality is one of these things) either does not exist or should not exist' (EEIP 1982, p. 4). Such statements alienated some homosexual activists in the Eastern Bloc, such as Christian Pulz and some East German groups, which adopted a more assimilationist rather than confrontational strategy for emancipation, and justified the groups' reluctance towards HOSI's initiatives.

The first EEIP report was quite remarkable for essentializing not only communist ideology, embodied in communist parties and states, but also Eastern Bloc societies. As Francesca Stella (2015, p. 7) reminds us, there has been a still persistent tendency to reify national cultures of the region and attribute inferior qualities to them, under such labels as the 'Soviet mindset' or the 'Balkan mentality'. In a similar vein, the authors of the first EEIP report pointed to the backwardness of some of the Eastern Bloc societies. Thus, the readers of the 1982 report could learn, for example, of Bulgaria that 'patriarchy rules supreme in this typical Balkan country' and that 'these people have just forgotten what freethinking, personal opinions and private lifestyles are' (p. 4); of Yugoslavia that 'the real barrier in the life of a homosexual is, as in Bulgaria, the Balkan mentality and its concept of the macho family man' (p. 13); and of Hungary that it was characterized by 'the relatively low cultural level of the average citizen' and by 'the proud "maleishness" of males (heterosexuals)' (p. 7). In the following report, the readers could additionally learn of East Germany that 'the attitudes concerning the situation of women are comparable to those which were common in the West ten or twenty years ago' (EEIP 1983, p. 8). The latter statement was notable because it not only pointed to the backwardness of East Germany but also juxtaposed it with the alleged progressiveness of the West. In that sense, it clearly exemplifies what Joanna Mizielińska and Robert Kulpa (2011, pp. 17–18) named a 'Western progress narrative', which makes the Western present the Eastern future to be achieved: 'whatever CEE became/is/will be, West had become/has already been/will have been'.

Finally, the EEIP reports indicated that communist regimes themselves tended to present homosexuality as a product of the Western bourgeoisie lifestyle and thus incompatible with communist ideals. Indeed, as Hekma et al. (1995, p. 8) explain, 'Socialists have repeatedly ascribed homosexuality to the "class enemy," contrasting the "manly" vigor and putative purity of the working-class with the emasculated degeneracy and moral turpitude of the aristocracy and haute bourgeoisie'. In EEIP reports, we can find even stronger statements, for example about Eastern Bloc homosexuals themselves internalizing the association of homosexuality with the West: 'Western lifestyle (and the degree of Western tolerance towards homosexuality) is considered evidence of Western decadence even by Bulgarian gays. Communist propaganda has done a good job!' (EEIP 1983, p. 3). In a special section on 'AIDS in Eastern Europe', HOSI additionally reported that not only homosexuality but also HIV/AIDS had been presented by some officials in the Eastern Bloc as a Western problem, which resulted in the denial of any HIV/AIDS cases in some countries in the region, particularly in the early 1980s. A case in point was an interview with the Soviet Union's Deputy Minister of Public Health, Piotr Burgasov, published in the trade union magazine *Trud* (Labour), where the official explained that 'This illness is a social problem that can be closely linked to the sexual freedom tolerated in some circles in the West which is, however, unnatural for our society' (EEIP 1986, p. 2). At this point, it is worth reminding that in the West too homosexuality happened to be attributed to those on the other side of the Iron Curtain, though never to the same extent as in the Eastern Bloc. The classic example is that of the Lavender Scare coupled with the Red Scare in the United States in the 1950s, when homosexuals were conflated with communists, even though most often just by the frequent co-occurrence of the two in the discourse of 'security risks' (Epstein 1994; Johnson 2006).

3.3   State Laws and Practices

The diversity of legal provisions concerning homosexuality in the Eastern Bloc probably best illustrates the complexity of the region in homosexuality-related issues. First of all, we should acknowledge different trajectories of those provisions throughout the time in particular countries. In Romania, for example, the general tendency was to strengthen the anti-homosexual laws as the Cold War progressed. Viviana Andreescu (2011, p. 212) explains that female and male same-sex acts, yet only those which produced a 'public scandal', were criminalized in the country in 1937, with the punishment of six months to two years of incarceration. In 1948, the state introduced punishments for public displays of homosexuality (two to five years of incarceration) and in 1957, it criminalized not only public but also private same-sex acts with the increased prison time of three to ten years, reduced in 1968 to one to five years (Andreescu 2011, p. 212). In East Germany, by contrast, there was a general tendency towards liberalization: while at first the communist state carried over the paragraph 175a of the Nazi legal code, which forbade 'unnatural desire' between men, in 1968 it decriminalized homosexuality by abolishing the infamous paragraph. Yet, at the same time it passed a new law which introduced an inequality in regard to age of consent: 14 for heterosexuals and 18 for homosexuals, both women and men (McLellan 2011, pp. 115–118). In Poland, in turn, same-sex acts were decriminalized as early as in 1932 and has not been recriminalized ever since (Płatek 2009).

The examples just quoted also point to the significant differences in homosexuality-related laws between different Eastern Bloc countries at particular moments in time. One of the aims of the EEIP reports, especially of their early editions, was to map these differences during the twilight of the Cold War. The information was first presented country by country, under the headline 'Legal information'. Most of the time, these sections were short and to the point: they included reprints from relevant legal documents and only sporadically were accompanied by a commentary. The focus was on the current situation concerning (1) the legal status of homosexuality and (2) the age of consent for same-sex acts versus opposite-sex acts.

Regarding the former, the distinction was made between 'simple homosexuality', not qualified in any respect, and 'special homosexuality', related to the laws on, for example, rape, prostitution or sex in public, which explicitly referred to homosexuality. According to the information presented in the first two EEIP reports, simple homosexuality was still illegal in the early 1980s in Romania (one to five years for both female and male same-sex acts), the Soviet Union (up to five years only for male same-sex acts) and parts of Yugoslavia (Kosovo, Macedonia, Serbia, and Bosnia and Herzegovina; up to one year only for male same-sex acts) but also, what was not stated in the reports, in Albania (Hildebrandt 2014; Torra 1998). Countries which did not criminalize homosexuality but provided tougher punishments for homosexuals than heterosexuals for different sex-related offences included Bulgaria, Czechoslovakia, East Germany, Hungary and parts of Yugoslavia (Croatia, Montenegro and Vojvodina). Poland and the Yugoslavia's Republic of Slovenia made no references to homosexuality in their legal documents, since 1932 for Poland and since 1977 for Slovenia, and thus established the strongest legal equality between heterosexuals and homosexuals among all the EEIP countries (for more details see Hildebrandt 2014; Torra 1998).

There were also differences between Eastern Bloc countries in the 1980s regarding the age of consent for same-sex acts. In Albania, Romania, the Soviet Union and parts of Yugoslavia homosexuality was illegal so the age of consent for homosexuals was not an issue, though, theoretically, the age of consent in Albania was set in 1977 at 14 for all sex acts (Torra 1998). Some other countries which had not delegalized same-sex acts as such set a higher age of consent for homosexuals than heterosexuals. For example, as reported in the first two EEIP reports, in Bulgaria the age of consent was set at 21 for homosexuals and 14 for heterosexuals, in Czechoslovakia at 18 and 15, in East Germany at 18 and 14, and in Hungary also at 18 and 14 respectively. In 1988, the Parliament of East Germany passed a change in the penal code evening out the age of consent for homosexuals and heterosexuals (EEIP 1989, p. 11). The Eastern Bloc countries which did not make any distinction in regard to age of consent between same-sex and opposite-sex acts in the early 1980s included Poland and Slovenia, with the age set at 15 and 16 respectively (see also Graupner 2000; Takács 2017; Torra 1998).

The differences in the legal treatment of homosexuals across the Eastern Bloc created a number of transnational problems in the region. One such problem arose when a citizen of Czechoslovakia, where homosexuality was legal except for a few special cases (Seidl 2016), was sentenced to five years of imprisonment for homosexuality during his stay in the Soviet Union, where male same-sex acts were severely punished. From the 1983 report we learn that 'His mother tried everything to help him. After two years her son was finally allowed to be transferred to a Czech prison where he is now serving out the rest of his sentence' (EEIP 1983, p. 11). Another case of transnational nature, though less related to legal provisions, also involved a Czechoslovakian citizen. He planned to go for holidays to the Bulgarian Black Sea coast, a popular summer destination for homosexuals in Eastern Bloc countries. However, when his mother found out about his homosexuality, she denounced him to the police suggesting that his plan was to escape from Bulgaria to Turkey with an inflatable boat. Consequently, as HOSI reported, the man was arrested, interrogated and his luggage searched: 'As it did not even contain an air mattress, he was finally released, but a prohibition to leave the country was imposed upon him because it would be against the Republic's interests that "such persons" represent the CSSR [Czechoslovakia] abroad' (EEIP 1983, p. 11).

The latter anecdote demonstrates that it was not only legal provisions but also very concrete state practices that strongly affected the lives of homosexuals in the Eastern Bloc. A common practice in the region was a surveillance of male homosexuals by police forces and the secret service. Already in the first EEIP report, the authors mentioned the heavy persecution of homosexuals in Romania, where the police officers in plainclothes were reported to 'go to the toilets and whip out their cocks in order to lure gays' (EEIP 1982, p. 10), as well as the formal registration of homosexuals in Poland, which resulted in the creation of state 'pink lists', or 'homosexual inventories' (EEIP 1982, p. 8). In Poland, the practice of registering homosexuals intensified in 1985, when it took a form of a systematic operation code-named 'Hyacinth' (EEIP 1986, p. 3; for more information see Chap. 4). Josie McLellan (2011, p. 134) discusses similar operations in East Germany, conducted in the 1980s by the Stasi under such cryptonyms as 'Operation Brother' or 'Operation After Shave', in response to the nascent homosexual movement in the country, and Denis Sweet (1995, p. 356) points to the existence of a special Stasi office for homosexual affairs in East Berlin, staffed by five full-time officers. Pink lists of suspected homosexuals existed also in Hungary (Takács 2015, 2017), the Soviet Union (Stella 2015, p. 34) and most likely in many other Eastern Bloc countries. Besides, the secret service was also using the technique of honey traps, sending young boys to seduce, and thus discredit or persecute, high-profile individuals such as French philosopher Michel Foucault, during his stay in Poland in the late 1950s (Macey 1993, pp. 86–87), Russian tenor Vadim Kozin (Healey 2014, p. 99) and East German vicar and homosexual activist Eduard Stapel (McLellan 2011, p. 132).

The intensity of authorities' surveillance and oppression of homosexuals differed from country to country. HOSI reported that in Hungary 'the authorities tolerate[d] the existence of the only gay café, and gay activities in steam baths and lavatories' (EEIP 1982, p. 7) as well as they had allowed the registration of the first officially recognized homosexual organization in the Eastern Bloc, Homeros Lambda, in March 1988 (EEIP 1988, p. 8; see also Kurimay and Takács 2016; Takács 2014). In Romania, by contrast, the persecution of homosexuals was particularly brutal. One case received special attention in EEIP reports:

> In July 1987 in the city of Arad, eight men were arrested. Through torture, police were able to get the names of gay friends of the arrested persons. Another 50 people were then arrested. One of the men committed suicide by jumping out of a window at the police station, the others awaited their trails. (EEIP 1988, p. 7)

HOSI continued the account by pointing to the overall tragic situation in the country regarding many aspects of sexuality (especially the pronatalist policies banning abortion and contraceptives, introduced in Romania in 1966 by the dictator Nicolae Ceaușescu, see e.g. Kligman 1992, 1998; Nachescu 2005) and demanding the intervention of ILGA in that particular case that had happened in Arad. ILGA complied and sent protest letters to Romanian authorities, including Romanian embassies in the West. The letters remained unanswered but the men arrested in Arad were released and the trials against them were cancelled (EEIP 1988, p. 8).

3.4   Homosexuality in Public Discourses

Not only the level of state, its laws and practices, but also that of society, its attitudes towards and perception of homosexuality in the Eastern Bloc, fell within the scope of the EEIP reports. There were, however, virtually no data available about the latter and hence HOSI turned to the content of mainstream media, which were believed to do both reflect and influence people's views on homosexuality. The EEIP reports regularly discussed articles, books and films, or the absence thereof, which dealt with homosexuality and were made available to Eastern Bloc audiences. Most of the time, the reports' authors complained about the scarcity of homosexuality-related media content in the region or about the prejudices and stereotypes reproduced in existing media representations. In the 1983 report, for example, they criticized Czechoslovakia for not showing films with homosexual themes—especially the US *Cabaret* (1972), which was reported to be popular in other Eastern Bloc countries—and, more broadly, for providing only limited and biased information about homosexuality: 'The only mention of homosexuality in the past two years in the media was an article in the magazine "100 ÷ 1" about the risks of Herpes, a disease that "is especially wide-spread in the homosexual milieu in Western Europe"' (EEIP 1983, p. 11). In the following reports, however, the authors pointed to some improvements in Czechoslovakia such as the publication of short stories 'with a very positive and open gay subject matter' (EEIP 1987, p. 2) and the appearance of a series of articles in the national youth daily *Mladá Fronta* (Young Front), initiated by an informal group Lambda Praha (EEIP 1989, p. 6). By contrast, East German media were constantly praised for particularly progressive reporting on homosexuality: 'Homosexuals in many Western countries would certainly be happy if their newspapers published such liberal and pro-gay/ lesbian articles as the GDR [East German] media does' (EEIP 1988, p. 4; see also Hillhouse 1990, p. 587).

The breakthroughs in representing homosexuality in mainstream media attracted special attention in the EEIP reports. For the Soviet Union, such a breakthrough was believed to come on 24 March 1987, when the youth magazine *Moskovsky Komsomolets* (Moscow Komsomol) published an article entitled 'Men prefer men', as a part of its series on sex education for young people (EEIP 1987, p. 2). The beginning of the same year also witnessed a boom of positive articles about homosexuality in Polish media, mainly in such weeklies as *Na Przełaj* (Cut Across), *Razem* (Together), *Sprawy i Ludzie* (Affairs and People), *Prawo i Życie* (Law and Life) and *Życie Literackie* (Literary Life) (EEIP 1987, p. 9). Especially the former, which was a Scout magazine, was praised for a series of articles entitled 'Rozgrzeszenie' (The Shrift), authored by Ewa Żychlinska and Mariusz Szczygieł, and motivated by an insufficient sex education in Poland. HOSI reported that

> The feedback was enormous. *Na Przełaj* alone received hundreds of letters from both girls and boys, who were becoming conscious of the fact that they are different, but they do not want to repress these feelings as others did in former generations. (EEIP 1987, p. 9; see also Szczygieł 2009; Więch 2005, p. 261)

In Slovenia, the breakthrough was the organization of the first 'gay culture week' in the Eastern Bloc, between 23 and 29 April 1984 in Ljubljana (EEIP 1984, p. 4). Entitled 'Magnus: Homoseksualnost in Kultura' (Magnus: Homosexuality and Culture), the culture week was organized by the Student Cultural Centre (ŠKUC) and was reported to receive extensive media coverage at both local and national levels (see also Kajinić 2016; Kuhar 2003).

Another crucial, and transnational, breakthrough was the release of the first mainstream film in the Eastern Bloc which openly featured homosexuality. Produced in Hungary and directed by Károly Makk, one of the Hungary's top director at that time, *Egymásra Nézve* (Another Way 1982) told the story of love between two women journalists (both roles played by Polish actresses) in the aftermath of the 1956 Hungarian revolution. The 1983 EEIP report provided detailed information about the film along with a two-page interview with one of the leading actresses, Jadwiga Jankowska-Cieślak, conducted by Selerowicz during one of his visits to Warsaw. In the interview, the actress expressed her scepticism about the tolerance of Polish society at that time, explaining that 'Poles are very prudish, religious and bound to tradition' but Selerowicz replied that the release of the film could serve as a good starting point for changing attitudes towards homosexuality and establishing a homosexual organization in Poland (EEIP 1983, p. 4). Scholars argue that the film used a lesbian plot only as a smokescreen for harsh criticism of the government, but despite that it achieved a cult status among lesbians in Hungary and, to a lesser extent, in some other Eastern Bloc countries (Moss 2007; Moss and Simić 2011; Takács 2014). It also received a great acclaim in the West: at the 1982 Cannes Film Festival, *Another Way* won the FIPRESCI critics' award and Jankowska-Cieślak, the best actress prize.

The first officially registered cases of HIV/AIDS in the Eastern Bloc in the mid-1980s turned HOSI's attention to the availability of relevant and reliable information on that matter in the region. In the early reports, the authors only briefly mentioned a growing number of references to HIV/AIDS in the mainstream media, especially in Poland but also in Czechoslovakia and Hungary (EEIP 1983, 1985). They pointed out that such references had either not mentioned homosexuality at all or attributed HIV/AIDS to the Western homosexuals and presented it as an evidence for 'just how rotten and decadent Western countries are' (EEIP 1983, p. 7). Interestingly, Kateřina Kolářová (2014) shows how a late Czechoslovakian film dealing with HIV and AIDS, *Kopytem Sem, Kopytem Tam* (A Tainted Horseplay 1988), reversed this narrative: it told a story of three heterosexual young men, all enjoying a lavish and carefree lifestyle, which led to one of them getting positively tested for AIDS (sic), and made their story, as well as AIDS itself, a metaphor for a moral and social decay not of the West but of the late communist Czechoslovakia.

Since mid-1980s, HOSI started to discuss HIV/AIDS more extensively. Notably, it ran a special series devoted exclusively to 'AIDS in Eastern Europe', included in three reports published between 1986 and 1988. In the first and longest one, the authors indicated a steady increase of mainstream reports on HIV/AIDS in the region, which helped to introduce the topic of homosexuality to the general public (EEIP 1986, pp. 2–5). Initial brief references to HIV/AIDS and homosexuality appeared in the least progressive countries, such as Bulgaria and the Soviet Union (the authors had no information about Romania), though they were reported to be overloaded with medical vocabulary and aimed at specialized audiences. More extensive and diverse coverage on the issue was provided in Czechoslovakia, East Germany, Hungary, Poland and Yugoslavia. Due to the lack of research on HIV/AIDS in the Eastern Bloc, the coverage was most often based on Western sources, such as the US *Newsweek* and *Time* as well as West German *Der Spiegel*. Consequently, as HOSI pointed out:

> full reports about gay life-style (in San Francisco for example) were published with photos of gay discos and various gay-pride events. For many peo-

ple in the East Bloc, this was the first confrontation with the subject of the
gay liberation movement and gay subculture in the West. (EEIP 1986, p. 2)

Finally, in the virtual absence of well-developed gay meeting places,
consisting mainly of informal and often unsafe cruising spots in parks,
baths and public toilets, as well as due to a very limited reach of a few
homosexual magazines in the region, personal ads in mainstream media
played an important role of connecting homosexuals. The 1985 EEIP
report described a case when such personal ads became a nationwide con-
troversy. At the end of 1983, the Warsaw mainstream monthly *Relaks*
(Relax) started publishing explicitly homosexual personal ads, which soon
became a well-known fact throughout the country and led to protests,
mainly in a form of angry letters to the editor. Threatened with the increase
of magazine prices—a warning coming from the Polish government but
originating in the Soviet embassy—*Relaks* decided to drop the section
with personal ads in July 1984 (EEIP 1985, pp. 8–9). Scholars report that
homosexual personal ads were also published in the mainstream media in
some other Eastern Bloc countries but they usually did not explicitly refer
to homosexuality and, thus, managed to escape the eye of the general public. Takács (2014, p. 196), for example, mentions that lesbians in Hungary
used as a code word the title of the cult film *Another Way*, discussed in a
previous paragraph. Véra Sokolová (2014, p. 99), in turn, points out that
Czechoslovakian lesbians coded their personal ads published in *Mladý Svét*
(Young World) by explaining in the ads that their intention was to 'enjoy
cultural experiences', 'teach a language/tongue' (the Czech *jazyk* means
both) as well as by mentioning the title of the acclaimed 1928 lesbian
novel *The Well of Loneliness* by the UK author Radclyffe Hall, published in
Czech in 1931 and 1969.

3.5 Homosexual Self-Organizing

Apart from reporting on state laws and practices as well as media coverage
related to homosexuality in Eastern Bloc countries, one of the key aims of
HOSI was to identify and support, or encourage to form, local homosexual groups. Therefore, the EEIP reports regularly discussed homosexual
initiatives in the region, particularly in East Germany, Poland and Slovenia
but also, in the late editions and only in individual special sections, in
Hungary (EEIP 1988) and Czechoslovakia (EEIP 1989). All homosexual
groups in Eastern Bloc countries, as attested by the reports, shared the

experience of being mistrusted by communist authorities, who seemed to be not much threatened by homosexuality itself but rather by the groups' potential to destabilize communist states (for the same argument regarding East Germany see McLellan 2011, p. 134, and regarding Poland, Fiedotow 2012, p. 244). The groups also benefited from the fact that HIV/AIDS became more often discussed in relation to homosexuality in the public discourses of many Eastern Bloc countries in the second half of the 1980s, which provided an ample justification for their existence as HIV/AIDS prevention groups (e.g. Kurimay and Takács 2016). Different national contexts, however, facilitated different conditions of formation and different trajectories of evolution of those groups. I will now discuss some of the most vivid attempts at homosexual self-organizing in the region at the twilight of the Cold War, with a deliberate omission of the Polish case, which will be analysed in detail in the following chapter.

The EEIP reports regularly praised East German homosexuals for creating the most active movement in the entire Eastern Bloc. While there were some initiatives undertaken in East Germany before 1980s, such as the Homosexual Interest Group Berlin (HIB) in the 1970s (Kleres 2001, p. 135; McLellan 2012), the movement gained its momentum in the early 1980s, when it found an important ally, the Evangelical Church. The activists were looking for a meeting room at that time and since some of them were members of the Church, they sought and gained the support of the institution. The first Homosexual Working Group within the Protestant Student Community officially began its work on 25 April 1982 in Leipzig (EEIP 1984, p. 3). Similar groups, tolerated but not officially recognized by the state, were soon formed in other cities and already in 1983 they organized their first national meeting. The 1988 EEIP report (p. 4) indicated that there were 16 homosexual groups operating within the Evangelical Church as well as four non-religious groups in East Germany at that time. Some women cooperated with men within those groups, others established their own groups Lesben in der Kirche (Lesbians in the Church), such as the one in Jena, formed in 1987, which started to publish an illegal magazine *Frau Anders* (Ms. Different or Different Woman) in January 1989 (EEIP 1989, p. 9; McLellan 2011, p. 127; Mittman 2007). The alliance of East German homosexual activists with the Church did influence their agenda, which included an organization of, for example, a lecture on 'Homosexuality in Theology, Church and Society' in 1982 and the first 'gay church service' in 1984 (EEIP 1984, p. 3). The establishment of homosexual church groups also sparked some controversial debates on homosexuality in the Church itself (EEIP 1987, p. 3).

Another homosexual movement praised in EEIP reports was that of the Republic of Slovenia, then part of Yugoslavia. In Slovenia, homosexuals found an ally not in the local church but at the Student Cultural Centre (ŠKUC) of the University of Ljubljana, and organized the first gay culture week in the Eastern Bloc in spring 1984 (EEIP 1984, p. 4), followed by the foundation of the first homosexual organization in Slovenia named Magnus, after Magnus Hirschfeld, in December the same year (Kuhar 2014). As in the case of East Germany, this particular alliance influenced the agenda of Slovenian activists, who focused on such cultural events as film screenings, poetry evenings and book exhibitions. The gay section of ŠKUC began to operate in April 1984 and a year later it published the first issue of its *Gayzine*, sold in Ljubljana, Belgrade and Zagreb (EEIP 1985, pp. 20–21). In 1988, a lesbian section of ŠKUC, LILIT, was formed and started publishing its own magazine titled *Lesbozine* (EEIP 1988, pp. 6–7; see also Greif 2005; Kajinić 2016; Takács 2003; Tratnik 2001). The first issue of the magazine was published in March 1988 thanks to the financial support of the Socialist Alliance of Slovenian Youth and, later on, also of Dutch homosexual organizations (EEIP 1988, p. 6). The Slovenian activists stayed closely in touch with Western activists. In an interview with HOSI, an organizer of the Magnus festival affirmed that 'From the very beginning we have been involved in international activities. Gay culture is international culture' (EEIP 1985, p. 22). Indeed, the members of ŠKUC gay and lesbian groups participated in annual ILGA conferences and, during the second edition of Magnus in 1985, they organized lectures with the representatives of Austrian organizations, HOSI and Rosa Lila Villa, as well as the screenings of three Austrian documentaries on homosexuality: *Inlandsreport: Homosexualität*, *Jetzt Reden Wir* and *Rosa Lila Villa* (EEIP 1985, p. 19).

The only officially registered homosexual organization in the Eastern Bloc was Hungarian Homeros Lambda. Istvan, one of the Homeros' co-founders, explained in an interview with HOSI that 'It started in the fall of 1985 when several gay men got together after hearing about the danger of AIDS' (EEIP 1988, p. 9). The activists first applied for the official recognition to the Ministry of the Interior in 1986. When their application was rejected, they submitted a new one to the Ministry of Health and Welfare in 1987. This time they were luckier and Homeros was officially registered in March 1988. Scott Long (1999, p. 251) explains that this registration was possible thanks to the introduction of the new Law on Associations in Hungary in 1988, which was originally meant for 'politics, not perverts', as some opponents of Homeros argued. The prime reason for creating the organization was to fight HIV/AIDS in cooperation with Hungarian health authorities, which included securing the availability of anonymous testing. Still, in a retrospective, the founders of Homeros admitted that they had also set some less pronounced aims such as the increase of the visibility of homosexuals in society and the facilitation of contacts between homosexuals, for example by opening in 1989 'the first fully gay bar', which was Lokál in Budapest (Takács 2014, p. 198). In 1989, Homeros started to publish its own magazine, *Mások* (Others) (Takács 2003). The first known homosexual magazine published in CEE was Czechoslovakian *Hlas Sexuální Menšiny* (The Voice of the Sexual Minority) and its successor *Nový Hlas:List pro Sexuální Reformu* (New Voice: Journal for Sexual Reform), published from 1931 to 1934 (with a short break), and clearly referring in its subtitles to the homophile movement and the World League for Sexual Reform (Huebner 2010).

Most of the homosexual groups formed in the Eastern Bloc in the 1980s, such as already discussed ŠKUC sections and Homeros Lambda, but also Czechoslovakian Lambda Praha (EEIP 1989, pp. 5–7) and Polish Etap (EEIP 1987, p. 8), closely cooperated with ILGA and HOSI. This cooperation involved sending local representatives to annual ILGA conferences and twinning with HOSI or other Western organizations. Besides, Western activists supported Eastern groups by attending their events and sending them magazines, books, films as well as condoms (e.g. EEIP 1989, pp. 10–11). When reporting to HOSI on the establishment of Lambda Praha in spring 1988, Jan Laný explained that the group aimed to become ILGA member and that he himself was already present at the ILGA conference in 1983 (EEIP 1989, p. 5). Interestingly, Long (1999, p. 247) points out that the local name of the organization was the Sociotherapeutic Club, but it presented itself to ILGA as Lambda Praha, possibly to downplay the close connection between homosexual activists and sexologists in Czechoslovakia (Sokolová 2014). ILGA also inspired the formation of the first informal groups in the most homophobic countries in the region such as the Soviet Union. Laurie Essig (1999, p. 58) reports that when a student in Leningrad, Aleksandr Zaremba, read about ILGA, he 'decided it was time to form a similar organisation in Russia. In 1984, Zaremba gathered about thirty persons together, four of whom were women, and founded the Gai Laboratoriia (Gay Laboratory)'.

The group, which aimed to abolish the 'anti-sodomy' law and educate homosexuals about the dangers of HIV and AIDS, soon got in touch with Finnish activists and became a member of ILGA. However, because of the harassment by the secret service, Gay Laboratory decided to disband in mid-1986 (Essig 1999, p. 58; Kon 1993, p. 103).

Most remarkably, ILGA and HOSI started to organize sub-regional conferences in order to foster the cooperation between homosexual groups in different Eastern Bloc countries. The first such conference took place in Budapest between 6 and 8 November in 1987, on the 70th anniversary of the October Revolution, as authors of the 1988 EEIP report pointed out. It included 30 activists from Czechoslovakia, East Germany, Hungary, Poland and Yugoslavia as well as the representatives of ILGA. HOSI reported, in a somewhat vague fashion, that 'Lesbian participation was higher than at other such international conferences' (EEIP 1988, p. 2). The key aims of the first meeting were to introduce different groups to each other and discuss the issues related to HIV and AIDS. The second conference was hosted by the Warsaw Homosexual Movement (WRH) in Warsaw between 16 and 17 April 1988 and the third one, by Homeros Lambda, again in Budapest, between 21 and 23 April 1989. The latter included 60 participants, 25 of whom were women (EEIP 1989, p. 2), together with representatives from Austria, Italy, the Netherlands and Switzerland (*Filo* 1989, 17, p. 3). Figure 3.2 reproduces the official Conference Statement from the 1989 meeting. After the fall of communism in Europe, the sub-regional conferences continued to be organized annually until 1996, when the Eastern and Western activists united under the umbrella of the newly founded ILGA-Europe (Ayoub and Paternotte 2012, p. 53; for details of all EEIP conferences see http://ilga.org/about-us/1978-2007-a-chronology/, last accessed 14 March 2017).

3.6 CONCLUSION

The EEIP reports reveal the great complexity of the Eastern Bloc in relation to homosexuality. The laws concerning the legal status of homosexuality and the age of consent for same-sex acts versus opposite-sex acts differed radically from country to country. State practices too ranged from systematic persecution of homosexuals in Romania to moderate tolerance of gay public spaces in Hungary; though the surveillance and registration of male homosexuals by the police forces or the secret service seemed to

CONFERENCE STATEMENT

Sixty lesbians and gay men from various groups in Czechoslovakia, the GDR, Hungary, Poland, and Yugoslavia, as well as several invited guests from non-Socialist countries gathered in Budapest, Hungary, from 21 to 23 April 1989 for the Third Regional Conference of Lesbians and Gay Men from Eastern and Southeastern Europe. The meeting was organized and hosted by the Hungarian national lesbian and gay association, HOMEROS λ.

In the first plenary session the individual groups reported about their activities and progress. From Czechoslovakia and Poland came the good news that the official registration of organizations in these countries is well under way. Twenty working groups affiliated with the Protestant Church and eleven gay & lesbian clubs are active in the GDR. One of their activities is the annual commemoration ceremony in former concentration camps for the homosexual victims of nazism. The host organization, HOMEROS λ, was proud to hold the conference in their newly-opened cultural center. Lesbians from Yugoslavia showed their dedication to strengthening the movement in their country.

In working groups, the topics AIDS, Bisexuality, Lesbian-Gay Cooperation, and Lesbians and Gays and their Children were discussed in detail. The AIDS workshop laid the framework for setting up an AIDS Network in the countries represented. A weekend meeting was planned in the GDR to elaborate on topics brought up in the workshop on bisexuality.

The participants decided on conference sites for the coming years: Budapest (1990), the GDR (1991), and Prague (1992). To coordinate activities between the conferences and to make concrete suggestions for establishing operating structures and conference topics, a committee with representatives from each country was set up.

The conference in Budapest established a new zenith for the aspiring lesbian and gay movement in Eastern Europe.

Fig. 3.2 Conference Statement of the third EEIP meeting in Budapest (EEIP 1989, p. 3). Courtesy of IHLIA Amsterdam

be common to most Eastern Bloc countries. Closely related to state laws and practices were also the coverage of homosexuality in the mainstream media and the capacity for homosexual self-organizing. Regarding the former, in Romania and the Soviet Union homosexuality was a taboo subject while in East Germany and Poland mainstream media provided extensive and diverse reports on the topic, especially in the second half of the 1980s. Regarding the latter, homosexual activists in the Soviet Union could not overcome the harassment of the state but those in Czechoslovakia, East

Germany, Hungary, Poland and Slovenia managed to create relatively strong groups. Besides, movements in different countries followed different trajectories of development, allying themselves with different segments of society or the state such as sexology in Czechoslovakia, Evangelical Church in East Germany, university in Slovenia or, alternatively, staying relatively independent, which was characteristic of Hungarian and Polish groups.

Moreover, the Pink Curtain, a homosexual version of the Iron Curtain, which hindered the flows of homosexuality-related information and travels of homosexuals between the Western and Eastern Blocs, was rusted. As the EEIP reports attest, the Pink Curtain was permeable, full of cracks and holes, which made CEE involved in the processes of the globalization of homosexuality—or possibly, more broadly, LGBT identities and politics—already before the fall of communism in Europe. Western films with homosexual themes, such as *Cabaret* (1972) (but also e.g. *Death in Venice* [1971] or *Hair* [1979]), found their way to the Eastern Bloc, and Eastern films, such as *Another Way* (1982), found their way to the Western Bloc. The UK novel *The Well of Loneliness* became so popular among Czechoslovakian lesbians that they used its title as a code word in personal ads sent to a mainstream magazine (Sokolová 2014). The media coverage on HIV and AIDS, which became more common and more diverse in some Eastern Bloc countries in the mid-1980s, relied much on the US and West German sources and thus, somewhat accidently, introduced Western gay cultures and movements to Eastern mainstream audiences. The EEIP reports abound in such examples of cultural products related to homosexuality which managed to cross the boundaries of countries and blocs during the last decade of the Cold War.

Travelling of people between the blocs was more difficult than travelling of cultural products. By no means, however, was it impossible. HOSI activists, some of whom were born in the Eastern Bloc and immigrated to the West (Selerowicz), regularly visited the countries behind the Iron Curtain in search of individuals and groups interested in the situation of homosexuals in their own countries. With the support of ILGA, the activists played an important role not only in gathering information about homosexuality in the Eastern Bloc but also in integrating, reinforcing and inspiring homosexual activists in the region. Their agenda was clear, to aid the formation of the homosexual movement in the Eastern Bloc 'according to the Western example' (EEIP 1983, p. 2). The first EEIP report revealed a good dose of prejudice on the part of HOSI members against communist ideology and Eastern Bloc societies. Yet, the Western activists seemed to tone down this initial attitude over time, especially after the dispute with East German activists (EEIP 1985), and managed to win the sympathy of many activists in the Eastern Bloc, surely in Czechoslovakia, Hungary, Poland, Slovenia and the Soviet Union. In that sense, ILGA and HOSI played a vital part in exporting a Western model of LGBT identities and politics to emerging movements in CEE. To be sure, this process was neither unidirectional nor total. Activists in the Eastern Bloc too eagerly travelled to ILGA annual conferences and, as will become clear in the second part of this book, selectively adopted as well as strategically and creatively adapted the elements of the Western model. In sum, it becomes clear that the ideas of a homogenous and essentialist attitude towards homosexuality in the Eastern Block as well as its near total isolation during the Cold War are myths.

BIBLIOGRAPHY

Altman, D. (1971[1974]). *Homosexual: Oppression and liberation.* London: Allen Lane.

Andreescu, V. (2011). From legal tolerance to social acceptance: Predictors of heterosexism in Romania. *Revista Romana de Sociologie, 22*(3/4), 209–231.

Ayoub, P. M., & Paternotte, D. (2012). Building Europe: The International Lesbian and Gay Association (ILGA) and LGBT activism in Central and Eastern Europe. *Perspectives on Europe, 42*(1), 51–56.

Ayoub, P. M., & Paternotte, D. (2014a). Challenging borders, imaging Europe: Transnational LGBT activism in a New Europe. In N. A. Naples & J. Bickham Mendez (Eds.), *Border politics: Social movements, collective identities, and globalization* (pp. 230–257). New York: New York University Press.

Ayoub, P. M., & Paternotte, D. (Eds.). (2014b). *LGBT activism and the making of Europe: A rainbow Europe?* Basingstoke: Palgrave Macmillan.

Bacchetta, P. (2002). Rescaling transnational "queerdom": Lesbian and "lesbian" identitary-positionalities in Delhi in the 1980s. *Antipode, 34*(5), 947–973.

Bracke, S. (2012). From "saving women" to "saving gays": Rescue narratives and their dis/continuities. *European Journal of Women's Studies, 19*(2), 237–252.

Brockmann, J. (1977). Antihomosexualität in Osteuropa. In R. Lautmann (Ed.), *Seminar: Gesellschaft und Homosexualität* (pp. 447–460). Frankfurt am Main: Suhrkamp.

Epstein, B. (1994). Anti-communism, homophobia, and the construction of masculinity in the postwar US. *Critical Sociology, 20*(3), 21–44.

Essig, L. (1999). *Queer in Russia: A story of sex, self, and the other.* Durham, NC: Duke University Press.

Fiedotow, A. (2012). Początki ruchu gejowskiego w Polsce (1981–1990). In P. Barański, A. Czajkowska, A. Fiedotow & A. Wochna-Tymińska (Eds.), *Kłopoty z seksem w PRL: Rodzenie nie całkiem po ludzku, aborcja, choroby, odmienności* (pp. 241–258). Warszawa: Wydawnictwa Uniwersytetu Warszawskiego.

Graupner, H. (2000). Sexual consent: The criminal law in Europe and overseas. *Archive of Sexual Behavior, 29*(5), 415–461.

Greif, T. (2005). The social status of lesbian women in Slovenia in the 1990s. In A. Štulhofer & T. Sandfort (Eds.), *Sexuality and gender in postcommunist Eastern Europe and Russia* (pp. 149–169). Binghamton: Haworth Press.

Hauer, G., Krickler, K., Marek, & Schmutzer, D. (1984). *Rosa Liebe unterm roten Stern: Zur Lage der Lesben und Schwulen in Osteuropa*. Frühlings Erwachen: Hamburg.

Healey, D. (2014). From Stalinist pariahs to subjects of "Managed Democracy": Queers in Moscow 1945 to the present. In M. Cook & J. V. Evans (Eds.), *Queer cities, queer cultures: Europe since 1945* (pp. 95–117). London: Bloomsbury.

Hekma, G., Oosterhuis, H., & Steakley, J. (1995). Leftist sexual politics and homosexuality: A historical overview. In G. Hekma, H. Oosterhuis, & J. Steakley (Eds.), *Gay men and the sexual history of the political Left* (pp. 1–40). New York: The Haworth Press.

Hildebrandt, A. (2014). Routes to decriminalization: A comparative analysis of the legalization of same-sex sexual acts. *Sexualities, 17*(1/2), 230–253.

Hillhouse, R. J. (1990). Out of the closet behind the wall: Sexual politics and social change in the GDR. *Slavic Review, 49*(4), 585–596.

Huebner, K. (2010). The whole world revolves around it: Sex education and sex reform in First Republic Czech print media. *Aspasia, 4*, 25–48.

Johnson, D. K. (2006). *The lavender scare: The Cold War persecution of gays and lesbians in the federal government*. Chicago: University of Chicago Press.

Kajinić, S. (2016). The first European festival of lesbian and gay film was Yugoslav: Dismantling the geotemporality of Europeanisation in Slovenia. In B. Bilić (Ed.), *LGBT activism and Europeanisation in the post-Yugoslav space: On the rainbow way to Europe* (pp. 59–80). London: Palgrave Macmillan.

Kleres, J. (2001). Cherries blossoming in East(ern) Germany? In H. Flam (Ed.), *Pink, purple, green: Women's, religious, environmental and gay/lesbian movements in Central Europe today* (pp. 120–131). New York: Columbia University Press.

Kligman, G. (1992). The politics of reproduction in Ceauşescu's Romania: A case study in political culture. *East European Politics and Societies, 6*(3), 364–418.

Kligman, G. (1998). *The politics of duplicity: Controlling reproduction in Ceausescu's Romania*. Berkeley: University of California Press.

Kolářová, K. (2014). The AIDSed *perestroika*: Discourses of gender in negotiations of ideological consensus in late-socialist Czechoslovakia. In H. Havelková

& L. Oates-Indruchová (Eds.), *The politics of gender culture under state social-ism: An expropriated voice* (pp. 234–256). London: Routledge.

Kon, I. (1993). Sexual minorities. In I. Kon & J. Riordan (Eds.), *Sex and Russian society* (pp. 89–115). London: Pluto.

Kuhar, R. (2003). *Media representations of homosexuality: An analysis of the print media in Slovenia, 1970–2000.* Ljubljana: Peace Institute.

Kuhar, R. (2014). Ljubljana: The tales from the queer margins of the city. In M. Cook & J. V. Evans (Eds.), *Queer cities, queer cultures: Europe since 1945* (pp. 135–150). London: Bloomsbury.

Kurimay, A., & Takács, J. (2016). Emergence of the Hungarian homosexual movement in late refrigerator socialism. *Sexualities.* Published online before print. Retrieved February 26, 2017, from http://journals.sagepub.com/doi/abs/10.1177/1363460716665786?journalCode=sexa

Lautmann, R. (Ed.). (1977). *Seminar: Gesellschaft und Homosexualität.* Frankfurt am.Main: Suhrkamp.

Long, S. (1999). Gay and lesbian movements in Eastern Europe: Romania, Hungary, and the Czech Republic. In B. D. Adam, J. W. Duyvendak, & A. Krouwel (Eds.), *The global emergence of gay and lesbian politics: National imprints of a worldwide movement* (pp. 242–265). Philadelphia: Temple University Press.

Macey, D. (1993). *The lives of Michel Foucault.* London: Hutchinson.

McLellan, J. (2011). *Love in the time of communism: Intimacy and sexuality in the GDR.* Cambridge: Cambridge University Press.

McLellan, J. (2012). Glad to be gay behind the wall: Gay and lesbian activism in 1970s East Germany. *History Workshop Journal, 74*(1), 105–130.

Mittman, E. (2007). Gender, citizenship, and the public sphere in postunification Germany: Experiments in feminist journalism. *Signs: Journal of Women and Culture in Society, 32*(3), 759–791.

Mizielińska, J., & Kulpa, R. (2011). "Contemporary peripheries": Queer studies, circulation of knowledge and East/West divide. In R. Kulpa & J. Mizielińska (Eds.), *De-centring Western sexualities: Central and Eastern European perspec-tives* (pp. 11–26). Farnham: Ashgate.

Moss, K. (2007). Queer as metaphor: Representations of LGBT people in Central and East European film. In R. Kuhar & J. Takács (Eds.), *Beyond the Pink Curtain: Everyday life of LGBT people in Eastern Europe* (pp. 249–267). Ljubljana: Peace Institute.

Moss, K., & Simić, M. (2011). Post-communist lavender menace: Lesbians in mainstream East European film. *Journal of Lesbian Studies, 15*(3), 271–283.

Nachescu, V. (2005). Hierarchies of difference: National identity, gay and lesbian rights, and the Church in postcommunist Romania. In A. Štulhofer & T. Sandfort (Eds.), *Sexuality and gender in postcommunist Eastern Europe and Russia* (pp. 57–77). Binghamton: Haworth Press.

O'Dwyer, C. (2013). Gay rights and political homophobia in postcommunist Europe: Is there an "EU effect"? In M. L. Weiss & M. J. Bosia (Eds.), *Global homophobia: States, movements and the politics of oppression* (pp. 103–126). Urbana: University of Illinois Press.

Paternotte, D., & Seckinelgin, H. (2015). "Lesbian and gay rights are human rights": Multiple globalizations and LGBTI activism. In D. Paternotte & M. Tremblay (Eds.), *The Ashgate research companion to lesbian and gay activism* (pp. 209–223). Farnham: Ashgate.

Płatek, M. (2009). Sytuacja osób homoseksualnych w prawie karnym. In R. Wieruszewski & M. Wyrzykowski (Eds.), *Orientacja seksualna i tożsamość płciowa* (pp. 49–81). Warszawa: Instytut Wydawniczy EuroPrawo.

Rupp, L. J. (2011). The persistence of transnational organizing: The case of the homophile movement. *The American Historical Review, 116*(4), 1014–1039.

Seidl, J. (2016). Decriminalization of homosexual acts in Czechoslovakia in 1961. In K. Vērdiņš & J. Ozoliņš (Eds.), *Queer stories of Europe* (pp. 174–194). Newcastle upon Tyne: Cambridge Scholars Publishing.

Sokolová, V. (2014). State approaches to homosexuality and non-heterosexual lives in Czechoslovakia during state socialism. In H. Havelková & L. Oates-Indruchová (Eds.), *The politics of gender culture under state socialism: An expropriated voice* (pp. 82–108). London: Routledge.

Stella, F. (2015). *Lesbian lives in Soviet and post-Soviet Russia: Post/socialism and gendered sexualities*. Basingstoke: Palgrave Macmillan.

Sweet, D. M. (1995). The Church, the Stasi, and socialist integration: Three stages of lesbian and gay emancipation in the former German Democratic Republic. In G. Hekma, H. Oosterhuis, & J. Steakley (Eds.), *Gay men and the sexual history of the political Left* (pp. 351–367). New York: The Haworth Press.

Szczygieł, M. (2009, May). Rozgrzeszenie w PRL. *Replika, 19*, 18–19.

Takács, J. (2003). Position, state of development and role of sexual minority media: Hungary, the Netherlands and Slovenia. Paper prepared for the Peace Institute Fellowship Program. Retrieved March 13, 2017, from http://core. ac.uk/download/pdf/11872025.pdf

Takács, J. (2014). Queering Budapest. In M. Cook & J. V. Evans (Eds.), *Queer cities, queer cultures: Europe since 1945* (pp. 191–210). London: Bloomsbury.

Takács, J. (2015). Disciplining gender and (homo)sexuality in state-socialist Hungary in the 1970s. *European Review of History: Revue européenne d'histoire, 22*(1), 161–175.

Takács, J. (2017). Listing homosexuals since the 1920s and under state socialism in Hungary. In C. Baker (Ed.), *Gender in twentieth-century Eastern Europe and the USSR* (pp. 157–170). London: Palgrave Macmillan.

Takács, J., & Kuhar, R. (2007). Introduction: What is beyond the Pink Curtain. In R. Kuhar & J. Takács (Eds.), *Beyond the Pink Curtain: Everyday life of LGBT people in Eastern Europe* (pp. 11–12). Ljubljana: Peace Institute.

Torra, M. J. (1998). Gay rights after the Iron Curtain. *The Fletcher Forum of World Affairs, 22*(2), 73–87.

Tratnik, S. (2001). II. Lesbian visibility in Slovenia. *The European Journal of Women's Studies, 8*(3), 373–380.

Więch, A. S. (2005). Różowy odcień PRL-u: Zarys badań nad mniejszościami seksualnymi w Polsce Ludowej. In K. Slany, B. Kowalska & M. Śmietana (Eds.), *Homoseksualizm: Perspektywa interdyscyplinarna* (pp. 257–264). Kraków: Nomos.

CHAPTER 4

Homosexual Activism in Communist Poland

The collapse of the Iron Curtain in 1989 is usually considered as the key moment enabling the emergence of homosexual—or lesbian, gay, bisexual and transgender (LGBT)—activism in Central and Eastern Europe (CEE). This is especially clear in Joanna Mizielińska and Robert Kulpa's (2011) own contribution to their collection *De-Centring Western Sexualities*, where the authors contrast the step-by-step development of the activism in the West ('time of sequence') with the all-at-once emergence of the activism in the East ('time of coincidence'), the latter only after the collapse of the Iron Curtain. Challenging the homogenizing and essentializing tendencies of the model in the context of Poland, Błażej Warkocki (2014) asks to historicize the Polish LGBT movement and proposes to divide it into three stages, where the collapse of the Iron Curtain too emerges as one of the critical thresholds but not as the beginning point of the movement. According to Warkocki (2014) (see also Warkocki and Sypniewski 2004), the first stage is that of early emancipation, situated between 1981 and 1990; the second one, of gay and lesbian emancipation, between 1990 and 2003; and the third one, of politicization of homophobia, which has started in 2003 and continues until present. Still, Agnés Chetaille (2011) and Conor O'Dwyer (2012) (see also O'Dwyer and Vermeersch 2016) present other periodizations of LGBT activism in Poland, as demonstrated in Fig. 4.1.

© The Author(s) 2018
L. Szulc, *Transnational Homosexuals in Communist Poland*,
Global Queer Politics, DOI 10.1007/978-3-319-58901-5_4

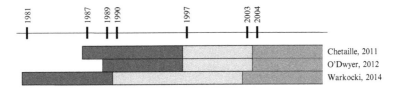

Fig. 4.1 Periodizations of the Polish LGBT activism.

I do not bring those different periodizations together to argue that they contradict each other: after all, authors divide Polish LGBT activism into stages only roughly and for the purpose of their own arguments. Instead, my aim is to reflect on the sheer process of creating periodizations and point to some consequences of dividing Polish LGBT activism into particular stages with particular beginnings. As briefly mentioned in Chap. 2, I consider the act of creating beginnings as consequential: 'a beginning *authorizes*: it constitutes an authorization for what follows from it' (Said 1975, p. 34), it establishes a radical difference between what was before and after, risking an overemphasis on discontinuity (Piontek 2006, p. 10), regardless of the true historical significance of the event considered as the beginning. In the case of Poland, some authors, like Chetaille (2011) and Warkocki (2014), locate the beginning point of the LGBT movement before the collapse of the Iron Curtain, though they differ in identifying this point: while Warkocki goes back to the publication of the first major articles and books on homosexuality in the mainstream media at the beginning of the 1980s, Chetaille starts with the destabilization of the communist regime and the emergence of the Warsaw Homosexual Movement (WRH) in 1987 (see also a more comprehensive account in Chetaille's [2015] doctoral thesis). Other authors, like O'Dwyer (2012) and O'Dwyer and Vermeersch (2016), simply start their discussion after the collapse of the Iron Curtain or, more generally, point to the crucial importance of the year 1989 for the emergence of LGBT movement in the country, only briefly (if at all) mentioning some self-organizational attempts under communism (see also Baer 2009; Frątczak 2012; Gruszczyńska 2009a; Kliszczyński 2001; Kowalska 2011; Stasińska 2012). This, of course, is not a problem in individual studies which have their own specific points of focus but, taken collectively, the scholarship largely recreates the impression that hardly any attempts at homosexual self-organizing were made in the People's Republic of Poland (PRL). Thus, 1989 becomes naturalized as the year of a wholesale rupture between (nearly) no homosexual activism in communist Poland and suddenly appearing LGBT movement in democratic Poland.

The key aim of this chapter is to challenge the ideas of the 1989 rupture and of the PRL's near total isolation by historicizing the development of LGBT activism in Poland as well as investigating its transnational nature already before the fall of communism in Europe. Therefore, my ambition here is to provide a contextualized and detailed account of homosexual self-organizing in communist Poland. To this end, I will draw on a rich variety of both primary and secondary sources listed in Chap. 1, especially the Eastern Europe Information Pool (EEIP) reports, documents from the Polish Institute of National Remembrance (IPN), interviews with activists and articles on homosexuality published in Poland in the 1980s. I will start the chapter by introducing the broader political and social context of Poland under communism, with a special focus on the role of the communist state, political opposition and Roman Catholic Church. Next, I will discuss some homosexuality-related issues in the PRL before 1980, particularly those regarding state laws and practices as well as public discourses. In the three following sections, I will detail the development of homosexual activism in late communist Poland in a chronological order: in the early, mid and late 1980s, pointing to the transnational origins of the activism, the importance of the police Operation Hyacinth for the mobilization of the activists as well as the role of HIV/AIDS discourses in framing the demands for official recognition of their groups.

4.1   THE STATE, OPPOSITION AND CHURCH

Even though the authorities of the PRL were consistently committed to the principles of first Stalinism and then Marxism-Leninism, the country did not develop into a fully consistent system. The relations of the state with the Soviet Union and the Roman Catholic Church, the strictness of state censorship or the treatment of political opposition, all varied under the rule of different key leaders of the Polish United Workers' Party (PZPR)—namely Bolesław Bierut (1948–1956), Władysław Gomułka (1956–1970), Edward Gierek (1970–1980) and Wojciech Jaruzelski (1981–1989)—as well as within their particular rules. The most profound changes took place after 1956: until then, Poland stayed under the direct control of Moscow, with the Marshal of the Soviet Union installed in Warsaw as the Minister of Defence, and went through the process of a severe Stalinization, which included the imposition of strict censorship and systematic persecution of the Church. As Norman Davies (1981) points out in his acclaimed *God's Playground: A History of Poland*, only after 1956 can we speak of 'Polish road to communism', characterized by a stronger independence of the PZPR, gained in the aftermath of Nikita Khrushchev's destalinization in the Soviet Union, and Gomułka's analogous process of reasserting Leninism in the PRL, including the dismissal of the Soviet Marshal.

The rules of Gomułka, up to 1970, and Gierek, up to 1980, went through a similar trajectory: from initial enthusiasm and optimism—coupled with some liberalizations in political and social life such as the relaxation of censorship and a greater tolerance towards the opposition and the Church—through economic and political crises, to the more relentless imposition of the party's ideology (Biskupski 2000; Davies 1981). At the same time, during those 30–35 years, Poland underwent profound social and economic changes: the population raised from 24 million in 1946 to 35 million in 1979 (with more than 10 million people migrating from country to city), much of the workforce moved from agriculture to industry, and the new class system emerged with the higher levels of the party and industrial management at the top, the industrial workforce in the middle and the peasants at the bottom (Davies 1981, pp. 595–600). Strikes against low wages, work conditions and, most importantly, food price rises broke out regularly, sometimes developing into mass and bloodily suppressed protests. These protests, however, did not translate into a strong, consolidated opposition until the second half of the 1970s, when new organizations were formed, especially the Workers' Defence Committee (KOR) in 1976 but also the Movement for Defence of Human and Civic Rights (ROPCiO) in 1977 (Sasanka 2011). The development of human rights organizations at that time was a broader regional phenomenon, a result of the Helsinki Accords, the final act of the Conference on Security and Co-operation in Europe, signed in 1975 by all European countries except for Albania (Biskupski 2000, p. 155; Davies 1981, p. 629).

The protests of March 1968 in Poland were unique because, unlike most of the other demonstrations, they were initiated by students instead of workers and against the violation of freedom of speech instead of the rise in food prices. The direct cause for the protests was the censorship of a theatre play based on the poem *Dziady* (Forefathers' Eve) by the most famous Polish national poet Adam Mickiewicz. Not disconnected from foreign protests against the US war in Vietnam as well as the military intervention of the Warsaw Pact in Czechoslovakia during the Prague Spring, the Polish 1968, nevertheless, lacked the component of sexual revolution (Eisler 1991, 2006; Falk 2003; Garsztecki 2008). In fact, the protesting students gained a firm support from the Church, conservative in gender- and sexuality-related issues. Already on 21 March but also on 3 May 1968, the Polish Episcopate issued pastoral letters condemning the regime's attacks on students (Garsztecki 2008, p. 183). As Sara Evans notes:

> Indeed, in places such as Poland, the institutional harbour for democratic hopes following the [1968] crackdown was the Catholic Church, which held out traditional gender roles within the family as a bulwark against intrusive and authoritarian state power. Students, who were reluctant at first to ally with the Church, nonetheless shared an inability to swallow the individualistic utopianism of Western student movements. (Evans 2009, p. 345)

The last decade of the PRL started with large strikes in Gdańsk and Szczecin in summer 1980 in opposition to the increased food prices. The protestors soon reached an agreement with the regime, which accepted the establishment of an independent trade union. On 17 September 1980 regional Inter-Factory Strike Committees united under the leadership of the soon-Nobel-Peace-Prize winner Lech Wałęsa and formed the Solidarity movement. Faced with the enormous popularity of Solidarity (10 million members at its peak, Biskupski 2000, p. 162) and (rather remote) possibility of Soviet military intervention, the new party leader, Wojciech Jaruzelski, declared the martial law in December 1981 and transferred all power to the established for that purpose Military Council of National Salvation (WRON). During the first days of the martial law the regime arrested nearly all Solidarity leaders, cut communications between Poland and the outside world, banned all public meetings, tightened censorship and imposed a curfew. Regaining his confidence after carrying out this well-planned and professionally executed manoeuvre, Jaruzelski gradually eased the tight control of the country: the martial law was suspended in December 1982 and lifted in July 1983. In 1986, he also granted amnesty to those arrested during the martial law and soon relaxed state censorship, echoing similar changes in the Soviet Union under its new progressive leader, Mikhail Gorbachev, especially his 1986 policy allowing freedom of discussion, known as glasnost (Biskupski 2000, p. 169; McNair 1991).

New strikes broke out in February 1988, again against the rise in food prices. The negotiations between the government, the party, Solidarity and the Church, known as the Round Table Talks, began in February

1989 and lasted two months. The main outcome of the talks was that the regime agreed to call a parliamentary election on 4 and 18 June 1989, which for the first time in communist Poland would be free, yet regulated by a curious voting formula: while all members to a newly established Senat, the upper house of the parliament, were to be chosen freely, the 65 per cent seats in Sejm, the lower house, were preserved exclusively for the PZPR and its satellite parties. Solidarity scored a stunning victory in the election, winning 99 of 100 seats in Senate and all 35 per cent of the available seats in Sejm. Thanks to a number of moves by Wałęsa, some of PZPR's satellite parties went over to the opposition, allowing Solidarity to secure majority in the lower house and install its own government. Soon after that, an actress Joanna Szczepkowska announced on TV in the major Polish news programme: 'Ladies and gentlemen, on 4 June 1989, communism in Poland had come to an end' (Lease 2016).

The important role of the Roman Catholic Church in breaking up the communist system in Poland is probably best illustrated by the fact that the Church was one of the principal factions at the Round Table Talks. In fact, the Church was the only public institution during the communist times in Poland that won a relative autonomy (Żaryn 2011). The party's attitude towards the Church was ambivalent: On the one hand, the party promoted the communist vision of atheist society and at times not only opposed but also oppressed the Church, particularly until 1956 but also later on. On the other hand, it could not ignore the enormous popularity of the Church among the people and tried to win its sympathy by occasional concessions. The Church, in turn, while mainly supporting political opposition, often functioned as the mediator between state and dissidents, taking on the role which Davies (1981, p. 614) describes as that of the 'loyal opposition'. Two figures in the history of the Polish Church helped to shape its image as the key patriotic institution in the PRL. The first one was cardinal Stefan Wyszyński, who was interned between 1953 and 1956 for his firm anti-communist stance, and the second one, pope John Paul II (elected in 1978), who preached patriotic sermons and referred to Solidarity symbolism during his pilgrimages to the communist Poland in 1979, 1983 and 1987 (Davies 1981, p. 615; Żaryn 2011, p. 107). The relationship between Solidarity and the Church strengthened during the martial law, when Solidarity was forced to go underground and found a refuge in the Church's infrastructure. This, in turn, influenced Solidarity's conservative attitudes towards gender and sexuality (Stanley 2010), as I will explain further in this chapter.

4.2   Homosexuality Before 1980

After regaining independence in 1918, or even before the First World War, Poland underwent what Kamil Janicki (2015, p. 40) asks to recognize as a 'moral' or 'sexual revolution': 'Sex in pre-war [Second World War] Warsaw or Cracow was everywhere. Polygamy, orgies, sex on a park bench and in a train car. But also the demands for abolishing monogamy and traditional institution of marriage altogether'. The origins of this revolution were versatile. First, Janicki (2015) notes the emergence of Polish sexology around the 1880s, which published some medical books dealing also with homosexuality, for example, by Leon Wachholz (1900), Stanisław Kurkiewicz (1913) and Antoni Mikulski (1920) (see also Gawin 2008; Kościańska 2016). Second, he indicates the development of a Polish feminist movement at roughly the same time, with such prominent figures as a more conservative Iza Moszczeńska (1904) and a more progressive Zofia Nałkowska, who at the Second Congress of Polish Women in 1907 demanded the recognition of women's sexuality by shouting out 'We want the whole life!' (Górnicka-Boratyńska 1999). Finally, Janicki (2015) also points to the impact of the Frist World War on bringing about the 'sexual revolution' in Poland through creating the atmosphere of the fragility of life and, thus, promoting the 'live in the here and now' attitude. Though, he argues that the end of the Great War also provoked a new rhetoric of 'moral renewal' for the post-war and independent Poland. In that context, homosexuals became in the interwar period the objects of interest to psychiatrists, sexologists and lawyers but also tabloid newspapers, which readily speculated about sexual orientation of prominent figures, such as the famous medical doctor Zofia Sadowska (Janicki 2015, pp. 387–392; Szot 2011a, b; Tomasik 2014, pp. 127–141; see also Agnieszka Weseli's online project www.sprawysadowskiej.pl).

Same-sex acts continued to be formally criminalized in Poland after the First World War, when the penal codes of the former occupants (Austro-Hungarian Empire, Imperial Russia and Prussia) remained in power (Płatek 2009). They mostly criminalized only male same-sex acts, though the Austro-Hungarian code included broader provisions against so-called 'same-sex fornication' and was indeed used also against women, at least in the Austro-Hungarian Empire (Kirchknopf 2013). The new penal code of the independent Poland from 1932 decriminalized consensual same-sex acts, which have not been recriminalized ever since. Besides, the age of consent in the penal code was set at 15 without the distinction between same-sex and opposite-sex acts. This new law, as Paweł Leszkowicz and Tomek Kitliński (2005, p. 50) explain, reflected the Napoleonic Code of 1804, which had been used as a model for the 1808 law of the Duchy of Warsaw, established by Napoleon Bonaparte in 1807 from the Polish lands ceded by Prussia. Janicki (2015, p. 397) adds that it was also influenced by the prominent Polish sexologists of that time, such as already mentioned Mikulski and Wachholz, who promoted the interpretation of homosexuality as innate. At the same time, Monika Płatek (2009) remarks that the 1932 penal code did criminalize same-sex prostitution, both for men and women, with the punishment of up to three years of incarceration. The most liberal provisions were introduced in communist Poland in 1969, when the new penal code (in force since 1970) did not mention homosexuality at all and, thus, decriminalized same-sex prostitution. The communist state also introduced some liberalization in other sexuality-related issues, most notably, it legalized abortion in 1956, which since that time until 1993 was allowed in Poland also because of 'difficult living conditions' of a pregnant woman (Czajkowska 2012).

The liberalization of homosexuality-related laws in the PRL did not translate into state's distinctly positive attitude towards homosexuals. In general, as Krzysztof Tomasik (2012, p. 17) points out, the PZPR did not have a clear stance on homosexuality, which enabled the party to adopt different approaches to homosexuals depends on different goals and circumstances. At least since the 1960s, the police forces and criminologists started to pay special attention to homosexuality, viewing it chiefly as a social pathology, related to such problems as same-sex prostitution and sex between men in prisons (Kurpios 2003; Szulc 2011). The secret service, in turn, saw homosexuality as an opportunity, a tool, which could help the agents to do their job. One way of operating was to use the information about homosexuality of prominent figures, or to fabricate it, to reach particular political goals, as it was the case with Michel Foucault, working for the French Embassy and the French Institute in Warsaw in the late 1950s, who was forced to leave Poland in 1959 after being caught up in a homosexual honey trap (Macey 1993, pp. 86–87). Similarly, when a homosexual writer Jerzy Andrzejewski signed an open letter in support of KOR in September 1976, the regime distributed a falsified letter in which the writer was supposedly demanding such 'controversial' rights for homosexuals as marriage equality (Tomasik 2012, p. 33). Another way of operating was to use the information about homosexuality of more or less prominent citizens to blackmail them into cooperation with the secret service. Partially for this purpose, police officers and secret service agents compiled extensive lists of homosexuals and create a kind of state 'pink archive'. Paweł Kurpios (2003) argues that this practice dates back in Poland to the 1970s and Agata Fiedotow (2012) that even to the 1960s, but its most clear manifestation was undoubtedly the 1985 Operation Hyacinth, which I will discuss in detail further in this chapter.

In the PRL's public discourse until 1980, male homosexuality was usually represented in stereotypical ways, either in a criminal context, especially in newspapers, or in a comical context, especially in films. Regarding the latter, homosexuality of male characters was usually coded by their effeminacy, declared misogyny as well as a keen interest in ancient Greece, fashion or ballet (Tomasik 2012). Not rarely, homosexuality was also depicted as characteristic of the perverse Western Bloc in contrast to the healthy Eastern Bloc: 'a foreign novelty, an imported disease, or the decadent hobby of the bored Western bourgeoisie' (Tomasik 2012 in Szulc 2015, p. 1019), particularly in the letters and reportages from abroad. Stanisław Cat-Mackiewicz, a Polish journalist who in 1956 returned to Poland from his few-years stay in England, disclosed soon after: 'I feel sick and sorrow but thank God I came back here. I remember emigration as a brothel of whores and pederasts to sell […]' (in Tomasik 2012, p. 27). Lesbians were in general absent from the public discourse of that time. When, however, they made it to the media, they too were discussed about mainly in a negative context: in newspapers, as criminals from prisons or youth custody centres, and in the memoirs by Poles who survived Nazi camps or Soviet gulags, as the ultimate symbols of the degeneration of humanity (Tomasik 2012, p. 266).

One notable exception to those stereotypical and overwhelmingly negative representations of homosexuality before 1980 was the first sociopolitical article in the Polish mainstream press which treated homosexuality seriously and sympathetically. Entitled 'Homosexuality and opinion' and published in 1974 by Tadeusz Gorgol in *Życie Literackie* (Literary Life), the article was exclusively devoted to homosexual men. It started with some explanations about the nature and origin of homosexuality, went through the histories of homosexuality in different cultures, and moved on to the discussions of miserable homosexual lives in Polish cities and towns. Some space was also devoted to the gay liberation movement in the West, especially in West Germany and the United States, including two paragraphs on the Stonewall Riots, where the author quoted a popular gay slogan in English: 'Two, four, six, eight—gay is just as good as straight'

(Gorgol 1974, p. 12). The most progressive parts of the article, however, were the passages where Gorgol emphasized the heterogeneity of homosexuals (among them there are both 'gentlemen and scoundrels', one could learn) and condemned the societal intolerance of and discrimination against homosexuals. As he pointed out at the end of the article, 'It is high time, if we aspire to be a cultural society, to start changing our social attitudes so homosexuality is no longer an object of unhealthy interest and public condemnation' (Gorgol 1974, p. 12). You can find this article as well as other texts about homosexuality published in Poland in the 1980s on the book's website www.transnationalhomosexuals.pl.

In all the materials I gathered, I did not find any traces of a more systematic homosexual self-organizing in Poland before 1980. One possible explanation for this is that 1968 never happened in Poland in the same way it did in the West. Surely, 1968 observed a unique student protests in the PRL, primarily against the regime's tightened censorship (Bren 2004), but the protests lacked the component of sexual revolution. Besides, none of my interviewees (Ryszard Kisiel, Paulina Pilch and Andrzej Selerowicz) recall much information about the sexual revolution in the West being available to them at that time and up to 1989, so the revolution could not provide Polish homosexual activists with great inspiration. Finally, as the EEIP reports attest (e.g. EEIP 1983, p. 2), homosexuals in the PRL seemed to be fairly satisfied with their relative freedoms. While some homosexuals in the West started to organize themselves against the laws criminalizing same-sex acts—still in force in the 1960s, for example, in the United Kingdom (Cook 2014) and West Germany (Moeller 2010)—in communist Poland such laws never existed. Moreover, without much pressure from below, the authorities themselves decriminalized same-sex prostitution in 1970. Clearly, the need for homosexual self-organizing was less urgent in Poland than in some Western countries at that time, at least as far as legal provisions on homosexuality were concerned.

4.3   EARLY 1980S: TRANSNATIONAL ORIGINS

The last decade of the communist Poland started with the formal recognition of an independent trade union Solidarity in September 1980 and the introduction of the martial law in December 1981, which lasted until July 1983. In his excellent essay on 'Sex and Solidarity', John Stanley (2010) argues that because the trade union was delegalized and forced to go underground during the marital law, it strengthened its relationship with the Roman Catholic Church, which was the only institution that could provide a safe haven for Solidarity at that time. This, Stanley (2010, p. 131) continues, explains the change in Solidarity's approach to gender- and sexuality-related issues from no clear take in the early 1980s to a distinctively conservative stance in the late 1980s, when Solidarity demanded, among other things, a ban on abortion. Though, we should remember that the Church was the most important ally of the political opposition throughout the communist rule in Poland (Żaryn 2011) and that most leaders of Solidarity, including Wałęsa, were religious and drew on religious nationalism from the beginning of Solidarity (Osa 1997). For that and other reasons, the authors of the first EEIP report (1982, p. 8) remained sceptical about the impact of Solidarity on homosexual emancipation in Poland: 'The liberalization which Solidarność [Solidarity] was working towards was aimed more in the direction of the social and political aspects of life. The movement was too shortlived to determine what effect it might have on public opinion concerning moral issues'. Nonetheless, despite its gender and sexual conservatism anchored in Roman Catholicism, Solidarity did provide a frame and ground for self-organizing of many other activists in Poland, for example, students, anti-militarists and environmentalists (Meardi 2005), and also feminists and LGBTs, for which Anna Gruszczyńska (2009b, p. 318) asks to recognize the 'conflicting legacy of Solidarity' in the Polish feminist and LGBT movements.

The introduction of the martial law had contradictory consequences for homosexuals in the PRL. On the one hand, we read in the 1982 EEIP report (p. 9) that, due to the tightening of censorship during the martial law, 'Polish gays are now forced to fight for their very survival. Any gay liberation activities have been abandoned for the time being'. On the other hand, we learn from the following report that 'Surprisingly enough, the gay movement in Poland under martial law has been strengthened. It seems that the authorities are having enough problems with political dissent so that, for the time being at least, repression of homosexuals has lessened' (EEIP 1983, p. 6). Similarly, the censorship of publications on homosexuality was reported to be relaxed in the early 1980s. For example, the 1983 EEIP report pointed to the publication of the book *Miazga* (The Pulp) by Andrzejewski in May 1982. Another example, not listed in the report, could be the article 'Gorzki fiolet' (Bitter violet) by Barbara Pietkiewicz, printed in the most popular weekly of that time, *Polityka* (Politics), in February 1981. Similarly to the already mentioned article in *Życie Literackie* from 1974, the one in *Polityka* treated homosexuality more seriously, presented it as an innate and fixed condition, and asked for the greater tolerance towards homosexuals in Poland. Though, it was not entirely free from prejudices and stereotypes: in one of the final passages Pietkiewicz (1981, p. 8) wrote that 'tolerance cannot equal acceptance or the granting of special rights'. The end of the martial law in the mid-1980s brought intensified surveillance and harassment of homosexuals by the police forces, which, as the 1985 EEIP report (p. 9) attests, 'suddenly remembered the gays'.

It is not clear what the authors of the first EEIP report (1982, p. 9) were referring to when they wrote about the suspension of Polish 'gay liberation activities' due to the introduction of the martial law. Some authors (Fiedotow 2012, p. 310; Krasicki 2001, p. 13) and primary sources (*Filo* 1989, 17, p. 19) do mention a number of homosexual initiatives at the very beginning of the 1980s, such as the Male Volunteer Sexual Service (MOPS), established already in 1980 in Piotrków Trybunalski, but they add that those were private, ephemeral and mainly focused on meeting new men for sexual and/or romantic purposes. Most likely, the EEIP reports were referring to the groups popping up thanks to the support of the Homosexual Initiative Vienna (HOSI), particularly Andrzej Selerowicz. Already in the second EEIP report (1983, p. 6), Selerowicz wrote that 'An informal group of gays that meets privately has expressed a willingness to work closely with the Eastern Europe Information Pool'. As Fiedotow (2012, p. 317) points out, it seems impossible to determine to what extent those early and more systematically organized groups in Poland were established thanks to the initiatives of HOSI. It is clear, however, that Selerowicz played a crucial role in supporting and consolidating the nascent homosexual movement in Poland. In March 1983, he started to distribute a short magazine in Polish, *Biuletyn/Etap* (EEIP 1983, p. 2; more about the magazine in the following chapter) and in the summer of the same year, he organized in Warsaw the first meeting of six Polish activists from different cities, all men (Mrok 1999). Similar meetings were also organized in the following years, surely in September 1984 and June 1985 (Mrok 1999; Selerowicz 1994).

In her analysis of selected letters from Polish homosexuals to Selerowicz, sent in response to *Biuletyn/Etap*, Fiedotow (2012, p. 261) points out that the most engaged activists were located in Gdańsk, Łódź, Warsaw and Wrocław; the last issue of the magazine additionally mentions groups in Cracow, Lublin and Żary (*Etap* 1987, 4, p. 1). One of the strongest, though still very informal, groups closely working with Selerowicz was Etap in Wrocław, with such key activists as Leszek Truchliński and Ryszard Ziobro (Fiedotow 2012; Mrok 1999). It was this group which took over the distribution of *Biuletyn* in 1986, since then circulated under the name *Etap*. Leaders of some other groups established in the second half of the 1980s also got to know about *Biuletyn/Etap* right after its creation in 1983 and soon got in touch with Selerowicz. Ryszard Kisiel, from the Gdańsk group Filo, recalls Selerowicz sending him Polish translations of Western books or plays with homoerotic themes, such as *Bent* by Martin Sherman and *Giovanni's Room* by James Baldwin, already by 1985 (Radziszewski and Kubara 2011; Szyk 2011). Waldemar Zboralski, one of the founders of the WRH, recollects that in 1983 he read an article about the International Gay Association (IGA, later ILGA) in West German *Der Spiegel*, asked the magazine for a contact address to the organization and thus started exchanging letters with Selerowicz (Kowalik 2013). *Etap* (1987, 1, p. 4) also mentioned a Łódź-based group Amiko as their contact address in Poland.

The HIV/AIDS epidemic, which broke out in the West at the very beginning of the 1980s, influenced the initiatives undertaken by Selerowicz, who in some issues of his magazine referred to the epidemic in order to encourage self-organizing of Polish homosexuals: 'Those critical moments, such as the AIDS epidemic, confirms the need for the existence of gay organizations' (*Biuletyn* 1985, 4, p. 1), he insisted. Still, as Jill Owczarzak (2009, p. 426) points out, 'From an epidemiological perspective, HIV/AIDS arrived in Poland relatively late (1985) and never reached the anticipated "epidemic" levels. In the years 1985, 1986, and 1987, for example, the number of newly detected HIV infections was 11, 9, and 32, respectively'. One important reason why there were no officially registered cases of HIV/AIDS in Poland before 1985 was the introduction of the martial law in 1981, which imposed stricter limitations on travelling abroad (Janiszewski 2013, p. 83). Still, the Polish press started reporting on HIV/AIDS already (or only) in 1983, with the first article published probably on 24 September that year in *Polityka*; it was an interview with a professor from the Medical School of Warsaw entitled 'AIDS znaczy strach' (AIDS means fear) (Mrok 1999). Some following articles adopted a similar medical approach to HIV/AIDS and simply reported on the state of knowledge about the virus and the disease at that time. Other articles took a more social approach but tended to present HIV/AIDS as an example of 'how rotten and decadent Western countries are' (EEIP 1983, p. 7) or scapegoat selected domestic groups such as homosexuals but also drug users, prostitutes as well as African, Arab and Latino students doing exchange programmes in Poland (Tomasik 2012, pp. 223–262).

Since 1985, when HIV/AIDS clearly became a Polish problem too, the number and diversity of publications on the topic increased dramatically, as the EEIP reports (1985–1989) attest. An important milestone in the visibility of homosexuals in Poland (and in relation to HIV/AIDS) was reached on 23 November 1985, when the *Polityka* weekly published an article 'Jesteśmy inni' (We are different), the first article in the Polish mainstream media authored by an openly homosexual person (see Fig. 4.2). Dariusz Prorok, under the pseudonym of Krzysztof T. Darski, started the article with the assertion that 'AIDS arrived in Poland. It is clear that homosexuals are the most affected group by the disease'. Yet, he quickly explained that because in Poland homosexuals were discriminated against and forced into heterosexual marriages, it was only a matter of time before HIV/AIDS would also become a problem of the heterosexual part of the society. In writing so, Prorok remained assertive and unapologetic, asking why, in this context, homosexuals should care about heterosexuals while the latter had never really cared about the former:

> Ridiculed and marginalized, discriminated against by all the social institutions and organizations without exception, haunted down by homophobes, insulted by cads, with the tacit consent of the prominent figures of the world, isolated and abandoned by the state, Church and sciences. And now suddenly it turns out that they [homosexuals] too are the citizens of the PRL. (Darski 1985, p. 8)

Finally, Prorok proposed a solution: the creation of an official organization which would cover the full range of homosexuality-related issues. The article evoked a nationwide discussion on homosexuality, joined also by the government's official spokesperson, Jerzy Urban (Tomasik 2012, pp. 244–251). In his reply to Prorok, published in *Polityka* two weeks later, Urban denied the accusations of discrimination against homosexuals in the PRL and ridiculed Prorok's demands for the establishment of a homosexual organization. He added that Poland did not need 'the Ministry for Pederasty' (EEIP 1986, p. 6).

Fig. 4.2 'Jesteśmy inni' (We are different) article in *Polityka* (23 November 1985, p. 8). Courtesy of *Polityka*

4.4   MID 1980S: OPERATION HYACINTH

The year 1985 was a watershed year for the nascent homosexual movement in the PRL. On 15 and 16 November, about three weeks before the Urban's official denial of discrimination against homosexuals, the police forces with the help of the secret service conducted undercover operation against homosexuals code-named 'Hyacinth' (Kurpios 2003; Mrok 1999; Szulc 2016a, b). The aim of the operation was to detain, interrogate and register both actual and alleged homosexuals in order to create a kind of state 'homosexual inventory', or 'pink archive'. The operation was relaunched at least twice, on 26–27 September 1986 and 16–17 November 1987 (IPN documents). It is estimated that altogether the police forces gathered around 11,000 files, the number which appeared in the 1988 letter from Professor Mikołaj Kozakiewicz to General Czesław Kiszczak, in which the former supported the official registration of a homosexual organization in Warsaw (Mrok 1999; more about the letter in the next section of this chapter).

Because Polish politicians and state institutions as well as the majority of Polish historians continue to ignore or silence the event, our knowledge about Operation Hyacinth remains limited to a few mentions in academic papers as well as journalistic accounts in the mainstream media and LGBT magazines. Most recently, on the 30th anniversary of the operation, the IPN released some limited data on the topic, specifically the internal-communication documents between the Polish Police Headquarters and its local branches in three cities: Szczecin (132 pages), Olsztyn (93 pages) and Tarnów (12 pages), which I consulted in the IPN's branch in Warsaw (see Fig. 4.3). Also on the occasion of the anniversary, two non-academic books were published in Polish: *Różowe Kartoteki* (The Pink Files) by Mikołaj Milcke (2015) and *Kryptonim 'Hiacynt'* (Code Name 'Hyacinth') by Selerowicz (2015). Both books adopt the genre of historical fiction, mixing real events with made-up stories, though Selerowicz assures me that his publication contains '90 per cent of facts' (interview with Selerowicz). Nevertheless, to date, conclusive information about many aspects of the operation remains elusive, including the way homosexuals were defined and identified, the real motivations behind the operation or the precise number and current location of personal files in the Polish pink archive.

Kisiel, from the Gdańsk group Filo, recalled his arrest in an interview for *DIK Fagazine*:

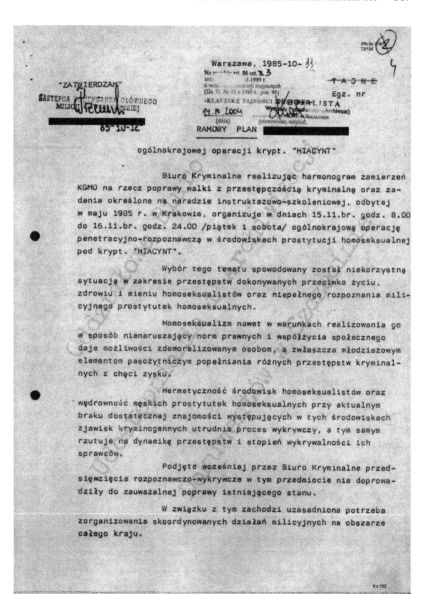

Fig. 4.3 First page of the framework plan for Operation Hyacinth (15–16 November 1985). Courtesy of the IPN

The police forces dragged us out of our homes and even from our workplaces and cafés. Someone simply rang my doorbell at six in the morning. I was really sleepy, as I had let a friend out from my apartment late at night … And I was so confused … Three security service guys barged into our hallway. I was still living with my parents back then. They called out my name … 'Please come with us …' They took me to the police station, where they tried to take my fingerprints and my photograph. In the beginning I tried to protest, but they intimidated me very quickly. (Radziszewski and Kubara 2011, p. 35)

Another activist, Waldemar Zboralski, the leader of the WRH, also described his arrest in an interview for the *Inaczej* (Differently) magazine:

They arrested me when I was at work (I was a nurse working in a hospital). During the interrogation the investigators filled in a document entitled 'The Dossier of a Homosexual' […] Above all, they asked for names. But also about sexual techniques, favourite sex positions and preferred types of lovers. (Wróblewski 1999, p. 5)

Some of the detained were also asked to sign the statement: 'I hereby declare that I, [name and surname], am a homosexual since birth. I had many sexual partners in my life, all of whom were adults. I am not interested in minors' (Kurpios 2003). They were threatened that unless they cooperated, their sexual orientation would be revealed to their family members, fellow students and/or colleagues. We do not know with certainty why the statement emphasized the natural character of homosexuality and differentiated between homosexuals and paedophiles. Kisiel suggested to me his belief that the interrogators used this innate definition of homosexuality to convince as many as possible to sign the statement, and then later blackmail them into cooperating with the secret service.

Some of the first to be detained, including the activists of the nascent Polish homosexual movement, were used by interrogators to identify other homosexuals. In an interview with *Replika* (Replica), Zboralski admitted that he involuntarily became an informant:

[At the time of the arrest] I was carrying a bag with a note book. I kept in it all the information from Andrzej Selerowicz about people with whom I wanted to cooperate. They searched me, found the note book and copied it. It was a mine of information about homosexual activists. (Kowalik 2013, p. 12)

Fiedotow (2012, p. 313) also points out that some homosexual activists based in Poland blamed Selerowicz himself for not being careful enough with handling their contact addresses, and few even accused him of cooperation with the Polish secret service. But the initial information about who, allegedly or not, was a homosexual came from the police's raids on gay meeting places such as cafés, baths, parks, public toilets and private houses, as well as from the archives of the PRL's institutions that had begun gathering information about homosexuals long before Operation Hyacinth was launched (Fiedotow 2012; Kurpios 2003). Additionally, there were a number of accidental sources. For example, in the 1985 EEIP report, published about six months before Operation Hyacinth, we read that

> When a homosexual was murdered in Gdańsk, the police found several hundred (!) letters in the victim's apartment which the man had received in answer to [personal] ads in *RELAKS*. All of the respondents were immediately brought in for questioning; their personal data, photos and fingerprints were taken and added to the militia's 'Pink Files' which expanded considerably. (EEIP 1985, p. 9)

The real motivations for launching the operation are still unclear. In fact, for some time, the authorities denied that the operation had ever taken place (Tomasik 2012, p. 43). Yet, an article published in the government weekly *W Służbie Narodu* (In the Nation's Service) in January 1986 relayed that 'the operation was not directed against homosexuals nor was it caused by the concern related to AIDS [...] It was directed against the parasitic and criminal elements operating within this social group' (Kopka 1986, p. 13). At least in the official version, then, the operation was justified by a desire to protect homosexuals (and those who happened to interact with them) against the criminals who indeed robbed, assaulted or even murdered them (see also Kirzyński 1986 in the same weekly). Kurpios (2003) points out, however, that one of the prime motivations for launching the operation could have been to intimidate the nascent social movement of homosexuals. The framework plans of Operation Hyacinth for the years 1985, 1986 and 1987, sent by the Polish Police Headquarters to its local branches, which I consulted in the IPN, do not support Kurpios' thesis. Though, they too give a somewhat ambiguous picture. On the one hand, the documents pointed out that the key aim of the operation was indeed to fight against criminal activities, and delegated the job accordingly to the criminal departments of local police branches. The reports sent back from the branches to the headquarters too primarily focused on criminal activity. On the other hand, however, the framework plans also mentioned, if only briefly, such aims as to prevent the spreading of HIV and to recruit secret informants. Additionally, in an update note sent by the headquarters only three days before launching the operation in 1985, the officers were further instructed to 'identify those homosexuals who are in touch with the international association of homosexuals based in Vienna' (IPN documents). This indicates that the headquarters were aware of and concerned about at least some aspects of the EEIP programme.

The greatest unknown regarding Operation Hyacinth, however, remains the precise number of personal files in the pink archive, as well as its current location. A small part of the collection has been found in the archives of the Polish Police Headquarters. Some are probably also stored in the IPN. Fiedotow (2012) suggests that most of the files remain scattered in the archives of local police stations. The information about the location of the personal files is of critical importance: there is a risk that those who continue to have access to the files will misuse the knowledge they contain. For that reason, in 2004, Campaign Against Homophobia (KPH), the largest Polish LGBT organization established in 2001, asked the Ministry of the Interior and Administration to destroy the personal pink files. Robert Biedroń, the leader of KPH at that time, explained that 'The files were used in the 1990s for political blackmail. This situation could be repeated' (Życie Warszawy 2004). However, the issue was abandoned because the files could not be located. While there is indeed the possibility of misusing the pink files, their destruction would once again render homosexuals invisible within the official version of the history of communist Poland. Therefore, I would rather suggest that Polish politicians and state institutions actively engage in locating and securing the pink files to eliminate the risk of misusing the knowledge they contain, but also to allow their thorough and careful examination by historians.

4.5   Late 1980s: Demands for Recognition

Operation Hyacinth was a shock for many Polish homosexuals, who could no longer have illusions about the secrecy of their homosexuality and the attitude of authorities towards homosexuals. Some of them withdrew even deeper into the closet, some fled abroad, as did Prorok, the author of the famous 'We are different' article in *Polityka* (Darski 1985).

Others, however, became outraged and responded with greater mobilization. For that reason, in one of my previous publications, I compared Operation Hyacinth to the Stonewall Riots (Szulc 2011, p. 162). Even though Operation Hyacinth did not trigger any organized protests or street riots, it did fuel new activist initiatives. Kisiel, for example, recollects in an interview with *DIK Fagazine* that 'the real reason behind creating *Filo* was the anti-gay militia campaign under the name "Hyacinth"' (Radziszewski and Kubara 2011, p. 30). The first issue of the *Filo* magazine was published in Gdańsk on 3 November 1986. For nearly a year, Kisiel was editing the magazine by himself, with some help of a friend who was a graphic designer. After a year, a student of journalism joined the project. Gradually, the magazine attracted other people, who soon formed one of the strongest homosexual groups in Poland in the second half of the 1980s, next to the Wrocław-based Etap and the Warsaw-based WRH. The last 'underground' (not officially registered) issue of *Filo*, dated May 1990, listed ten people involved in the magazine, including one woman, Paulina Pilch, an editor-in-chief of the lesbian section. I will provide more details about the magazine in the following chapter.

Operation Hyacinth also outraged Zboralski, who, as mentioned before, already since 1983 stayed in touch with Selerowicz. Right after his interrogation in November 1985, Zboralski sent a letter to Selerowicz about the operation. As he recalls in an interview for *Replika*: 'I thought that now [after the interrogation], when everybody knows everything about me, I need to put all my anger, rebellion and energy to good use' (Kowalik 2013, p. 13). Zboralski, hailed by Tomasik (2012, p. 12) as 'the gay Wałęsa', moved from his hometown Nowa Sól to Warsaw, where he started organizing the WRH, together with such prominent activists as Sławek Starosta and Krzysztof Garwatowski. The first meeting of the WRH is reported to take place on 24 January 1987 (Mrok 1999; Zboralski 1991), though Starosta recollects that some meetings were held already in 1986 (Kowalik 2012, p. 12). In June 1987, the group started publishing its own magazine, *Efebos*, but the project was soon abandoned after publishing only one or, possibly, two issues of the magazine. One of the aims of the group was to increase the visibility of homosexuals in public discourse. Therefore, the leaders of the WRH, particularly Zboralski, took part in TV and radio programmes on homosexuality, such as *Rozmowy Intymne* (Intimate talks) aired on the Polish Radio on 18 December 1987 (Mrok 1999; Zboralski 1991), though still under pseudonyms and placed with their backs to the camera.

In the late 1980s, Polish homosexuals also took first steps to officially register their groups. One such attempt was made by Truchliński, from the Wrocław group Etap, who enquired about the possibility to register the group at the local voivodship office but received a negative reply (EEIP 1987, p. 8; *Filo* 1989, 16, p. 16). More controversial in public discourse was the case of the WRH. To meet all the requirements of the registration, the Warsaw group officially chose its leaders as well as adopted its name, statute and logo, the latter being a male version of the Mermaid of Warsaw, the city's coat of arms (see Fig. 4.4). On 24 March 1988, the activists submitted their application to the Warsaw City Council (Mrok 1999; Selerowicz 1994). Importantly, they received the support of some prominent public figures, in the form of an open letter to the Ministry of Internal Affairs, written by Kozakiewicz, who at that time was also a Member of Parliament. The letter was signed by, among other people, the sexologist Kazimierz Imieliński, film director Jerzy Kawalerowicz and *Polityka*'s journalists Barbara Pietkiewicz and Daniel Passent. Zboralski (1991) reports that right after submitting the application for the registration of the WRH, he became an object of meticulous attention from the secret service, which was trying to exhort him to withdraw the application. Because of these persecutions, Zboralski decided to immigrate to Denmark.

Just as the article by Prorok in *Polityka* in 1985, so too the first applications for the official recognition of homosexual organizations in Poland heavily drew on the discourse of HIV and AIDS. The statute adopted by the WRH started with the following words:

> For many reasons of social and cultural nature, but most importantly because of the spreading of the AIDS disease, convinced that there is a necessity to reach as many homosexual people as possible—who are one of the increased risk groups—we would like to officially register our activity under the name of 'Homosexual Movement'. (Kołodziejski 1987, p. 22)

Similarly, the letter of support written by Kozakiewicz referred to HIV/ AIDS already in the first paragraph. The author explained that during last ten months of 1987 the official number of people infected with the 'AIDS virus' (sic) increased in Poland from 24 to nearly 60; that homosexuals were one of the 'increased risk groups'; and that because of their social isolation, they were very difficult to reach. Therefore, in order to (1) promote safer sex among homosexuals, (2) protect their dignity and (3)

Fig. 4.4 Logo of the Warsaw Homosexual Movement. Courtesy of Waldemar Zboralski

reduce the crime rate within 'homosexual milieu', Kozakiewicz requested to allow homosexuals to organize themselves. It becomes clear, then, that the spread of HIV/AIDS to the Eastern Bloc in the second half of the 1980s not only led to the greater visibility of Polish homosexuals, as well as the visibility of Western gay and lesbian cultures and movements in Poland (Więch 2005), but also provided Polish activists with a framework within which they could formulate their demands beyond the discourse of minority rights: HIV/AIDS was presented as a soon-to-become nation-wide problem, which would affect heterosexuals as much as homosexuals.

Still, all the attempts at the official registration of a homosexual organization in the PRL failed. Although the WRH never received an official reply to their application, *Polityka* informed on 29 October 1988 that 'the Warsaw Homosexual Movement was refused registration because its activity would violate the rules of public morality' (p. 2). The support for homosexuals in society at large seemed to be indeed very low at the end of the 1980s. In November 1988, the Polish Public Opinion Research Centre (CBOS) published a report on 'Opinions about homosexuality: Tolerance or condemnation?'. CBOS explained that the main reason for conducting the survey was 'the increased activity of homosexuals, manifested by their aspirations to create and register their own association' (p. 2). Thirty-eight per cent of the respondents considered 'the problem of homosexuality in Poland' as either petty or non-existent, 31 per cent as serious and another 31 per cent answered that it was difficult to say. Furthermore, over the half of the respondents concurred with the idea that the authorities should not allow the registration of a homosexual organization, a quarter took the contrary view, and another quarter did not have a clear opinion about it. Most scarily, however, nearly a half of the respondents thought that the state should 'fight' homosexuals and only 6.6 per cent answered that the state should 'protect' them. It is not clear if the authorities had commissioned the survey or if they had known about its results before they denied an official registration of the WRH. The reliability of the survey is also difficult to assess. Nonetheless, the report was clearly working to the advantage of the state, which decided to dismiss the request of homosexual activists.

Additional, unofficial, reasons for refusing the registration of homosexual organizations in the PRL were supposed to be the state's fear of the Church's negative reaction as well as the activists' contacts with Western organizations (Kowalik 2012; Mrok 1999). Regarding the latter, homosexual groups in Poland indeed started to tighten their relationship with activists on the other side of the Iron Curtain in the second half of the 1980s. The representatives of Etap and the WRH took part in the annual ILGA conference for the first time in May 1987, in Cologne, where the two groups were also accepted as official ILGA members; Filo joined ILGA in 1989 (Fiedotow 2012; Mrok 1999). Besides, Polish activists took part in the sub-regional conferences organized by ILGA and HOSI: in November 1987 in Budapest, in May 1988 in Warsaw and in

April 1989 again in Budapest. Since 1988, the Polish groups also twinned with Western organizations: the WRH started to cooperate with the Swiss HACH and Filo with the Norwegian Tupilak (Fiedotow 2012, p. 312) as well as the Swedish RFSL Stockholm (interview with Kisiel). Importantly, at least some of these transnational connections were known to the general public and the authorities. For example, an article entitled 'Inny homo' (Different homo), published in the weekly *Argumenty* (Arguments) in 1987, explained that Polish homosexual activists

> follow the example of foreign gay movements, which have their own 'official' clubs, publications and even an international association. Representatives of two Polish groups from Warsaw and Wrocław joined ILGA (International Lesbian and Gay Association), and laid a foundation for their own organizations. (Tumiłowicz 1987, p. 6; for other examples see Selerowicz 1994, p. 23)

I have also pointed out that the information about HOSI was mentioned in some police documents regarding Operation Hyacinth. Therefore, it seems plausible that the transnational contacts of the Polish activists with their Western counterparts influenced the authorities' negative decision regarding the registration of homosexual groups.

4.6   CONCLUSION

The year 1989 did bring about far-reaching political and social changes in Poland. It also marked a new era in Polish homosexual activism: in the end, it was only after the fall of communism in Europe when the first Polish homosexual organization was officially recognized by the state. The organization was named the Association of Lambda Groups and was registered in 1990 (Adamska 1998; Gruszczyńska 2009b). Yet, it did not come out of nowhere. Its declaration of aims, reprinted in the last underground issue of *Filo*, had been signed by three groups formed already in the 1980s: Wrocław-based Etap, Gdańsk-based Filo and Warsaw-based WRH. This as well as all other versatile sources presented in this chapter attests that homosexual self-organizing in Poland began already before 1989. First homosexual groups were formed at the beginning of the 1980s and a more systematically organized activism dates back at least to the mid-1980s, when the activists outraged by Operation Hyacinth intensified their efforts and demanded official recognition. For that reason, Operation

Hyacinth could be considered as a 'catalytic event' (Darsey 1991) of the Polish homosexual movement, similar to the Stonewall Riots (Szulc 2011, p. 162). Though, the comparison to Stonewall may be unnecessary here, and not only because it perpetuates the privileged position of the United States in the history of LGBT activism: after all, as I point out elsewhere, 'If Stonewall is a history that is *made* [Piontek 2006], what does it mean to search for the Polish equivalent? In the end, it becomes a search for a copy with no original, a simulacrum' (Szulc 2014).

The spread of the HIV/AIDS epidemic to the Eastern Bloc and the proliferation of public discourses on this topic in Poland in the mid-1980s provided homosexual activists with an important framework within which they were able to pursue their objectives. As Arkadiusz Więch (2005, p. 261) points out 'It may sound like a paradox, but it was thanks to AIDS that a homosexual in the PRL saw the light of day'. It was also the discourses of HIV and AIDS that helped Polish activists to justify the need for the establishment and registration of their groups and to gain support for their demands from some prominent public figures. Like their counterparts in some other Eastern Bloc countries, the Polish activists did not directly challenge the communist state but tried to work within and with the system to address the HIV/AIDS problem and to create a space for homosexual movement. One of the postulates in the WRH's statute was 'to cooperate with the authorities in the areas of [HIV/AIDS] prevention, hygiene and health propaganda, as well as the protection of homosexuals against crime groups' (Kołodziejski 1987, p. 22). Unlike their counterparts in some other Eastern Bloc countries, however, the Polish activists could not count much on the major institutional support of such segments of society or the state as church, university, sexologists or health authorities. Reluctant to cooperate with the conservative Polish Roman Catholic Church ('deviation should not form a coalition with devoutness', as Kisiel joked during our interview) or with the political opposition, especially the Solidarity movement (much due to its alliance with the Church), homosexual activists in Poland remained relatively independent. Because of that, as well as thanks to the active involvement of Selerowicz in the EEIP programme, Polish homosexual activists strongly relied on their cross-border partnership with ILGA, but also with other national organizations in the West (particularly HOSI), from the very beginning of their existence.

I have just proposed that Operation Hyacinth could be considered as a 'catalytic event', possibly a beginning point, of the Polish homosexual movement. But some authors (Kurpios 2003) and primary sources (IPN documents) suggest that one of the secondary aims of Operation Hyacinth was to weaken the already existing, even though informal, homosexual groups in Poland. Therefore, an alternative proposition for establishing the beginning point of Polish homosexual activism could be the year 1983, when Selerowicz started to publish *Biuletyn/Etap* and facilitated the creation of more systematically organized groups among some readers of the magazine, especially in Wrocław. This transnational intervention from the West played a key role in motivating, integrating and mobilizing Polish homosexuals, who until then seemed to be satisfied with their relative freedoms, at least with the progressive (for that time and compared to some Western countries) legislation related to homosexuality. However, to push the discussion still a bit further we may acknowledge that some arguments for the acceptance of homosexuality were made in public already in the interwar Poland, for example, by the famous writer Tadeusz Boy-Żeleński (Janicki 2015; Tomasik 2014). The interwar period, thus, could also possibly serve as the beginning point of a (more sporadic and informal) homosexual activism in Poland. Of course, I discuss those different propositions not to establish a new mythical beginning of the Polish homosexual movement but to reflect on the processes of beginning making. In the end, while not denying the special importance of the year 1989, my central aim in this chapter was to challenge the idea that the fall of communism in Poland, as much as the Stonewall Riots in the United States, was a 'unifying and originary historical moment' (Bravmann 1997, p. 85) for the emergence of homosexual activism.

BIBLIOGRAPHY

Adamska, K. (1998). *Ludzie obok: Lesbijki i geje w Polsce*. Toruń: Pracownia Duszycki.

Baer, M. (2009). "Let Them Hear Us!" The politics of same-sex transgression in contemporary Poland. In H. Donnan & F. Magowan (Eds.), *Transgressive sex: Subversion and control in erotic encounters* (pp. 131–150). New York: Berghahn Books.

Biskupski, M. B. (2000). *The history of Poland*. Westport, CT: Greenwood Press.

Bravmann, S. (1997). *Queer fictions of the past: History, culture, and difference*. Cambridge: Cambridge University Press.

Bren, P. (2004). 1968 East and West: Visions of political change and student protest from across the Iron Curtain. In G.-R. Horn & P. Kenney (Eds.), *Transnational moments of change: Europe 1945, 1968, 1989* (pp. 119–135). Lanham: Rowman & Littlefield.

Chetaille, A. (2011). Poland: Sovereignty and sexuality in post-socialist times. In M. Tremblay, D. Paternotte, & C. Johnson (Eds.), *The lesbian and gay movement and the state: Comparative insights into a transformed relationship* (pp. 119–133). Farnham: Ashgate.

Chetaille, A. (2015). *Les paradoxes d'une histoire sans transition: Entre l'Ouest et la nation, les mobilisations gaies et lesbiennes en Pologne (1980–2010).* Doctoral dissertation. École des Hautes Études en Sciences Sociales.

Cook, M. (2014). Sexual revolution(s) in Britain. In G. Hekma & A. Giami (Eds.), *Sexual revolutions* (pp. 121–140). Basingstoke: Palgrave Macmillan.

Czajkowska, A. (2012). O dopuszczalności przerywania ciąży: Ustawa z dnia 27 kwietnia 1956 r. i towarzyszące jej dyskusje. In P. Barański, A. Czajkowska, A. Fiedotow & A. Wochna-Tymińska (Eds.), *Kłopoty z seksem w PRL: Rodzenie nie całkiem po ludzku, aborcja, choroby, odmienności* (pp. 99–186). Warszawa: Wydawnictwa Uniwersytetu Warszawskiego.

Darsey, J. (1991). From "Gay is Good" to the scourge of AIDS: The evolution of gay liberation rhetoric, 1977–1990. *Communication Studies, 42*(1), 43–66.

Darski, K. T. (1985, November 23). Jesteśmy inni: Czy homoseksualiści mają prawa? *Polityka, 47,* 8.

Davies, N. (1981[1991]). *God's playground: A history of Poland. Volume II: 1795 to the present.* Oxford: Clarendon Press.

Eisler, J. (1991). *Marzec 1968: Geneza, przebieg, konsekwencje.* Warszawa: PWN.

Eisler, J. (2006). *Polski rok 1968.* Warszawa: IPN.

Evans, S. M. (2009). Sons, daughters, and patriarchy: Gender and the 1968 generation. *The American Historical Review, 114*(2), 331–347.

Falk, B. (2003). *The dilemmas of dissidence in East-Central Europe.* Budapest: CEU Press.

Fiedotow, A. (2012). Początki ruchu gejowskiego w Polsce (1981–1990). In P. Barański, A. Czajkowska, A. Fiedotow & A. Wochna-Tymińska (Eds.), *Kłopoty z seksem w PRL: Rodzenie nie całkiem po ludzku, aborcja, choroby, odmienności* (pp. 241–258). Warszawa: Wydawnictwa Uniwersytetu Warszawskiego.

Frątczak, A. (2012). Polish feminist and LGBT press: Twenty years of emancipation. In K. Pokorna-Ignatowicz (Ed.), *The Polish media system 1989–2011* (pp. 157–179). Kraków: Krakow Society for Education, AFM Publishing House.

Garsztecki, S. (2008). Poland. In M. Klimke & J. Scharloth (Eds.), *1968 in Europe: A history of protests and activism, 1956–1977* (pp. 179–187). Basingstoke: Palgrave Macmillan.

Gawin, M. (2008). The sex reform movement and eugenics in interwar Poland. *Studies in History and Philosophy of Biological and Biomedical Sciences, 39,* 181–186.

Gorgol, T. (1974, April 28 and May 5). Homoseksualizm a opinia. *Życie Literackie, 17 and 18,* 12 and 12.

Górnicka-Boratyńska, A. (Ed.). (1999). *Chcemy całego życia. Antologia polskich tekstów feministycznych z lat 1870–1939*. Warszawa: Res Publika.

Gruszczyńska, A. (2009a). *Queer enough? Contested terrains of identity deployment in the context of gay and lesbian public activism in Poland.* Doctoral dissertation. Aston University.

Gruszczyńska, A. (2009b). Sowing the seeds of solidarity in public space: Case study of the Poznan March of Equality. *Sexualities, 12*(3), 312–333.

Janicki, K. (2015). *Epoka hipokryzji: Seks i erotyka w przedwojennej Polsce*. Kraków: Znak.

Janiszewski, J. (2013). *Kto w Polsce ma HIV?* Warszawa: Wydawnictwo Krytyki Politycznej.

Kirchknopf, J. K. (2013). Ausmaß und Intensität der Verfolgung weiblicher Homosexualität in Wien während der NS-Zeit. Rechtshistorische und quantitative Perspektiven auf Dokumente der Verfolgungsbehörden. *Invertito: Jahrbuch für die Geschichte der Homosexualitäten, 15*, 75–112.

Kirzyński, J. (1986, July 12). W męskim gronie. *W Służbie Narodu, 49*, 16 and 21.

Kliszczyński, K. (2001). A child of a young democracy: The Polish gay movement, 1989–1999. In H. Flam (Ed.), *Pink, purple, green: Women's, religious, environmental and gay/lesbian movements in Central Europe today* (pp. 161–168). New York: Columbia University Press.

Kołodziejski, A. (1987). Różowy trójkąt. *Pan, 2*, 22.

Kopka, S. (1986, January 12). Hiacynt. *W Służbie Narodu, 2*(1661), 11 and 13.

Kościańska, A. (2016). Sex on equal terms. Polish sexology on women's emancipation and "good sex" from the 1970s to the present. *Sexualities, 19*(1/2), 236–256.

Kowalik, W. (2012, September). Gej Sławek Pierwszy. An interview with Sławek Starosta, *Replika, 39*, 12–13.

Kowalik, W. (2013, July). Moja karta homoseksualisty. An interview with Waldemar Zboralski, *Replika, 44*, 12–13.

Kowalska, A. (2011). Polish queer lesbianism: Sexual identity without a lesbian community. *Journal of Lesbian Studies, 15*(3), 324–336.

Krasicki, A. C. (2001, April 22). Gej znaczy przeklęty, *Przekrój, 16*, 10–13.

Kurkiewicz, S. (1913). *Słownik płciowy: Zbiór wyrażeń o płciowych właściwościach, przypadłościach i t.p.* Kraków: Nakładem autora.

Kurpios, P. (2003). Poszukiwani, poszukiwane. Geje i lesbijki a rzeczywistość PRL. *Zeszyty Kulturoznawcze, 1*, 27–34.

Lease, B. (2016). In Warsaw's New York: Krzysztof Warlikowski's queer interventions. In A. Campbell & S. Farrier (Eds.), *Queer dramaturgies: International perspectives on where performance leads queer* (pp. 35–50). Basingstoke: Palgrave Macmillan.

Leszkowicz, P., & Kitliński, T. (2005). *Miłość i demokracja: Rozważania o kwestii homoseksualnej w Polsce*. Kraków: Aureus.

Macey, D. (1993). *The lives of Michel Foucault*. London: Hutchinson.
McNair, B. (1991). *Glasnost, perestroika and the Soviet media*. London: Routledge.
Meardi, G. (2005). The legacy of solidarity: Class, democracy, culture and subjectivity in the Polish social movement. *Social Movement Studies, 4*(3), 261–280.
Mikulski, A. (1920). *Homoseksualizm ze stanowiska medycyny i prawa*. Warszawa: Gazeta Lekarska.
Milcke, M. (2015). *Różowe kartoteki*. Słupsk: Wydawnictwo Dobra Literatura.
Mizielińska, J., & Kulpa, R. (2011). "Contemporary peripheries": Queer studies, circulation of knowledge and East/West divide. In R. Kulpa & J. Mizielińska (Eds.), *De-centring Western sexualities: Central and Eastern European perspectives* (pp. 11–26). Farnham: Ashgate.
Moeller, R. G. (2010). Private acts, public anxieties, and the fight to decriminalize male homosexuality in West Germany. *Feminist Studies, 36*(3), 528–552.
Moszczeńska, I. (1904). *Czego nie wiemy o naszych synach*. Warszawa: Księgarnia Naukowa.
Mrok, M. (1999). *Ruch gejowski w Polsce od 1989 (PRL) oraz ruch gejowski w III Rzeczpospolitej po 1989 do 1999*. Gdańsk: G-Eye Team.
O'Dwyer, C. (2012). Does the EU help or hinder gay-rights movements in post-communist Europe? The case of Poland. *East European Politics, 28*(4), 332–352.
O'Dwyer, C., & Vermeersch, P. (2016). From pride to politics: Niche-party politics and LGBT rights in Poland. In K. Slootmaeckers, H. Touquet, & P. Vermeersch (Eds.), *The EU enlargement and gay politics: The impact of Eastern enlargement on rights, activism and prejudice* (pp. 123–145). London: Palgrave Macmillan.
Osa, M. (1997). Creating Solidarity: The religious foundations of the Polish Social Movement. *East European Politics and Societies, 11*(2), 339–365.
Owczarzak, J. (2009). Defining democracy and the terms of engagement with the postsocialist Polish state: Insights from HIV/AIDS. *East European Politics and Societies, 23*(3), 421–445.
Pietkiewicz, B. (1981, February 21). Gorzki fiolet. *Polityka, 8*, 8.
Piontek, T. (2006). *Queering gay and lesbian studies*. Urbana: University of Illinois Press.
Płatek, M. (2009). Sytuacja osób homoseksualnych w prawie karnym. In R. Wieruszewski & M. Wyrzykowski (Eds.), *Orientacja seksualna i tożsamość płciowa* (pp. 49–81). Warszawa: Instytut Wydawniczy EuroPrawo.
Radziszewski, K., & Kubara, P. (2011, September). Interview with Ryszard Kisiel. *DIK Fagazine, 8*, 30–39.
Said, E. (1975). *Beginnings: Intention and method*. New York: Basic Books.
Sasanka, P. (2011). Polska Gierka—Dekada przerwana czy zmarnowana? In K. Persak & P. Machcewicz (Eds.), *PRL od grudnia 70 do czerwca 89* (pp. 7–34). Warszawa: Bellona.

Selerowicz, A. (1994). *Leksykon kochających inaczej: Fakty, daty, nazwiska*. Poznań: Softpress.

Selerowicz, A. (2015). *Kryptonim 'Hiacynt'*. Kraków: Wydawnictwo Queermedia. pl.

Stanley, J. (2010). Sex and Solidarity, 1980–1990. *Canadian Slavonic Papers: Revue Canadienne des Slavistes, 52*(1–2), 131–151.

Stasińska, A. (2012). Od "Niech nas zobaczą" do "Miłość nie wyklucza": Jak zmieniła się polityczna strategia LGBT w Polsce w ostatnich latach? In M. Kłosowska, M. Drozdowski & A. Stasińska (Eds.), *Strategie queer: Od teorii do praktyki* (pp. 94–114). Warszawa: Difin.

Szot, W. (2011a). Zofia Sadowska w relacjach prasy brukowej (1). *Homiki.pl*. Retrieved April 5, 2017, from http://homiki.pl/index.php/2011/11/zofia-sadowska-w-relacjach-prasy-brukowej-1/

Szot, W. (2011b). Zofia Sadowska w relacjach prasy brukowej (2). *Homiki.pl*. Retrieved April 5, 2017, from http://homiki.pl/index.php/2011/11/zofia-sadowska-w-relacjach-prasy-brukowej-2/

Szulc, L. (2011). Queer in Poland: Under construction. In L. Downing & R. Gillett (Eds.), *Queer in Europe: Contemporary case studies* (pp. 159–172). Farnham: Ashgate.

Szulc, L. (2014). Making the Polish Stonewall. *Notches: (Re)marks on the History of Sexuality*. Retrieved June 4, 2016, from http://notchesblog.com/2014/02/21/making-the-polish-stonewall/

Szulc, L. (2015). Book review. Krzysztof Tomasik, Gejerel: Mniejszości Seksualne w PRL-u. *Sexualities, 18*(8), 1018–1019.

Szulc, L. (2016a). Niespodziewane efekty akcji "Hiacynt". *Ale Historia, 47*(201), 14–15.

Szulc, L. (2016b). Operation Hyacinth and Poland's pink files. *Notches: (Re)marks on the History of Sexuality*. Retrieved March 17, 2016, from http://notchesblog.com/2016/02/02/operation-hyacinth-and-polands-pink-files/

Szyk, A. (2011, March). Mają państwo w domu zboka. An interview with Ryszard Kisiel. *Replika, 30*, 8–9.

Tomasik, K. (2012). *Gejerel: Mniejszości Seksualne w PRL-u*. Warszawa: Wydawnictwo Krytyki Politycznej.

Tomasik, K. (2014). *Homobiografie*. Warszawa: Wydawnictwo Krytyki Politycznej.

Tumiłowicz, B. (1987). Inny homo. *Argumenty, 42*, 6.

Wachholz, L. (1900). Krytyczne uwagi w sprawie uranicznego poczucia płciowego. *Krytyka Lekarska*, 7–8.

Warkocki, B. (2014). Trzy fale emancypacji homoseksualnej w Polsce. *Porównania, 15*, 121–132.

Warkocki, B., & Sypniewski, Z. (2004). Wstęp. In Z. Sypniewski & B. Warkocki (Eds.), *Homofobia po Polsku* (pp. 5–13). Warszawa: Wydawnictwo Sic!.

Więch, A. S. (2005). Różowy odcień PRL-u: Zarys badań nad mniejszościami seksualnymi w Polsce Ludowej. In K. Slany, B. Kowalska & M. Śmietana (Eds.), *Homoseksualizm: Perspektywa interdyscyplinarna* (pp. 257–264). Kraków: Nomos.

Wróblewski, S. (1999, October). Pytaniami deptano najintymniejszą sferę człowieka. An interview with Waldemar Zboralski, *Inaczej, 10*, 5 and 10.

Żaryn, J. (2011). Państwo-Kościół katolicki w Polsce 1956–1989 (wybrane zagadnienia). In K. Persak & P. Machcewicz (Eds.), *PRL od grudnia 70 do czerwca 89* (pp. 35–122). Warszawa: Bellona.

Zboralski, W. (1991, February). Wspomnienia weterana. *Inaczej, 9*, 2–3 and 5.

Życie Warszawy. (2004, August 11). Akta Hiacynta pilnie poszukiwane. Retrieved March 8, 2017, from http://www.zw.com.pl/artykul/152842.html?print=tak

PART II

Transnationalism in Gay and Lesbian Magazines

CHAPTER 5

Polish Gay and Lesbian Magazines

Gay and lesbian magazines played a crucial role in the emergence of Western homosexual activism at the end of the eighteenth and through the nineteenth century. As Roger Streitmatter points out in his extensive history of the US gay and lesbian press:

> Russian revolutionary Vladimir Lenin observed that a newspaper is one of the best political organizers, and that is especially true with respect to the emergence of a self-conscious gay community. Because we exist everywhere but each of us must consciously identify himself or herself as a gay person, newspapers and magazines are uniquely important in our social movement. (Streitmatter 1995, p. xiii)

In this sense, the significance of gay and lesbian press for activism lies not only in its capacity to challenge mainstream discourses and, ultimately, to transform societies and cultures but also in its ability to create a sense of common identity around which it is possible to form a group, community or movement. The history of homosexual publishing proves that gay and lesbian press was indeed key for the establishing of both the homophile movement, originating in Germany (e.g. Marhoefer 2015a, b; Oosterhuis 1992), and gay liberation, originating in the United States (e.g. Baim 2012b; Streitmatter 1995). History also teaches us that gay and lesbian press became a key medium of transnational communication between

© The Author(s) 2018
L. Szulc, *Transnational Homosexuals in Communist Poland*,
Global Queer Politics, DOI 10.1007/978-3-319-58901-5_5

homosexual activists in different Western countries, at least until the popularization of the internet and invention of the World Wide Web.

In Poland too, first more systematic attempts at homosexual self-organizing, described in the previous chapter, were closely intertwined with the publishing of magazines. In fact, two out of the three main homosexual groups formed in Poland in the 1980s were created around a magazine. The Etap group from Wrocław emerged thanks to the collaboration of Polish activists with Andrzej Selerowicz, who started to produce what was most likely the first Polish gay magazine called *Biuletyn* (later renamed *Etap*) in 1983 in Vienna, and who needed help to photocopy and distribute it in Poland. The Filo group from Gdańsk also emerged around a magazine, entitled *Filo*, first published in 1986 by Ryszard Kisiel. The two titles turned out to be the most successful cases of gay and lesbian press in communist Poland, each published relatively regularly for about four years (see Table 5.1). Other groups also produced their magazines but those proved either short-lived or were set up in the very late 1980s. The activists in Warsaw, for example, published only one or, possibly, two issues of *Efebos* in 1987 and the activists in Łódź started to produce *Kabaret* in December 1989. With their authors speaking Western languages, Polish magazines, at least *Biuletyn/Etap* and *Filo*, abounded in transnational information, primarily originating in Western gay and lesbian magazines, to which Selerowicz had access in Vienna and which Kisiel, and other authors of *Filo*, were receiving from sailors and travellers or by mail.

In this chapter, my aim is to present a brief history, production context and general content of the two most successful gay and lesbian magazines in communist Poland, *Biuletyn/Etap* and *Filo*. Before doing so, however, I will provide additional theoretical and contextual information, which will help to understand the emergence of these magazines. First, I will review some conceptual frameworks for defining and analysing 'alternative media' and discuss their importance for social movements. Second, I will trace the history of gay and lesbian publishing in the West, pointing to its crucial role in both creating national homosexual movements and connecting their activists transnationally, but also—as will become evident later in this chapter—in inspiring authors of *Biuletyn/Etap* and *Filo*. Third, I will focus on the Polish publishing context in the 1980s, when the first gay and lesbian magazines emerged despite communist censorship and in opposition to the core of the underground publishing. Finally, in the last two sections, I will zoom in on *Biuletyn/Etap* and *Filo*, detailing their history and emphasizing their transnational dimensions. The chapter will be based primarily on my three in-depth and face-to-face interviews

Table 5.1 List of issues and number of pages of *Biuletyn/Etap* and *Filo* (original numbering, size approximate; M stands for 'Missing' and SI for 'Special Issue')

Biuletyn/Etap		Year	Filo	
Size	Issue		Issue	Size
1.5	1	1983		
1.5	2			
M	3			
1	4			
1	1	1984		
M	2			
M	3			
2	4			
2	1	1985		
2	2			
2	3			
4	4			
2	1	1986		
2	2			
4	3		1	1
4	4		2	4
4	1	1987	3	6
4	2		4	4
4	3		5–6	8
4	4		7–8	8
			9–10	8
			11–12	8
		1988	13	8
			14	12
			15	20
		1989	16	16
			SI	4
			17	28
			18	32
		1990	19	44
			20	54
45		Total		265

with the editors-in-chief of *Biuletyn/Etap* and *Filo*, Selerowicz and Kisiel respectively, as well as Paulina Pilch, the only regular female contributor to *Filo*. As mentioned in Chap. 1, the interviews were filmed and longer excerpts from them are available in Polish with English subtitles on the book's website: www.transnationalhomosexuals.pl. Some additional information comes from analysing the magazines' content.

5.1   Alternative Media and Social Movements

Alternative media is a broad and debated term encompassing different media technologies, modes of media production and distribution as well as media content (Atton 2002, 2015; Downing 2015). Many definitions of alternative media focus on the production process, which is considered to be, in contrast to the mainstream media, deprofessionalized, deinstitutionalized and decapitalized (Hamilton 2001 in Atton 2002, p. 25; Williams 1980). While some authors propose stricter criteria, for example by requiring 'a democratic/collectivist process of production' (O'Sullivan et al. 1994, p. 205), others broaden up the scope of alternative media production, for example by including commercial media (Bailey et al. 2008). Still others ask to recognize the unique modes of not only production but also distribution of alternative media. Chris Atton (2002, pp. 42–49), for one, discusses such alternative strategies of 'distributive use' as anticopyright (i.e. reusing already existing media content without permission, either in an original or photomontage version) and open copyright (i.e. encouraging one's readers as well as other media to freely reproduce and distribute their own content). Atton (2002) additionally points out that before the internet age, the wider distribution of alternative media strongly relied on mail and stamps instead of newsagents and actual money.

Focusing mainly on production process and distribution strategies, most definitions of alternative media neglect their content, as Atton (2015, p. 8) notes in the introduction to his recent *Routledge Companion to Alternative and Community Media*. The author encourages us to think of the importance of an 'alternative' subject matter in the media and points to a definition suggested by the Royal Commission of the Press in 1977, which recognized that alternative media (1) deal with the opinions of a small minority, (2) express attitudes hostile to widely held beliefs, and (3) espouse views or deal with subjects not given regular coverage (Atton 2002, p. 12). Such alternative content does not necessarily need to be radical, in the sense that it challenges the established social order. While the history of alternative media usually dates back to the US and UK underground press of the 1960s (Atton 2002, p. 1), the archetype of alternative media became the fanzines (or fan magazines) of the 1970s. Their content, usually devoted to the meticulous discussion of a tiny segment of, for example, art, music, literature sports or hobbies, surely provided an alternative to the discourses available in the mainstream but did not always offer radical reconsiderations of those discourses. Similarly, the explosion of fanzines as well as zines (simply 'any self-published or small circulation periodical[s]', Atton 2011, p. 566) in the 1980s, did not necessarily trigger an explosion of radical social views.

Radicalism, in turn, often becomes a characteristic of alternative media created by social movements, for instance, environmentalists, anarchists, leftists, feminists as well as LGBTs. Hence, some authors, especially John Downing (1984, 2001), prefer to call social movement media 'radical' rather than 'alternative'. The common denominator of radical media would be the fact that, in Downing's (2001, p. xi) words, 'they break somebody's rules, although rarely all of them in every respect.' Such conceptualizations of alternative media recognize radical content as their cornerstone and draw on the discussions of democracy, public sphere and media power to identify alternative media as a crucial component of democracy: a 'subaltern counter-public' (Fraser 1992), a part of civil society independent of both the state and the market (Bailey et al. 2008; Couldry and Curran 2003). As Roger Silverstone (1999, p. 103) points out, alternative media 'have created new spaces for alternative voices that provide the focus both for specific community interests as well as for the contrary and the subversive'. Yet, it is not only that alternative media create a space for alternative discourses of social movements but also that their emergence is often virtually inseparable from the actualization of those social movements; in some cases to the extent that 'the medium becomes the space, the community forms itself within and around the medium [...] the medium creates a community from a previously dispersed and atomised group of individuals' (Atton 2015, p. 6).

In this sense, the chief function of alternative media created by social movements is to create and sustain the movement's identity. The focus is on the self: self-definition, self-representation and self-expression of a particular group, community or movement. Some, of course, may argue that authors of social movement media should go beyond the self and aim to get their voices heard beyond the narrow group of their enthusiastic readers in order to impact mainstream discourses. The Minority Press Group, known as Comedia, for example, asserts that a usually low circulation of (mainly pre-internet) alternative media—often a result of their commitment to break away from capitalism and managerialism—dooms these media to alternative ghettos, 'an existence so marginal as to be irrelevant' (in Atton 2002, p. 34). For me, and many other authors, however, the key relevance of alternative media lies not in their impact on the mainstream but in their ability to validate a marginalized identity as well as facilitate the formation and consolidation of a community. From this perspective, the volume of circulation or size of audience is only a side issue. Some groups may indeed dedicate their media to get their message across to the society at large. Other groups may keep their audiences small, either implicitly, for example by providing a highly specialized content, or explicitly, for example to avoid state control or preserve an aura of exclusivity (Atton 2015, p. 8).

In their book *Understanding Alternative Media*, Olga Bailey, Bart Cammaerts and Nico Carpentier (2008, p. xi) additionally argue that the problem with the limited social impact of individual alternative media is alleviated by their collective contribution to the democratization of information and communication. The authors come up with a model encompassing four approaches to alternative media. The first approach recognizes the prime function of the media as serving a community. The second one identifies alternative media as a supplement to the mainstream media, 'a counter-hegemonic critique of the mainstream' (Bailey et al. 2008, p. 15). The third one emphasizes the role of this type of media as a part of civil society and a stimulator of micro-participation. The fourth one draws on the metaphor of rhizome, introduced by Gilles Deleuze and Félix Guattari (1987), and focuses on the elusiveness of these media, their linkages with diverse democratic struggles but also their interconnections with the state and the market. While Bailey et al. (2008, p. 30) themselves favour the forth approach, they explain that the approaches are not mutually exclusive and propose to apply them simultaneously. In conclusion, they again emphasize the collective power of diverse alternative media: 'From this panoptic perspective, alternative media should be seen as a multiplicity of public spaces, a colorful—but at times also contentious—myriad of media initiatives as diversified as society itself' (Bailey et al. 2008, p. 153).

5.2   TRANSNATIONAL NETWORK OF GAY AND LESBIAN MAGAZINES

Alternative media proved to be the mainstay of early attempts at homosexual self-organizing in the West. One important reason for that was that, historically, mainstream media either ignored homosexuals, as well as other LGBTs, or represented them in a much stereotypical and prejudiced fashion. For example, the rare coverage of homosexuals in the US press in the late nineteenth century focused mainly on their gender nonconformity, and in the early twentieth century, on their supposedly strong criminal inclinations (Baim 2012a). In TV and cinematic representations, homosexuals have long shared a common fate of 'invisibility, stereotyping, and confinement in restricted secondary roles' (Gross and Woods 1999, p. 4; Gross 2001). Regarding stereotyping in films, homosexuals, if represented at all, tended to be depicted as 'weak and silly, or evil and corrupt' (Gross 1998, p. 92), sissies and tomboys, who towards the end of the film most likely either killed themselves or killed others (e.g. Dyer 1984; Russo 1987; Tyler 1972). One strategy against such non- and misrepresentations was to adopt the practice of so-called queer reading, that is, reading mainstream media 'against the grain' by decoding potentially hidden references to homosexuality or simply reading homosexual themes into popular media texts (e.g. Doty 1993; Dyer 1986; Feuer 1989). Another strategy for homosexuals was to create their own representations in their own media, even if the latter could only be, at least at the start, small-scale, non-profit and non-professional ventures.

The origins of homosexual publishing go back to the end of the nineteenth century in Germany, where, as explained in Chap. 2, Magnus Hirschfeld created the Scientific Humanitarian Committee (WhK) in 1897 and thus established the first homosexual rights movement in the world (Hekma 2015, p. 21). Among the activities of the WhK, as well as other German groups in the late nineteenth and early twentieth century, was the production of many activist and academic publications, both periodicals and non-periodicals, which inspired activists in other countries (Marhoefer 2015a, b; Steakley 1975). One example is the WhK's pamphlet *Wass soll das Volk vom dritten Geschlecht wissen?* (What should the people know about the third sex?), published in 1901 (Steakley 1975, pp. 30–32). As Hekma (2015, p. 21) notes, this document was translated into Dutch in 1913 and into English in 1915, which illustrates the transnational connections between homosexual activists in Europe before and during the Weimar Republic (1918–1933) as well as the leading role of Germany in homosexual activism at that time. Another example, already mentioned in Chap. 3, is the Czechoslovakian magazine *Hlas* (Voice; later *Nový Hlas* [New Voice]), published from 1931 to 1934 and connected to Czechoslovakian branch of the World League for Sexual Reform (Huebner 2010). In turn, the German periodical *Der Eigene* (The Special One or, more loosely translated, The Self-Owner), which is considered to be the first homosexual magazine in the world, was founded by Hirschfeld's chief rival, the twenty-one-year-old Adolf Brand, who published the magazine with interruptions from 1896 to 1931 (Oosterhuis 1992, p. 2; Whisnant

2016, p. 7). *Der Eigene* had an anarchist tone and focused largely on culture and literature, taking on such subtitles as 'Magazine for Friendship and Freedom' or 'Journal for Male Culture, Art and Literature'. In 1903, Brand and other men involved in the magazine created their own group named Gemeinschaft der Eigenen (Community of the Special) (Marhoefer 2015a, p. 24; Whisnant 2016, p. 7).

The influence of German activists extended to the other side of the Atlantic Ocean. The precursor of the gay and lesbian press in the United States was Henry Gerber, who in 1924 published two issues of the magazine *Friendship and Freedom* (Streitmatter 2000, p. 565), the title being a direct translation of one of the subtitles of *Der Eigene* (Baim 2012b, p. 81). However, another precursor of the US gay and lesbian press, Edith Eyde (also known as Lisa Ben), started her magazine independently and considered it as a private rather than public or political endeavour, born out of the feelings of isolation and loneliness (Streitmatter 1995, pp. 1–16). In 1947 and 1948 in Los Angeles, Eyde produced nine issues of *Vice Versa*, which is believed to be the first lesbian publication in the world (Baim 2012b, p. 83). As Streitmatter (1995, pp. 1–16) points out in *Unspeakable: The Rise of the Gay and Lesbian Press in America*, she published editorials, poetry, short stories and letters to the editor as well as book and film reviews to promote such values as positive self-image for lesbians, homosexual separatism and feminine grooming and fashion. Working as a secretary, Eyde typed 12 copies of each *Vice Versa*'s issue in her office and then handed or posted most of them to her friends, distributing the rest at local gay and lesbian bars. The history of the magazine ended when Eyde found a new job, which did not allow her to continue her publishing activity.

The German homosexual rights movement and its press were dismantled in 1933, when the Nazis raised to power (Marhoefer 2015a). Their legacy, however, lived on. For one thing, as mentioned in Chap. 2, the equivalents of the WhK were formed abroad. The Dutch WhK published for a short time a magazine called *Levensrecht* (Right to Live), which was revived by one of the magazine's editors, Nico Engelschman, in 1946 under the title *Vriendschap* (Friendship) (Jackson 2015, p. 32). German legacy was also continued by the magazine *Der Kreis* (The Circle), published under different names from 1932 to 1967 in Zurich, thanks to Swiss neutrality during the Second World War (Kennedy 1999). The magazine was set up by Laura Thoma after her visit to Berlin and was long edited by Karl 'Rolf' Meier, who had worked as an actor in Germany between 1924 and 1934 (Jackson 2015, p. 32; Kennedy 1999, p. 7). In his detailed history of the magazine, *The Ideal Gay Man: The Story of Der Kreis*, Huber Kennedy (1999, p. 1) emphasizes the strong transnational aspect of the magazine, which consistently included contributions in three languages: German, French and English. Finally, it was Germans that provided much inspiration for the post-war homophile movement, which abounded in magazines that shared the common goal of assimilation and, for the first time in history, achieved wider popularity. Examples include such titles as German *Die Freund, Die Gefährten, Hellas, Die Insel, Der Ring* and *Du und Ich* (Rehberg 2016; Whisnant 2012, p. 92), US *The Ladder* (an exceptional lesbian publication), *Mattachine Review* and *One Magazine* (Soares 1998; White 2012), French *Arcadie* and *Futur* (Jablonski 2002), Danish *Vennen* (Jackson 2015, p. 31) as well as the already mentioned Dutch *Vriendschap* and Swiss *Der Kreis*. David Churchill (2008) details strong transnational connections between the magazines, for example, in the form of reprinting each other's content, posting other magazines' advertisements and organizing joint business meetings.

While the influence of German activists was gradually fading away, the new powerful impetus for homosexual activism and publishing came from the United States. As discussed in Chap. 2, after the Stonewall Riots in June 1969, US activists set up new militant organizations, such as the Gay Liberation Front (GLF) and Gay Activist Alliance (GAA), which rejected the assimilationist strategies of the homophile movement (Weeks 2015). Importantly, the riots also provoked the surge of 'in-your-face newspapers [...]——voicing outrage, demanding justice, and shrieking at the top of their lungs' (Streitmatter 1995, p. 116). Emerging from the movement itself, like *Come Out!, Gay Flames, Gay Sunshine* and *Gay Times*, or set up by straight entrepreneurs, like *GAY*, the new magazines combined anarchistic ideals with tabloid headlines. Owning to the 1968 sexual revolution, they also celebrated sexual liberation, publishing articles and columns under such headlines as 'What's Wrong with Sucking?', 'How to Get Fucked (and Like It)' or 'Hornyscope' (Streitmatter 1995, pp. 116–153). As Lucy Robinson (2007, p. 65) points out '[t]here is no doubt that the publicity attached to the riots brought international attention to the possibilities of the politics of sexuality.' Activists in other Western countries soon followed their US counterparts: for example, the London GLF published *Come Together* (later, its former members also founded *Gay News* and *Gay Left*) (Power 1995; Robinson 2007) and the French Homosexual Front for Revolutionary Action (FHAR) published *Le Fléau Social* and *L'Antinorm* (Sibalis 2005, 2009).

The HIV/AIDS epidemic, in turn, dominated the content of the majority of Western homosexual publications in the 1980s, even if some gay and lesbian magazines at first trivialized or ignored the problem. In the United States, the *New York Native*, created in December 1980, took a lead with detailed medical reports by Lawrence Mass and angry manifestos against both institutional inertia and gay promiscuity by Larry Kramer (Streitmatter 1995, pp. 243–275). In the United Kingdom, 'reporting of the [HIV/AIDS] crisis was consistent but relatively low-key', notes Sharif Mowlabocus (2010, pp. 41), pointing to such important titles as *Capital Gay*, *Gay Times* and *Him Monthly*. In the Netherlands, the leading magazines informing about the epidemic in the 1980s were *De Gay Krant* and *SEK* (Hospers and Blom 1998, p. 51). At the same time, and even more so in the 1990s, gay press in the West set the trend towards commercialization, depoliticization and sexualization (Sender 2004), with such internationally popular magazines as *Advocate* in the United States (Sender 2001), *Attitude* in the United Kingdom (Mowlabocus 2010, pp. 42–44) and *Gai Pied* in France (Duyvendak and Duyves 1993). The last 20 or 25 years have marked a steep decline of gay and lesbian printed media, mainly due to the popularization of the internet and invention of the World Wide Web (Baim 2012c; Scott 2011). However, while the internet provided a new terrain for transnational communication between homosexuals, or more broadly LGBTs, it also relegated their subcultures to a new age of e-invisibility: as Travers Scott (2011, p. 96) points out, while magazines, books or bars can be accidentally stumbled upon by strangers, 'queer e-resources are typically only seen by those who look for them.'

5.3   PUBLISHING UNDERGROUND IN COMMUNIST POLAND

The major difference between the Western and Eastern Blocs, in terms of political context in which gay and lesbian publications were produced during the Cold War, lay in the intensity of censorship. While in the West the censorship was relatively light after the Second World War, in communist Europe it became one of the pillars of the new regimes, though practised to a different extent in different countries and at different times. In Poland, the Ministry of Information and Propaganda was formed already in 1944 and the Main Office for the Control of the Press, Publications and Public Performances (GUKPPiW) in 1946 (Bates 2004; Mielczarek 2011). The former functioned for less than three years, the latter until 1990. Comparing the GUKPPiW to the George Orwell's 'Ministry of Truth', Norman Davies (1981, p. 593) points out that it imposed a tight system of preventive censorship, 'not merely to manipulate information but actually to manufacture it, to process it, and to classify it'. John Bates (2004, p. 143) explains that apart from creating the GUKPPiW, Polish communist authorities 'rapidly took over print works and the distribution of paper supplies after WWII [Second World War], and continually cleared public and academic libraries of reading matter they deemed "undesirable"'. Furthermore, they also imposed a strict post-publication censorship of books and periodicals printed abroad: 'custom officers not only searched tourists' luggage, but——jointly with the Polish Postal Services—— opened packages sent to Poland from abroad, while a censor on duty would decide what printed/filmed/taped matter should be confiscated' (Remmer 1989, p. 418). At the beginning of the 1980s, the authorities somewhat relaxed censorship and adopted a new, less restrictive Censorship Law (Bates 2004; Goban-Klas 1990). A more aggressive approach to publishing was reintroduced during the martial law period (1981–1983) but censorship was relaxed again in 1986, echoing similar changes in the Soviet Union, especially the Mikhail Gorbachev's policy of glasnost (Biskupski 2000, p. 169; McNair 1991).

The apparatus of censorship in communist Poland was never leak-proof and some non-state-controlled publications were officially allowed to be printed and distributed in the country as long as they were published by 'collectives'—institutions and organizations—but not private companies (Pokorna-Ignatowicz 2012, p. 11). This is why Karol Jakubowicz (1991) speaks of three public spheres in late communist Poland: the official, 'alternative' and 'opposition' ones. The alternative public sphere, he explains, existed since at least 1956 and was connected to the Roman Catholic Church. At the end of the 1980s, it comprised some 50 newspapers and periodicals published by the Church or Catholic organizations, with a total circulation of about two millions. The opposition public sphere was established in 1976 by the political opposition, first mainly by the Workers' Defence Committee (KOR) and then largely by Solidarity. Between 1980 and 1981, it included about 1,000 Solidarity periodicals (national and regional weeklies, factory bulletins, etc.). After the introduction of the martial law at the end of 1981, the number of these publications doubled and their circulation soon reached 80,000 copies. Jakubowicz (1991, p. 158) argues that the key difference between the two non-official public spheres lay in their approach to the communist state and ideology: while the Church-connected alternative press 'has been prevented by censorship, and probably by the policy of the Church itself [...], from openly questioning the fundamental tenets of the system or advocating its overthrow', the opposition press was committed to fighting communism and intended to draw a road map for a new political system in Poland.

All the publications connected either to the Church or to the opposition printed and distributed in communist Poland without authorities' permission constituted what many scholars call a 'second circulation', that is, a professionally organized publishing underground (e.g. Bereś 1990; Bielska 2013; Jastrzębski and Krysiak 1993; Sowiński 2011). Despite its independence from the state, second circulation publications remained either directly connected to or strongly influenced by the Roman Catholic Church. As I explained in the previous chapter, while some KOR members tried to distance themselves from the Church, Solidarity and its leaders—themselves usually religious Catholics—strongly relied on the Church's infrastructure, especially after Solidarity's delegalization in December 1981 (Osa 1997; Stanley 2010). Consequently, Solidarity embraced the discourse of moral superiority over communists and the publications of the second circulation reflected values such as religious nationalism, social conservatism and patriarchal structures. This, in turn, resulted in a number of what Bates calls 'blank spaces', or taboo topics, that existed in the second circulation:

> homosexuality, women's rights, and to a lesser extent ethnicity (above all, Polish/Jewish relations) [...] To an extent, these deficiencies reflected the hegemony of a different concept of liberty in the final years of communist rule—the collectivist ethos embodied in Solidarity, which essentially deferred consideration of individual liberty for the sake of the general cause. (Bates 2004, pp. 163–164)

Do-it-yourself and counterculture magazines provided an alternative to the publications of both first and second circulations, and therefore became collectively named the 'third circulation' (Bielska 2013; Głowacki 2010). Their origins go back to the 1970s and are related to the emergence of a punk rock subculture in late communist Poland, especially to the establishment of the National Festival of the Music of the Young Generation, first organized in Jarocin in 1980 (Bielska 2013, p. 196). The third circulation consisted primarily of fanzines, their number being estimated at about 100 titles in the late 1980s (Bielska 2013, p. 198), including one of the most popular *QQRYQ*, published in Warsaw, and *Antena Krzyku* (Scream Aerial), published in Wrocław (Głowacki 2010, p. 38; also mentioned in *Filo* 1988, 15, p. 14). Additionally, some groups organized concerts and recorded and distributed rock music on compact cassettes. The fanzines of the third circulation fit into Atton's (2002) definition of alternative media: their production was deprofessionalized, deinstitutionalized and decapital-ized; their distribution was limited to mail and concerts; and their con-tent touched upon topics virtually non-existent in either first or second circulations. Besides, because their reach was very limited (circulation usually did not go beyond 100 copies), they were ignored by, if not simply invisible to, the state and could therefore enjoy a considerable independence from the censorship apparatus.

While the magazines of the third circulation most often focused on music, they also provided radical perspectives on many aspects of politi-cal and social life. Regarding politics, authors expressed their criticism towards both communism and capitalism (be it conservative or liberal), and saw their future in a somewhat vaguely defined 'third way', mostly inspired by the ideas of anarchism. Very quickly they also became distrust-ful of Solidarity, as one of the third-circulation authors, Tomasz Lipiński, explains:

> Since the beginning of 1981 we saw in Solidarity the new establishment, largely subordinate to the Church, which didn't leave us with much hope. On the other hand, Solidarity in itself, as a movement with clear anarchist inclinations, was acceptable for us. As long as Solidarity was anarchist, we shared some common ground. (in Bielska 2013, p. 197)

Regarding social matters, Katarzyna Bielska (2013, p. 198) points out that the authors of the third circulation 'often trampled traditional val-ues, social conservatism and religion'. In their music magazines they published not only reports from concerts, interviews with musicians and descriptions of punk subcultures abroad but also, as it was in the case of *QQRYQ*, information about vegetarianism, squatting and alternatives to compulsory military service (Głowacki 2010, p. 39). Other magazines also discussed such topics, non-existent in the publications of the first and second circulations, as anarchism, pacifism, ecology, anticlericalism as well as feminism and homosexuality (Głowacki 2010, p. 42).

The gay and lesbian magazines produced in Poland in the 1980s, such as *Biuletyn/Etap* and *Filo*, shared many characteristics with other publications of the third circulation, as I will explain in detail in the rest of this chapter. Therefore, it seems clear to me that these magazines should be counted as a valid component of the third circulation's countercultural publishing activity in communist Poland. However, none of the recent academic, artistic or cultural projects about the third circulation which I was able to locate discuss, or even mention, Polish gay and lesbian magazines of the 1980s. The state-sponsored project Independent Culture (www.kultura-niezalezna.pl) focuses mainly on the publications of the second circulation and provides no information about gay and lesbian cultural production, either before or after 1989. Zine Library (www.zinelibrary.pl), a project by Michał Schneck, exclusively devoted to Polish counterculture, does not list any gay and lesbian publications either. The only, and usually very brief, information which I was able to find was in academic and non-academic publications on homosexuality in communist Poland (e.g. Fiedotow 2012; Mrok 1999; Więch 2005 as well as the *Replika* magazine). A most notable exception is the work of the artist Karol Radziszewski, who in one issue of *DIK Fagazine* reprinted selected pages of *Filo*, along with an interview with its editor-in-chief, and continues to organize exhibitions and make films on the topic (see e.g. *Kisieland* [2012], www.karolradziszewski.com). Building on the latter works, in the rest of the book, I will offer a thorough analysis of the gay and lesbian magazines' production context and content.

5.4 *BIULETYN/ETAP* MAGAZINE

The story of the first Polish gay (but not lesbian) magazine is the story of one man, Andrzej Selerowicz. Born in 1948 and brought up in Bełchatów, at that time a tiny village in central Poland, Selerowicz moved first to Łódź for studies and then to Warsaw for work. In the 1970s, he was an average employee in a company specializing in foreign trade, which enabled him to get in touch with many foreigners as well as to sporadically travel abroad, though mainly to other countries of the Eastern Bloc. In the late 1970s, however, he was invited by a friend to spend his holidays in France and managed to obtain a passport for that visit. This proved to be the turning point in his life:

> It was in France where I realized that I wasn't satisfied with my life in Poland and that there was little room for improvement. Although I had an interesting job, I got paid peanuts. I didn't own a flat and could not afford one for the next 15 years. (Interview with Selerowicz)

Because his passport was still valid for six months, he decided to stay in the West to earn some money. He chose Vienna for a couple of reasons: mainly because Polish citizens were not required visas in Austria but also because he was fluent in German and had a very good friend in the city, also a Pole, who had moved there five years before Selerowicz and encouraged him to do the same. When asked if his homosexuality influenced his decision to immigrate, Selerowicz replies: 'Absolutely not! My living conditions were a thousand times more important. These issues didn't even cross my mind.'

Selerowicz managed to find a job in Vienna immediately after his arrival. He started to work for a foreign trade company, which aimed to expand its reach to Eastern Bloc countries, especially Hungary and Czechoslovakia but also Poland. Soon, he also found a boyfriend, US citizen John Clark, who turned out to be his life partner. As Selerowicz explains: 'After two years together, we realized that our relationship was stable enough so we could get more involved in the life and society around us.' This is why, they decided to attend a meeting of a newly established gay and lesbian organization Homosexual Initiative Vienna (HOSI) in 1981. The same year, one of the leading member of HOSI, Kurt Krickler, came back from the conference organized by the International Gay Association (IGA, later ILGA) in Turin with the idea to create the Eastern Europe Information Pool (EEIP) programme. Selerowicz was the perfect person for the job: a native speaker of Polish with 'insider' knowledge of the region, who regularly travelled to Eastern Bloc countries for work. His partner, Clark, also joined the team: as a native speaker of English, he was mainly responsible for writing and editing the English-language output of the group. When travelling for work to Poland, Selerowicz started to reach out to Polish homosexuals: the people he had known before immigrating to Austria but also their friends and some other men met coincidently. He started corresponding with about ten Polish homosexuals at that time: 'It was clear from my first contacts that those people knew very little about the gay movement and how it was developing in the West. How could they know, really?', explains Selerowicz. In order to inform, but also to integrate, Polish homosexuals, he decided to start producing a short newsletter (*Biuletyn* 1983, 1, p. 1).

Biuletyn was published regularly, four times a year, since March 1983 until December 1987 in the form of a letter, starting with the words *Mój drogi* (My dear) or *Drogi przyjacielu* (Dear friend), where the word friend often worked as a euphemism for a homosexual at that time in Poland (Szulc 2012). In total, Selerowicz produced 20 issues of the magazine, each consisting of one, two or four pages (see Table 5.1). The entire production process was carried out in Vienna, in Selerowicz's office and home. The first step was to type the content of the magazine using a typewriter available at his work. Because the typewriter did not have Polish fonts, the second step was to manually add all the dots and dashes required by some Polish characters such as ę, ś or ż. The effects of this manual work are clearly visible in the *Biuletyn*'s content. The third step was to copy the magazine using a photocopier, again the one Selerowicz had access to at work. Usually, he created about 50–100 copies of each issue. All the costs associated with the production and distribution of the magazine were covered first by Selerowicz himself and later also by his collaborators in Poland. Therefore, in one of the issues he appealed to his readers to financially support the magazine:

> When you receive a copy of *Biuletyn* you should realize that somebody had to pay for photocopying and mailing it to you from their own, most likely very small, salary. Are you able to return the favour, for example by sending a couple of stamps to the return address? We have really not been financed by the CIA [Central Intelligence Agency], and there is no sign of it happening soon. (*Biuletyn* 1985, 2, p. 1)

Selerowicz started to distribute the magazine by simply handing it to the people he met during his stays in Poland. Alternatively, and more commonly in fact, he was posting copies of *Biuletyn* to about 50 addresses in Poland, which he had managed to collect by the mid-1980s. However, he sent the mails not from Vienna but from Budapest. This was because he travelled to Hungary more often than to Poland and because mail between Eastern Bloc countries was less suspicious for the Polish Postal Services—as well as cheaper for Selerowicz—than letters from the West. At one point, Selerowicz started to collaborate with activists from Wrocław, first Leszek Truchliński and then Ryszard Ziobro, who helped him to distribute the magazine. Over time, the activists actually took over the entire distribution of *Biuletyn* as well as some parts of its photocopying, though the creation of content remained solely in Selerowicz' hands. The activists also came up with a new title for the magazine, *Etap:*

Gazetka Gejowska (Stage: A Gay News-Sheet), which was adopted for the first time at the end of 1986 (see Fig. 5.1). The title *Etap*, which was supposed to indicate that the publishing activity was another stage in homosexual activism in Poland, was later adopted as the official name of the Wrocław group itself.

The content of *Biuletyn/Etap* was very diverse. Often, it included information about the development of the homosexual movement in the West, including news from HOSI and ILGA, but also from Poland and other countries of the Eastern Bloc. Information about HIV/AIDS was quite commonly featured in the magazine, though this time with the majority of articles focused on the West. Lists of homosexuality-related articles in the mainstream media as well as books, films, pop songs and theatre plays which became available in Poland or in the West could also be found in numerous issues of the magazine. From time to time, Selerowicz additionally published translations of homoerotic poems and reprinted homosexual drawings, for example from the *Tom of Finland*'s *Kake* series, without obtaining any permissions for their reproduction, which is typical for alternative media (Atton 2002). Although he was initially sceptical about including personal ads—the prime function of the magazine was to motivate Polish homosexuals to start organizing themselves—Selerowicz did include some of them after the personal ads section had been dropped from the mainstream monthly *Relaks* in 1984 (see Chap. 4). Finally, *Biuletyn/Etap* included many personal tips from Selerowicz on a diverse range of topics such as rights of homosexual people in Poland, gay travel destinations (both in the Eastern and Western Blocs), coming out as well as sex and romantic life (especially a four-part 'Sexual guide for gay men' series). Not rarely, giving the tips, Selerowicz played the role of an expert in the Western gay lifestyle, explaining, for example, what Western gay men wear (1985, 4, p. 3) and how Polish gay men should deal with their Western 'friends' (1987, 4, p. 4). The entire content of *Biuletyn/Etap* was focused on men only. As Selerowicz explains in the interview: 'I didn't feel able and I didn't want to participate in the lesbian movement because I knew very well that I was completely unfit for this job. So I left it to somebody else.'

HOSI's EEIP programme was the key information source for *Biuletyn/Etap*, a fact occasionally explicitly mentioned in the magazine. Not surprisingly, therefore, the magazine included a lot of information also provided in the EEIP reports, for example about the gay culture week in Ljubljana (*Biuletyn* 1985, 3, p. 1) or the first ILGA's sub-regional con-

Fig. 5.1   First page of *Etap* at the end of 1986. Courtesy of Lambda Warszawa

ference in Budapest (*Etap* 1987, 4, p. 2). The majority of 'world news' was about the West in general, and German-language countries and the United States in particular, which was most likely related to Selerowicz' fluency in German and his relationship with a US citizen. At the same time, the bulk of information about Poland came from the magazine's readership. In *Biuletyn/Etap*, Selerowicz regularly thanked his readers for sending him news from Poland, sometimes accompanied by press cuttings from Polish newspapers and magazines, for example about HIV and AIDS (*Biuletyn* 1986, 1, p. 1) or Operation Hyacinth (*Biuletyn* 1986, 1, p. 1). As he explained in one issue, 'the main objective of the magazine is to provide you with information about important issues for the homosexual community in the West in exchange for your news from the country' (*Biuletyn* 1985, 2, p. 1). The last issue of *Biuletyn/Etap* was published in December 1987. Selerowicz explained that he decided to stop his publishing activity because its

> primary aim—to mobilize homosexuals—has been in my opinion reached. Group consciousness has grown and first organizations have been formed. It is their job now to take responsibility for the future of the gay movement in Poland, including its publishing activities. (*Etap* 1987, 4, p. 4)

5.5 *FILO* MAGAZINE

Similarly to *Biuletyn/Etap*, *Filo* started as a one-man project. Ryszard Kisiel, born in 1948, spent most of his life in Gdańsk, one of the biggest Polish cities. He met his first homosexual friends and partners at nudist beaches and other homosexual meeting points in the Tri-City area, consisting of Gdańsk, Gdynia and Sopot, located right next to each other at the Baltic Sea. Because of the cities' location at the coast, Kisiel had regular contacts with homosexual sailors, mainly Poles but also foreigners, who were bringing him gay magazines from the West. In our interview, he recalls a meeting with a Finnish sailor: 'It was difficult to communicate with him because my English was bad. But he gave me what was in fact shreds of a Finish magazine, not a pornographic one, barely a couple of pages. Its title was *Seta*, I think' (for information about *Seta* see Fitzgerald 1980; Stålström and Nieminen 2000). Inspired by Western magazines, Kisiel was thinking about setting up a similar magazine in Poland already before the 1980s. He realized that such a publication would never pass Polish censors so he decided to look for an alternative way of producing the magazine. He thought it would be helpful if he had a job in publishing so he found employment first in a printing house and then in a copy shop. However, the direct trigger to set up *Filo* was Operation Hyacinth: 'Especially because the operation was illegal, even according to the communist law then in power [...], I realized we [homosexuals] needed more information; not just pornography but information' (interview with Kisiel).

Filo was published in its underground form since November 1986 until May 1990, altogether 17 issues (including some double issues) consisting of a different number of pages (see Table 5.1). Kisiel came up with the name of the magazine while writing letters to his lover. He normally started the letters with the headline 'Dear Friend' but when his aunt intercepted one such letter, she noted that it sounded like two of them were lovers. Kisiel decided to better encrypt his message and came up with the word *filo*, which he later used as the title of his magazine (see Fig. 5.2). At first, he was publishing only 30–50 copies of *Filo*, later on even up to 1000. Officially, however, the circulation indicated in the magazine never exceeded 100 copies. That was because Kisiel had learnt during his work in a printing house that according to the 1981 Censorship Law all self-published documents up to 100 copies were exempt from censorship. The first issues of *Filo* were very short and authored entirely by Kisiel himself, with a little help from his friend, Henryk Tapitz, who was a graphic designer. Over time, however, the project attracted other people: some came and went, others joined the core of the editorial team, which for the most time consisted of five or six people. While Kisiel remained the publisher of the magazine for its entire existence, he handed over his position of editor-in-chief first to Remigiusz Placyd (since *Filo* 1988, 15) and then to Artur Jeffmanski (since *Filo* 1989, 18). There were no women involved in the magazine during the first years of *Filo* but Kisiel did sporadically include some information related to lesbians (e.g. 1987, 3, p. 4). The only regular female author was Warsaw-based Paulina Pilch, who started sending her articles to Gdańsk in June 1989, when she was only 16 years old. Thus, compared to *Biuletyn/Etap*, *Filo* became a much more collaborative project, trying to appeal to both men and women, even if to a much lesser extent to women than men.

The production and distribution of *Filo* was similar to that of other alternative media in general, and other publications of the Polish third circulation in particular. In fact, for some time, in the masthead of the magazine, Kisiel wrote that *Filo* was published by a 'Third Circulation Press', an invention of his own, and in some other issues *Filo* was called a 'zine'.

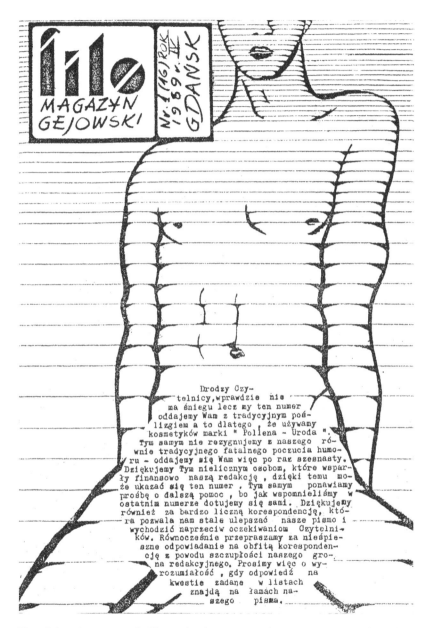

Fig. 5.2 First page of *Filo* at the beginning of 1989. Courtesy of Lambda Warszawa

The content was produced on a typewriter and photocopied by Kisiel at his work in a copy shop. The magazine was then posted to people in different cities in Poland as well as abroad, both in the Eastern and Western Blocs. Like *Biuletyn/Etap*, *Filo* was self-financed and non-profit, and was supported by donations from readers, which at one point were made obligatory. Unlike Selerowicz, however, Kisiel needed not only stamps and envelops, but also paper, distribution of which was controlled by communist authorities. He obtained some paper from readers and got the rest from his former colleagues still working in a printing house. Access to a typewriter, or even to typewriter tape (*Filo* 1988, 11, p. 20), was also not easy in communist Poland. At the beginning, Kisiel was using a very old German typewriter (with Polish fonts), which he had got as a present from his father a long time before. Later, however, the typewriter began to break apart and Kisiel received a new one from a friend of a friend who happened to work in a factory producing typewriters (interview with Kisiel). Pilch, in turn, had access to a typewriter at home thanks to her parents who both were working as academics (interview with Pilch).

The diversity of *Filo*'s content was increasing proportionally to the increase in its size. In the first, one-page issue, there was only a short list of books, films and theatre plays of interest to a homosexual reader. Information about homoerotic, as well as explicitly homosexual, art, film, music and literature continued to constitute a significant part of the magazine, though, over time, it transformed from brief general news to more extensive critical reviews. Another popular topic was HIV and AIDS, with coverage of the latest medical developments, statistics from Eastern Bloc countries and tips on safer sex. For Kisiel, the information on HIV/AIDS additionally worked as a legal protection against potential restrictions from the state: 'I could always argue that we do AIDS prevention work and it is those who obstruct such work, not those who do it, that commit an offence,' he explains (interview with Kisiel). *Filo* also provided much information about homosexual activism in the Eastern and Western Blocs, including Poland, encouraging its readers to organize small homosexual groups around the country so they could later unite and create a strong nationwide organization (*Filo* 1987, 7, p. 1). Apart from that, some issues of *Filo* discussed selected social issues, such as religion and homosexuality or army service, and provided practical information, for example about cruising spots, as well as personal ads. In the magazine, we can also find many pictures and drawings, often made by *Filo*'s own Henryk Tapitz or reprinted artworks by such artists as Aubrey Beardsley, Ralf König and Tom of Finland (with or without permission).

As acknowledged in the interviews with Kisiel and Pilch, but also some-times indicated in the magazine itself, a large part of information in *Filo* came from abroad. Western gay and lesbian magazines were one of the first and key foreign information sources. At the beginning, Kisiel received the magazines mainly through Polish sailors or friends travelling to or living in the West. After setting up *Filo*, however, he established contacts with Western publishers, simply by sending them copies of *Filo* and asking for the copies of their magazines in return. Because he was fluent in French, Kisiel established the strongest contacts with French-language magazines. He admits that the most popular title in his archive was French *Gai Pied* but also mentions, for example, Swiss *Dialogue*. His German-speaking friend was responsible for contacts with German- and Dutch-language magazines such as German *Rosa Flieder*, Swiss *Anderschume Kontiki* and Dutch *De Gay Krant*. A student of English philology, in turn, helped to translate articles from the UK *Capital Gay* and *Gay Times* as well as the US *Advocate*. Besides, Kisiel also mentions a number of Scandinavian titles such as Swedish *Kom Ut!* and *Reporter* (Rosqvist 2012) or Danish *Pan* (interview with Kisiel). Pilch too had access to foreign magazines, until 1990 mainly to the German ones, as she was able to read German better than English at that time. She met a new friend in Warsaw who was regularly receiving a feminist-lesbian magazine from West Berlin, the title of which she cannot recall. As she explains in the interview: 'Most of the articles I wrote [for *Filo* before 1990] were translations of German articles. Or, on their basis, I wrote my own pieces about, for example, the history of the lesbian movement in Germany.'

Another important source of foreign information was located in Vienna, where Selerowicz focused much of his activist work at HOSI on Poland. Kisiel recalls, for example, that Selerowicz was regularly sending him Austrian *Lambda Nachrichten* (Lambda News), which provided much information on Eastern Bloc countries, supplied by the HOSI's EEIP pro-gramme. Thanks to Selerowicz, the Filo group also established new inter-national contacts, both in the East (especially with homosexual groups in East Germany) and in the West (especially with Norwegian Tupilak, Swedish RFSL Stockholm and ILGA), which resulted in the exchange of information and magazines. The annual conferences of ILGA and EEIP too became important information sources, particularly since Polish rep-resentatives started to attend the events. Pilch says that even though she did not participate in any of the events herself, the Polish activists who did attend them were bringing her relevant leaflets, documents and magazines.

Other, less common sources of foreign information included, for example, foreign students who stayed in Poland on an exchange (Kisiel mentions collaboration with Cuban and Panamanian students) or Westerners travelling to Poland (Pilch recollects two female journalists from the United Kingdom who came to Warsaw to make a documentary for the Channel 4 about homosexuality and who provided her with some information on homosexuality in the country). Besides, Kisiel himself was travelling to other Eastern Bloc countries, especially to Bulgaria and Czechoslovakia, where, with some help from the *Spartacus International Gay Guide*, he met new friends and asked them about homosexuality-related issues in their countries (interview with Kisiel). *Filo* was published in its underground version until the second half of 1990, when the magazine was officially registered as well as get professionalized and commercialized; available in colour for the first time in its history.

5.6   Conclusion

Just as the first gay and lesbian magazines in the West, so too their Polish counterparts played an essential role in the emergence of homosexual activism. Both *Biuletyn/Etap* and *Filo* provided Polish homosexuals with relevant information, advice and contacts, thus creating a community of interests among their readers. With their limited circulation, the magazines did not aim to challenge dominant discourses of sexuality in Polish society. Instead, they enjoyed their virtual invisibility from the state and society at large in order to freely define, represent and express themselves. Similarly to alternative media published by other social movements, Polish gay and lesbian magazines were breaking hegemonic social rules (Downing 2001, p. xi), in that case the rules of the rampant heteronormativity in late communist Poland. The aim was to create a new safe space where they could define and discuss their issues. Moreover, *Biuletyn/Etap* and *Filo*, turned out to be the cornerstones of the first homosexual groups in Poland. It was the magazines that attracted new members as well as integrated and mobilized them so they could soon, for example, apply for the official recognition of their groups. Atton (2015, p. 6) correctly recognized the potential of alternative media when he wrote that for social movements often 'the medium becomes the space': Polish gay and lesbian magazines did not only play the role of a key communication channel for homosexual activists but also created an actual space within and around which formed the first more systematically organized homosexual groups in Poland.

Biuletyn/Etap and *Filo*, as much as any other media, were products of their place and time (Hall 1990, p. 222). They were created in the context of censorship in late communist Poland and in opposition to the main publishing underground, the latter governed chiefly by the Roman Catholic Church and Solidarity. They were founded in times of growing homosexual visibility in the mainstream media and first officially registered cases of HIV/AIDS in the Eastern Bloc. They were also printed and distributed in the pre-internet age, when access to paper, typewriters and postal services in Poland was regulated by communist authorities. But the sheer emergence of those magazines was also the outcome of a series of fortunate coincidences which happened to particular people. Both magazines were created as one-man projects by motivated individuals, Selerowicz and Kisiel, who, apart from their knowledge, skills and dedication, turned out to be the right people in the right place at the right time. After all, those magazines resulted from the unique combination of authors' geographical conditions (migrating to Vienna or living at the Polish coast), professional trajectories (working for a foreign trade company or in a publishing house and a copy shop) and language skills (fluency in German or French). As deprofessionalized, deinstitutionalized and decapitalized media ventures, presenting radically different content from the media of the first and second circulations, those magazines fit well into popular definitions of alternative media (e.g. Atton 2002; Bailey et al. 2008) and should be recognized as a vital part of the Polish third-circulation counterculture.

Furthermore, Polish gay and lesbian magazines also managed to overcome national and regional boundaries, including the Iron Curtain. *Biuletyn/Etap* was produced in Vienna by a Pole embedded in a Western activist network through his collaboration with HOSI and ILGA. It was then brought to Poland by Selerowicz or sent by mail from Budapest, and was distributed in the country by activists from Wrocław. *Filo*, in turn, was born out of the fascination of Kisiel with Western gay magazines, which he was receiving from homosexual sailors and travellers. Western gay and lesbian magazines as well as Western organizations and conferences were key sources of information for him and Pilch. But the flow of magazines was not all in one direction: Kisiel also used to send *Filo* to his Polish friends living in the Eastern and Western Blocs, as well as to gay and lesbian publishers in the West in exchange for their own magazines. As we read in one issue of *Filo* (1990, 19, p. 38), the magazine was also featured in gay and lesbian press in the West, for example in the UK *Capital Gay* and *Gay Times* as well as Canadian *X-tra*. Besides, *Biuletyn/Etap* and *Filo* must have reached some other Westerners too, since both magazines published a number of personal ads requesting a reply in a Western language. In fact, *Filo* had a separate section with personal ads from abroad, published usually in Polish, English or German and submitted by people from all over Europe as well as Australia and the United States. Certainly, both magazines were part of a transnational network of gay and lesbian magazines, authors of which were reading, or at least skimming through, each other's publications. Much influenced by their Western counterparts, the Polish magazines took similar forms, discussed a lot of similar topics and, in some cases, simply translated Western texts and reproduced Western images. Nonetheless, as will become clear in the next two chapters, the final result was a combination of international influences, regional and national realities as well as personal choices.

BIBLIOGRAPHY

Atton, C. (2002). *Alternative media*. London: Sage.

Atton, C. (2011). Zines. In J. D. H. Downing (Ed.), *Encyclopedia of social movement media* (pp. 565–567). Los Angeles, CA: Sage.

Atton, C. (2015). Introduction: Problems and positions in alternative and community media. In C. Atton (Ed.), *The Routledge companion to alternative and community media* (pp. 1–18). London: Rutledge.

Bailey, O. G., Cammaerts, B., & Carpentier, N. (2008). *Understanding alternative media*. Maidenhead: Open University Press and McGraw Hill.

Baim, T. (2012a). All the news that's not fit to print. In T. Baim (Ed.), *Gay press, gay power: The growth of LGBT community newspapers in America* (pp. 15–77). Chicago: Prairie Avenue Productions and Windy City Media Group.

Baim, T. (2012b). Gay news: In the beginning. In T. Baim (Ed.), *Gay press, gay power: The growth of LGBT community newspapers in America* (pp. 79–140). Chicago: Prairie Avenue Productions and Windy City Media Group.

Baim, T. (2012c). The future of queer newspapers. In T. Baim (Ed.), *Gay press, gay power: The growth of LGBT community newspapers in America* (pp. 438–447). Chicago: Prairie Avenue Productions and Windy City Media Group.

Bates, J. M. (2004). From state monopoly to a free market of ideas? Censorship in Poland, 1976–1989. In M. Díaz-Sacke (Ed.), *Censorship & cultural regulation in the modern age* (pp. 141–167). Amsterdam: Rodopi.

Bereś, W. (1990). Drugi obieg: Historia, sława, zmierzch. *Kultura, 11*(518), 100–107.

Bielska, K. (2013). Trzeci obieg wydawniczy w PRL oraz drugi obieg w latach 70. i 80. *Pedagogia Ojcostwa, 6*(1), 194–201.

Biskupski, M. B. (2000). *The history of Poland*. Westport, CT: Greenwood Press.

Churchill, D. S. (2008). Transnationalism and homophile political culture in the postwar decades. *GLQ: A Journal of Lesbian and Gay Studies, 15*(1), 31–66.

Couldry, N., & Curran, J. (2003). The paradox of media power. In N. Couldry & J. Curran (Eds.), *Contesting media power: Alternative media in a networked world* (pp. 3–15). Lanham: Rowman and Littlefield.

Davies, N. (1981[1991]). *God's playground: A history of Poland. Volume II: 1795 to the present*. Oxford: Clarendon Press.

Deleuze, G., & Guattari, F. (1987). *A thousand plateaus. Capitalism and schizophrenia*. Minneapolis: University of Minnesota Press.

Doty, A. (1993). *Making things perfectly queer: Interpreting mass culture*. Minneapolis: University of Minnesota Press.

Downing, J. D. H. (1984). *Radical media: The political experience of alternative communication*. Boston, MA: South End.

Downing, J. D. H. (2001). *Radical media: Rebellious communication and social movements*. Thousand Oaks, CA: Sage.

Downing, J. D. H. (2015). Conceptualising social movement media: A fresh metaphor? In C. Atton (Ed.), *The Routledge companion to alternative and community media* (pp. 100–110). London: Routledge.

Duyvendak, J. W., & Duyves, M. (1993). Gai Pied after ten years. *Journal of Homosexuality, 25*(1–2), 205–213.

Dyer, R. (1984). *Gays and film*. New York: Zoetrope.

Dyer, R. (1986). Judy Garland and gay men. In R. Dyer (Ed.), *Heavenly bodies: Film stars and society* (pp. 141–194). London: Routledge.

Feuer, J. (1989). Reading Dynasty: Television and reception theory. *South Atlantic Quarterly, 88*(2), 443–459.

Fiedotow, A. (2012). Początki ruchu gejowskiego w Polsce (1981–1990). In P. Barański, A. Czajkowska, A. Fiedotow & A. Wochna-Tymińska (Eds.), *Kłopoty z seksem w PRL: Rodzenie nie całkiem po ludzku, aborcja, choroby, odmienności* (pp. 241–258). Warszawa: Wydawnictwa Uniwersytetu Warszawskiego.

Fitzgerald, T. (1980). Gay self-help groups in Sweden and Finland. *International Review of Modern Sociology, 10*(2), 191–200.

Fraser, N. (1992). Rethinking the public sphere – A contribution to the critique of actually existing democracy. In C. Calhoun (Ed.), *Habermas and the public sphere* (pp. 109–142). Cambridge, MA: MIT.

Głowacki, B. (2010). Prasa trzeciego obiegu w okresie przełomu. *Kultura-Media-Teologia, 3*, 33–43.

Goban-Klas, T. (1990). Making media policy in Poland. *Journal of Communication, 40*(1), 50–54.

Gross, L. (1998). Minorities, majorities and the media. In T. Liebes & J. Curran (Eds.), *Media, ritual and identity* (pp. 87–102). London: Routledge.

Gross, L. (2001). *Up from invisibility: Lesbians, gay men, and the media in America.* New York: Columbia University Press.

Gross, L., & Woods, J. D. (1999). Introduction: Being gay in American media and society. In L. Gross & J. D. Woods (Eds.), *The Columbia reader on lesbians and gay men in media, society, and politics* (pp. 3–22). New York: Columbia University Press.

Hall, S. (1990). Cultural identity and diaspora. In J. Rutherford (Ed.), *Identity: community, culture and distance* (pp. 222–237). London: Lawrence & Wishart.

Hekma, G. (2015). Sodomy, effeminacy, identity: Mobilizations for same-sexual loves and practices before the Second World War. In D. Paternotte & M. Tremblay (Eds.), *The Ashgate research companion to lesbian and gay activism* (pp. 1–29). Farnham: Ashgate.

Hospers, H., & Blom, C. (1998). HIV prevention activities for gay men in the Netherlands 1983–93. In T. Sandfort (Ed.), *The Dutch response to HIV: Pragmatism and consensus* (pp. 40–60). London: UCL Press.

Huebner, K. (2010). The whole world revolves around it: Sex education and sex reform in First Republic Czech print media. *Aspasia, 4,* 25–48.

Jablonski, O. (2002). The birth of a French homosexual press in the 1950s. *Journal of Homosexuality, 41*(3–4), 233–248.

Jackson, J. (2015). The homophile movement. In D. Paternotte & M. Tremblay (Eds.), *The Ashgate research companion to lesbian and gay activism* (pp. 31–44). Farnham: Ashgate.

Jakubowicz, K. (1991). Musical chairs? The three public spheres in Poland. In P. Dahlgren & C. Sparks (Eds.), *Communication and citizenship: Journalism and the public sphere* (pp. 153–173). London: Routledge.

Jastrzębski, M., & Krysiak, E. (1993). Avoiding censorship: The "second circulation" of books in Poland. *Journal of Reading, 36*(6), 470–473.

Kennedy, H. (1999). *The ideal gay man: The story of Der Kreis.* Binghamton, NY: The Haworth Press.

Marhoefer, L. (2015a). *Sex and the Weimar Republic: German homosexual emancipation and the rise of the Nazis.* Toronto: University of Toronto Press.

Marhoefer, L. (2015b). "The book was a revelation, I recognized myself in it": Lesbian sexuality, censorship, and the queer press in Weimar-era Germany. *Journal of Women's History, 27*(2), 62–86.

McNair, B. (1991). *Glasnost, perestroika and the Soviet media.* London: Routledge.

Mielczarek, T. (2011). Kultura i polityka: Kultura, życie umysłowe, media 1944–1989. In K. Persak & P. Machcewicz (Eds.), *PRL od grudnia 70 do czerwca 89* (pp. 259–300). Warszawa: Bellona.

Mowlabocus, S. (2010). *Gaydar culture: Gay men, technology and embodiment in the digital age.* Farnham: Ashgate.

Mrok, M. (1999). *Ruch gejowski w Polsce od 1989 (PRL) oraz ruch gejowski w III Rzeczpospolitej po 1989 do 1999.* Gdańsk: G-Eye Team.

Oosterhuis, H. (1992). Homosexual emancipation in Germany before 1933. *Journal of Homosexuality, 22*(1–2), 1–28.

Osa, M. (1997). Creating Solidarity: The religious foundations of the Polish Social Movement. *East European Politics and Societies, 11*(2), 339–365.

O'Sullivan, T., Dutton, B., & Rayner, P. (1994). *Studying the media: An introduction.* London: Arnold.

Pokorna-Ignatowicz, K. (2012). From the communist doctrine of media to free media. The concept of a new information order in the Round Table Agreements. In K. Pokorna-Ignatowicz (Ed.), *The Polish media system 1989–2011* (pp. 11–21). Kraków: Krakow Society for Education: AFM Publishing House.

Power, L. (1995). *No bath but plenty of bubbles: An oral history of the Gay Liberation Front 1970–1973.* London: Cassell.

Rehberg, P. (2016). "Männer wie Du und Ich": Gay magazines from the national to the transnational. *German History, 34*(3), 468–485.

Remmer, A. (1989). A note on post-publication censorship in Poland 1980–1987. *Soviet Studies, XLI*(3), 415–425.

Robinson, L. (2007). *Gay men and the left in post-war Britain: How the personal got political.* Manchester: Manchester University Press.

Rosqvist, H. B. (2012). A special kind of married man: Notions of marriage and married men in the Swedish gay press, 1954–1986. *Journal of Historical Sociology, 25*(1), 106–125.

Russo, V. (1987). *The celluloid closet: Homosexuality in the movies.* New York: Harper and Row.

Scott, D. T. (2011). Queer media studies in the age of the e-invisibility. *International Journal of Communication, 5,* 95–100.

Sender, K. (2001). Gay readers, consumers, and a dominant gay habitus: 25 years of the Advocate magazine. *Journal of Communication, 51*(1), 73–99.

Sender, K. (2004). *Business, not politics: The making of the gay market.* New York: Columbia University Press.

Sibalis, M. (2005). Gay liberation comes to France: The Front Homosexuel d'Action Révolutionnaire (FHAR). In I. Coller, H. Davies, & J. Kalman (Eds.), *French history and civilization: Papers from the George Rudé Seminar* (pp. 265–276). Retrieved July 29, 2016, from http://www.h-france.net/rude/2005conference/rudecomplete.pdf.

Sibalis, M. (2009). The spirit of May '68 and the origins of the gay liberation movement in France. In L. J. Frazier & D. Cohen (Eds.), *Gender and sexuality in 1968: Transformative politics in the cultural imagination* (pp. 235–253). New York: Palgrave Macmillan.

Silverstone, R. (1999). *Why study the media?* London: Sage.

Soares, M. (1998). The purloined *Ladder:* Its place in lesbian history. *Journal of Homosexuality, 34*(3–4), 27–49.

Sowiński, P. (2011). *Zakazana książka. Uczestnicy drugiego obiegu 1977–1989.* Warszawa: ISP PAN.

Stålström, O., & Nieminen, J. (2000). Seta: Finnish gay and lesbian movement's fight for sexual and human rights. In I. Lottes & O. Kontula (Eds.), *New views on sexual health. The case of Finland* (pp. 119–139). Helsinki: Population Research Institute.

Stanley, J. (2010). Sex and solidarity, 1980–1990. *Canadian Slavonic Papers: Revue Canadienne des Slavistes, 52*(1-2), 131–151.

Steakley, J. D. (1975). *The homosexual emancipation movement in Germany.* New York: Arno.

Streitmatter, R. (1995). *Unspeakable: The rise of the gay and lesbian press in America.* Boston: Faber and Faber.

Streitmatter, R. (2000[2005]). Gay and lesbian press. In G. E. Haggerty (Ed.), *Gay histories and cultures* (pp. 565–567). New York: Garland Publishing.

Szulc, L. (2012). From queer to gay to Queer.pl: The names we dare to speak in Poland. *Lambda Nordica, 17*(4), 65–98.

Tyler, P. (1972). *Screening the sexes: Homosexuality in the movies.* New York: Holt, Rinehart and Winston.

Weeks, J. (2015). Gay liberation and its legacies. In D. Paternotte & M. Tremblay (Eds.), *The Ashgate research companion to lesbian and gay activism* (pp. 45–57). Farnham: Ashgate.

Whisnant, C. J. (2012). *Male homosexuality in West Germany: Between persecution and freedom, 1945–69.* Basingstoke: Palgrave Macmillan.

Whisnant, C. J. (2016). *Queer identities and politics in Germany: A history 1880–1945.* New York: Harrington Park Press.

White, T. (2012). Drama, power and politics: *One* magazine, *Mattachine Review* and *The Ladder* in the era of homophile activism. In T. Baim (Ed.), *Gay press, gay power: The growth of LGBT community newspapers in America* (pp. 141–151). Chicago: Prairie Avenue Productions and Windy City Media Group.

Więch, A. S. (2005). Różowy odcień PRL-u: Zarys badań nad mniejszościami seksualnymi w Polsce Ludowej. In K. Slany, B. Kowalska & M. Śmietana (Eds.), *Homoseksualizm: Perspektywa interdyscyplinarna* (pp. 257–264). Kraków: Nomos.

Williams, R. (1980). *Problems in materialism and culture: Selected essays.* London: Verso.

CHAPTER 6

(Re)constructing Identities

Same-sex desires and practices do not necessarily translate into homosexual identities: much research shows, for example, that men may voluntarily have sex with other men or be romantically or sexually attracted to them while not identifying as homosexuals (see the classic study by Kinsey et al. 1948; and also, e.g. Copen et al. 2016; Ward 2012). According to social constructivist approach to the study of sexuality, adopted in this book, the divide between heterosexuality and homosexuality is not based on essential reality but is first and foremost cultural and historical in nature (Weeks 2011, pp. 204–208). From this perspective, the questions about the possible biological, psychological or sociological *causes* of homosexuality are irrelevant and, most likely, insoluble. The questions which do matter deal with the *meanings* of same-sex desires and practices in general, and the *origins* and *contents* of the dominant modern ideas of homosexual identities in particular. In other words, social constructivist approach focuses chiefly on when, where and how same-sex desires and practices have become to be understood as a key component of the self rather than, for example, as a crime or sin (McIntosh 1968; Foucault 1978), as well as which values have been inscribed in the dominant ideas about who modern homosexuals are and what they do (e.g. Altman 1996, 1997; Halperin 2012; Plummer 1981).

Additionally, as I detailed in Chap. 2, the growing body of research looks into the processes of the globalization of sexuality, including the

© The Author(s) 2018
L. Szulc, *Transnational Homosexuals in Communist Poland*,
Global Queer Politics, DOI 10.1007/978-3-319-58901-5_6

worldwide proliferation of the dominant models of modern homosexual, or LGBT, identities, originating in the West and dating back to the Industrial Revolution with its hallmarks of urbanization, secularization and indi- vidualization (D'Emilio 1992). Scholars show how those identities have been imposed by the West on the Rest by means of political and economic neocolonialism and cultural imperialism—largely due to the rise of human rights discourses, global media products and transnational LGBT politics (e.g. Altman 2001; Massad 2007; Petchesky 2000)—and also how same- sex practitioners in the non-West adopt, adapt or resist those identities (e.g. Boellstorff 2003; Enteen 2010; Martin 2009; Özbay 2010). However, I also pointed out that the scholarship heavily focuses on the relationship between the 'First' and 'Third' Worlds, between 'Western' and 'develop- ing' or 'postcolonial' countries. The 'Second' World enters the debates on the globalization of homosexuality virtually only after it falls apart in 1989, as if there was no travelling of cultural products and people, and thus no exchange of homosexuality-related ideas, between the West and the East before the collapse of the Iron Curtain and the fall of the Berlin Wall.

In this chapter, I will further challenge the idea of the near total iso- lation of the Eastern Bloc, particularly focusing on cross-border flows of identity paradigms. Drawing on my qualitative content analysis of *Biuletyn/Etap* and *Filo*, I will discuss how homosexuality was understood in the magazines: What kind of model of homosexual identity (individual and collective) was constructed there? And to what extent did that model reconstruct Western concepts of the globalized modern homosexual, the global gay (Altman 1997) and the cosmopolitan queer (Weeks 2011)? First, I will point to the prevalence of the 'born this way' narrative in both magazines, which was employed as an identity resource anchoring homo- sexuality in the realm of the natural, transhistorical and transcultural. Second, I will look into the discourses promoting the 'out and proud' model of homosexuality, which strongly encouraged self-awareness, self- acceptance and, ultimately, coming out, while explicitly drawing on such Western terms as 'gay' and indeed 'coming out'. In the next two sections, I will move on from the level of an individual to the level of relationships between individuals and investigate the values which the magazines advo- cated in relation to love and sex, and the role which HIV/AIDS epidemic played in the formulation of those values. Finally, in the last section, I will focus on the (re)constructions of the collective self, that is, on the mak- ing of a homosexual community of interest with basic ideas about what homosexuals should read, watch, listen to and wear.

6.1   Born This Way

Is homosexuality natural—innate and fixed—or is it unnatural—acquired, temporary and thus susceptible to change? *Filo* expressed somewhat ambivalent opinions on the subject. In one of the first issues of the magazine, the authors explained in a piece on paedophilia that, according to a growing body of research, being subjected to a 'homosexual seduction' in childhood does not translate into taking on a 'homosexual role' in adulthood: 'It turns out', the authors continued, clearly drawing on psychoanalytical ideas on the subject at that time, 'that the biggest influence comes from family environment (the upbringing), and is particularly a consequence of a lack of a father figure (physical or only mental), an unacceptable image of a father or an overprotective or strict mother' (*Filo* 1987, 3, p. 3). At the same time, the last issue of the magazine included two articles, both translations from English, which argued that there are two types of homosexuals. In the first article, we read that male homosexuality could be either innate and permanent or acquired and temporary, the latter being characteristic of closed homosocial environments such as army, prisons, monasteries or boarding schools, and normally fading away spontaneously after a 'homogenic' environment is abandoned (*Filo* 1990, 20, pp. 19–22). In the second article, we find out that apart from 'natural lesbians', there are also women who look for the company of other women, temporarily or permanently, because of the understanding and support they can find in women, especially needed after having previous traumatic experiences with men (*Filo* 1990, 20, pp. 31–33).

Nevertheless, the idea of homosexuality as natural dominated the pages of the two analysed magazines overwhelmingly. For example, *Biuletyn/ Etap*, while recommending its readers to come out to their families, suggested to support such an announcement by explaining that 'This is not my fault. I was born this way and I'm sure I'll never change' (1984, 4, p. 1). *Filo*, in turn, listed a few examples of sexual diversity among animals (1989, 17, p. 27) as well as asserted that (male) homosexuality cannot be 'caught' by watching homosexual pornography (1987, 5–6, p. 2) or changed by having sex with women (1988, 14, p. 5). Both magazines also provided a number of arguments supporting the idea of natural homosexuality. Similarly to the homophile movement and gay liberation (Churchill 2008; Weeks 2015), the Polish magazines most often drew on scientific discourses: Andrzej Selerowicz, for instance, explained in *Biuletyn* (1984, 4, p. 1) that 'numerous scientific publications of Polish sexologists prove that homosexuality is an equally normal way of satisfying sexual drive [compared to heterosexuality] and can no longer be viewed as a perversion,' and Paulina Pilch pointed out in *Filo* (1990, 19, p. 26) that psychologists, psychiatrists and sexologists, with few exceptions, 'have now no doubts that homosexuality, both in men and in women, is innate'. As Churchill (2008, p. 50) explains in his work on the homophile movement, by using the authority of science 'homophiles sought to create cultural legitimacy and legal standing for same-sex sexual subjects'. In the Polish case, however, the authority of science was evoked in alternative media aimed exclusively at homosexuals, which suggests that its prime function was not to legitimize homosexuality in society at large but rather to convince homosexuals themselves of the natural character of homosexuality.

Strikingly, a few times *Filo* compared homosexuals to black people. Already in the third issue, while discussing anti-discrimination articles of the Polish Constitution at that time, Kisiel argued that a provision protecting people against discrimination based on 'social position' included 'any social minority, also homosexuals', and explained that 'our social position is similar to the one of black people: just as there is no pill to change skin colour, so too there is no medicine to change homosexual orientation' (*Filo* 1987, 3, p. 2). Homosexuality was compared to being black also in other issues of *Filo* (e.g. 1987, 7–8, p. 5 and 1988, 13, p. 3), where homosexuals and black people were both framed as social 'others', particularly as 'minority groups', the very phrase being used in the magazine in literal translation. Though, at one point, writing about the discrimination of black people, or more broadly people of colour, in Poland in the context of some local moral panics around the HIV/AIDS epidemic, *Filo* (1988, 14, p. 3) noted that unlike people of colour, homosexuals could hide their otherness in the public. I called the comparisons of homosexuals to black people (or people of colour) striking because of the general invisibility of the latter in communist Poland: even today about 95 per cent of Poland's residents define their ethnicity as 'exclusively Polish' (GUS 2013, p. 90) and there have been only a few attempts at self-organizing of people of colour in the country so far (Omolo 2017). Therefore, the comparisons in *Filo* demonstrate rather how strongly its authors were influenced by the rhetoric of the US gay liberation, itself indeed much inspired by the black struggle: 'gay power', as Weeks (2011, p. 66) reminds us, echoed 'black power'.

Another fairly common strategy employed in the magazines to naturalize homosexuality was to show that homosexuals, or at least same-sex practitioners, have existed throughout time and in all corners of the world, thus proving that homosexuality is a truly transhistorical and transcultural phenomenon. Again in line with corresponding discourses in the West (Bravmann 1997; Halperin 1990), the Polish magazines most heavily exploited the theme of homosexuality in ancient Greece. In *Etap* (1986, 4, p. 4), we can find a Polish translation of a poem by a twentieth-century Greek poet, Constantine P. Cavafy, whose works, as Selerowicz explained, 'interweave homoeroticism with a fondness for the Hellenic past'. *Filo* drew on the theme in its very title—written first in Greek (*φίλο*) and later in Latin alphabet—which was chosen 'because, first, the culture of the ancient Greek cities favoured homosexuality, second, "filo" has multiple meanings in Greek, including "a friend" but also "a lover", and third, the word contains the letter λ (lambda), an international gay symbol' (*Filo* 1987, 3, p. 1). *Filo* also made other references to male homosexuality in ancient Greece, for example when discussing the life and work of the famous Polish composer Karol Szymanowski, who, like Greeks, supposedly had a liking for pedagogic erotic relationships with younger men and considered love between men as of a higher order than that between a man and a woman, since the former could go beyond the simple biological drive for procreation (*Filo* 1990, 20, pp. 27–29). I also found in *Filo* one reference to female homosexuality in ancient Greece: introducing a number of poems sent by a reader who used the pseudonym of Giovanna, Pilch described her as a 'true student of Sappho' (*Filo* 1990, 20, p. 33).

As Scott Bravmann (1997, p. 49) notes, references to ancient Greece in the discussions on homosexuality are 'neither historically inevitable nor politically innocent'. Pointing to a larger cultural project of employing a particular version of the Greek history as 'the pure origin of Western civilization', 'the epitome of Europe', the author argues that privileging the 'Greek love' discourse in homosexual politics is marked by implicit racism and continental chauvinism. Both magazines under scrutiny did not draw much on the histories of same-sex desires or practices in other cultural contexts, apart from a few exceptions, for example the discussions on homosexuality in 'biblical times' (*Filo* 1989. 16, p. 9) or among Chinese emperors (*Filo* 1990, 19, p. 32). They did, however, dig deeper into Polish history. *Biuletyn/Etap* and *Filo* regularly published pieces about homosexuality, or same-sex experiences, of Polish poets, writers, singers, composers, actors, film-makers and politicians. *Filo* additionally looked into same-sex relationships of Polish kings, naming the rulers 'suspected of homosexuality' (1988, 15, p. 16) and criticizing what we would call today the heterosexism of historians of Poland who 'list female lovers of Casimir the Great or Stanislaw August meticulously and with great relish [...] but remain utterly silent on the topic of sexual inversion' (1989, 18, p. 11). This practice—a sort of homosexing of the Polish history, showing that homosexuality could be found not only at any point of time and in any part of the world but also *here*, in *our* history—countered these communist narratives which had depicted homosexuality as a product of the West.

Along with putting forward the idea of homosexuality as natural, transhistorical and transcultural, *Filo* declared it indestructible and, thus, everlasting. Sometimes, the magazine published just a general statement like the one in a letter to the editor: 'we [homosexuals] did exist, do exist and will exist as long as humanity exists on Earth' (*Filo* 1988, 14, p. 8). Other times, it provided more concrete examples of homo-survivability in the face of brutal oppression, usually with reference to the Inquisition or Nazism, for instance: 'Until the eighteenth century, homosexuals were burned at the stake but despite such punishment, they existed and conducted their sexual lives. Those died, but new ones were born' (*Filo* 1988, 15, p. 12) and 'Neither the Inquisition nor the Hitler's concentration camps managed to kill off all homosexuals' (*Filo* 1988, 14, p. 1). A few examples, though much less common, also concerned the oppression of homosexuals under the most authoritarian communist regimes in Europe such as those of Romania and the Soviet Union, for instance: 'a more-than-a-50-year-long ban on homosexuality [in the Soviet Union] did not suppress it' (*Filo* 1989, 17, p. 6). This way, the authors once again conveyed to their readers the idea of homosexuality as natural, but also as eternal; homosexuality as an inseparable—if not yet properly recognized, often oppressed—part of humanity.

6.2   OUT AND PROUD

While establishing that homosexuality, at least the 'real' one, is natural, innate and fixed, both magazines emphasized the importance of self-awareness and self-acceptance. One of the central problems of many, indeed 'too many', Polish homosexuals, as defined in *Biuletyn* (1984, 4, p. 1), was that they 'treat themselves as degenerates, perverts and the propagators of evil who deserve punishment'. *Filo* (1988, 14, p. 5) added that Polish homosexuals 'are absolute past masters at deceiving themselves [...] They just don't want to accept the fact that they are homosexuals' and continue making unsuccessful 'attempts at heterosexualization'. Not surprisingly, the authors of the magazines criticized such negative self-conceptualizations. For example, in reply to a letter to the editor on difficulties of being a homosexual in Poland, especially in the countryside, the editor wrote: 'A thought "I'm a homosexual" should never provoke a wave of self-destruction, like: "I hate myself, I'm worse than others, defective, what if others find out?" Why shall we think this way, falling into depression and anxiety?' (*Filo* 1989, 17, p. 18). Similarly, Pilch encouraged lesbian self-awareness and self-acceptance: 'This should be our starting point: to understand and to like ourselves [...] to tell ourselves: "I'm a lesbian and I'm proud of it"' (*Filo* 1989, 18, p. 10).

The Western inspirations for this rhetoric of homosexual affirmation are clear in the word choice of *Biuletyn/Etap* and *Filo*. Even though some scholars argue that the words 'gay' and 'lesbian' arrived in Central and Eastern Europe only after 1989 (e.g. Frątczak 2012, p. 171, Long 1999, p. 242; Sokolová 2014, p. 103), both magazines started to use them quite regularly (usually interchangeably with the word 'homosexual') soon after being founded and in much the same way as gay liberation did: to affirm the 'out and proud' version of homosexuality (Weeks 2011, pp. 63–68). Most often, the magazines adopted the words in their Polish version, *gej* and *lesbijka*, but they also used the original spelling occasionally. In addition, a couple of times the authors of *Filo* became highly self-reflexive about their choice of names, particularly about the word 'gay'. For example, they expressed their indignation at the Polish Public Broadcaster for wrongly translating 'gay' as *pederasta* (pederast) in a programme about AIDS, explaining that 'the word gay was introduced to replace the vulgar and pejorative names for homosexuality' (*Filo* 1987, 7–8, p. 3). In one of the following issues, they actually provided a definition of 'gay', drawing on *Eros i Film* (Kornatowska 1986), a book inspired by Western feminist theories and gay and lesbian studies and much praised in *Filo*. They wrote that gay means 'the struggle for a new awareness, self-contained identity as well as social recognition' (in *Filo* 1987, 11–12, p. 2; see also Fig. 6.1). Similarly, in one of the letters to the editor we read that

> Not every faggot [*pedał*], not every poofter [*ciota*] is a gay, but only the one who accepts himself and tries to come out or has already done it. We may also define gay as a self-aware faggot who is ready to fight for his rights and propagate tolerance, who is involved in the movement. (*Filo* 1988, 14, p. 12)

Darkrooms   i   krzaki

Powstanie tzw. darkrooms w USA i
innych krajach wynikło z potrzeb
(normalnych - seksualnych) środowisk
gejów,potrzeb nawiązywania bezpiecz-
nych kontaktów .Często się zdarza,
że zaproszony przez geja partner,
już w jego mieszkaniu dokona rabunku,
kradzieży czy nawet mordu.
Dlatego właśnie aby uniknąć takich
niebezpiecznych sytuacji powstała
instytucja "darkrooms"w kawiarniach,
przede wszystkim w łaźniach,gdzie
stosunek z poznanym przed chwilą
partnerem odbywa się na miejscu bez
konieczności zapraszania go do domu.
Ograbienie partnera w takim miejscu
nie jest już możliwe gdyż są wokół
najczęściej przyjaciele i znajomi
potencjalnej ofiary,którzy wszyscy
się znają i mogą uniemożliwić taką
grabież.Dziś w dobie AIDS te właśnie
darkrooms przyczyniają się do roz-
przestrzeniania tej choroby prowadzą-
cej do śmierci a miały chronić przed
śmiercią z rąk lujów.
Takie darkrooms chroniły również
przed wścibskimi sąsiadami czy rodziną.
Ktoś do,którego często przychodzili
mężczyźni był brany na języki ,gdy
prawda wychodziła na jaw musiał się
wyprowadzać.W przypadku korzystania
z darkroomów całymi latami można
mieszkać samemu i nie mieć żadnych
gości i nikt z sąsiadów nawet nie
będzie podejrzewać takiego faceta
o homoseksualizm.
W Polsce i nie tylko,w każdym bądź
razie w krajach gdzie jest kryzys
mieszkaniowy rolę "darkroomów" pełnią
krzaki.Mają też wzięcie ci starsi
panowie,którzy już mają mieszkanie
i tu właśnie są narażeni na rabunek bo
nie ma u nas "darkroomów" ani nawet
tanich hotelików z pokojami na godziny.
2

W ogóle brak hoteli i nawet jak pójdzie-
my do recepcji to okazuje się,że brak
miejsc bo trzeba je rezerwować z kilku-
dniowym wyprzedzeniem.
Tymczasem w Stanach Zjednoczonych *
Walka o prawa mniejszości seksualnych potraktowana została jako część
generalnej walki politycznej o prawa
wszelkiego rodzaju mniejszości (np.
Murzynów w USA), o prawo jednostki
do swobodnej samorealizacji, do bycia
sobą w społeczeństwie.
Wówczas też w początkach lat siedem-
dziesiątych ruch homoseksualistów
w USA propaguje rozpowszechnienie
słowa "gay", które powinno wyrugować
z użytku słowa wulgarne,pejoratywne
w swej wymowie na określenie homoseksualistów.
                                    * *
Gay - w odniesieniu do homoseksualistów
obojga płci - oznacza "walkę o nową
świadomość,niezależną tożsamość i spo-
łeczne uznanie".Sformułowania progra-
mowe ruchów tzw. mniejszości seksualnych odzwierciedlają "nową świadomość
rzeczy". Lewacka retoryka zdobi obficie
wystąpienia bojowników ruchu.Mniejszo-
ści wszelkiego rodzaju- od młodzieży
i Murzynów począwszy,a na lesbijkach
i homoseksualistach - kończąc - łączą
się we wspólnym froncie przeciwko
opartemu na ucisku i dyskryminacji
ładowi społecznemu.Bardzo to znamienne
dla epoki zjawisko.

* Marla Kornatowska , Eros i film .
* * tamże.

Fig. 6.1   Discussions of the Western darkroom culture and the word 'gay' in *Filo*
(1987, 11–12, p. 2). Courtesy of Lambda Warszawa

Just as in the gay liberation's model of the 'out and proud' homosexuality, so too in *Biuletyn/Etap* and *Filo* self-awareness and self-acceptance should be followed by coming out, especially to family and friends. The authors of the magazines were aware that coming out was not easy in late communist Poland, pointing to such particular difficulties as, at the more abstract level, a highly prejudiced (also because deeply religious) society (*Filo* 1990, 20, p. 37) and, at the more practical level, a problem with securing housing in case coming out would mean losing a roof over one's head (*Filo* 1989, 18, p. 12). Nevertheless, they insisted that coming out is inevitable for any homosexual who aims to live a happy life, a life without shame and stress, without the constant fear of being unintentionally found out or intentionally outed (*Filo* 1990, 19, p. 40). Selerowicz (*Etap* 1987, 2, p. 3) also pointed out the advantages of coming out for homosexuals being detained and interrogated by the police forces or the secret service during such actions as Operation Hyacinth. He explained that when being out to their family, friends and colleagues, homosexuals cannot be subjected to blackmail and forced into cooperation, which usually involved betraying homosexual friends and lovers. *Filo*, in turn, stressed that coming out, both gay and lesbian, is a good test of 'parental love' and 'true friendship': 'For every normal intelligent person, it is people's personality that counts, not who they sleep with. Really. A person who will turn away from you when the truth comes to light must be slightly handicapped' (1989, 18, p. 10; see also 1990, 20, p. 37).

Additionally, to encourage their readers to come out, both magazines published countless words of warning, stories with tragic endings (in the form of reportages, short stories, film reviews and letters to the editor) of homosexuals who, as one character in the 1970 film *The Conformist*, 'wanted to be just like others at any price, was running away from freedom and from being who he really was' (*Filo* 1987, 4, p. 3). At the same time, they provided many positive examples of homosexuals living their lives 'in the truth', especially of openly gay celebrities (mainly in the West) such as Jean Genet (*Filo* 1987, 7–8, p. 3), Truman Capote, Yukio Mishima (*Filo* 1988, 13, p. 5) or Salvador Dali, the latter described as 'living his life to the fullest, without stressing out or hiding his passions' (*Filo* 1989, 17, p. 27). In *Filo*, other positive examples included coming out success stories in the form of letters to the editor—hence, much closer to the realities of the magazine's readers than celebrity stories—where the readers attested that, for example, their coming out to family and friends did not trigger rejection (1990, 19, p. 40) but 'gave the absolutely incredible feeling of mental comfort' (1990, 20, p. 51). Pilch additionally presented one success story of lesbians coming out to the local community. This, however, was a story from abroad, of Bente and Helga who decided to live an openly lesbian life in a small Norwegian town (*Filo* 1989, 17, pp. 27–28). The story demonstrated the possibility for ordinary homosexuals to live an openly gay or lesbian life in the public, the life supposedly already lived in the West if not yet attainable in Poland.

Also in support of its readers' coming out, in one of the early issues of *Biuletyn* (1984, 4, pp. 1–2), Selerowicz published a two-page article with tips for coming out to family. He started the article by suggesting the order in which family members should be approached—first brother or sister, then mother and finally father—and continued by detailing how to come out to a mother. He advised to make meticulous preparations in advance: to compile a list of key arguments and draft a text of the speech, to choose the right time and place (so not to be disturbed during the talk), and even to do some household chores right before the talk (so to make your mother feel sympathetic towards you). While there is a lot to be said about the gendered nature of this advice that reflects heteropatriarchal structures, what cannot be denied is its very detailed and practical character. In the article, we can also find a sample text of the speech, where Selerowicz proposed to explain to a mother that homosexuality is natural and normal; that there are plenty of homosexuals in the world, including 'many famous people who played a pivotal role in the progress of human civilization' (*Biuletyn* 1984, 4, p. 1); and that homosexuals can be valuable and happy people. Taking into consideration the specificities of the Polish context, he also offered some counterarguments to the potential questions relating to 'religious morality', as he called it: 'If God wanted me to be born homosexual, then he also needs to find a place for me in this world. After all, isn't Christianity about the love of one's neighbour and the forgiveness of sins?' (*Biuletyn* 1984, 4, p. 2).

The word choice is again indicative of the source of inspiration for the magazines when writing about coming out. Both magazines routinely used the phrase 'coming out' in English as well as explicitly reflected on its meaning. Selerowicz, for example, explained that '"coming out" means to realize (and be open about) the fact that being a homosexual does not mean to be a second-category person, sick pervert or crazy lunatic' (*Biuletyn* 1983, 2, p. 1). *Filo*, in turn, used the phrase in an article encouraging to establish 'coming out support groups' across Poland (*Filo* 1990, 19, p. 12) and in a piece on homosexuality in cinema, where the author mentioned East German film *Coming Out*, with the title being originally in English, not German (*Filo* 1990, 20, p. 20; for more about the film see McLellan 2011, pp. 136–137). Additionally, *Filo* included a two-issue series entitled 'Coming Out' (1988, 13 and 14), where (this time) the authors discussed the importance of self-acceptance rather than the act of coming out itself and reflected on the meaning of the phrase. Acknowledging their source, which was a piece published in the US *Advocate*, they explained the origin of the phrase (in the US culture of presenting a 14-year-old girl to the community) and pointed out that 'the American movement of homosexuals adopted it to indicate the process from discovering your same-sex orientation to accepting your homosexuality' (*Filo* 1988, 13, p. 4). They also proposed to translate 'coming out' into Polish as *wyjście na zewnątrz* (going outside). Thus, similarly to the previous discussions on the word 'gay' in *Filo*, here too authors of both magazines introduced a new English term, reflecting on its importance, meaning and possible equivalents in Polish.

6.3   THE ROMANTIC SELF

Not only self-hatred or 'living in the lie' but also loneliness emerged in the magazines as a major source of homosexual sorrow. Still, the loneliness was most often framed as a direct consequence of living the secret life and presented as the most tragic possible outcome of life in old age. In a particularly depressing fictional story published in the last issue of *Filo*, the author outlined a vision of such a lifelong closet:

> Months pass by, turn into years [...] but you still don't accept yourself, still look for a girlfriend who would cure you [...] and then you turn forty, fifty, sixty years old [...] your life is already over even though you still move, eat, drink, smoke and, most of all, want to love. But the only thing left is your paralyzing fear of loneliness, which by now has become an irreversible fact. (1990, 20, pp. 35–37)

The theme of loneliness was also employed in some personal ads in *Filo*, where the readers expressed that they were 'very lonely' (1989, 18, p. 19) or were living 'on the glass mountain of loneliness' (1990, 20, p. 46), and was even more prominent in the *Filo*'s series entitled 'Encounters with love', where both authors and readers of the magazine presented romantic-erotic poems and short stories, occasionally accompanied by

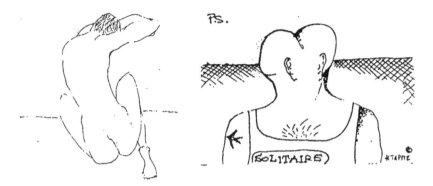

Fig. 6.2 Images of loneliness in *Filo* (1988, 13, pp. 6 and 8). Courtesy of Lambda Warszawa

images equally full of romance and loneliness. Figure 6.2 shows two such images, one of which (on the right) aptly demonstrates the combination of the concept of loneliness with the idea of life in the closet, resulting in an inner conflict and double life.

To overcome the loneliness, both *Biuletyn/Etap* and *Filo* recommended first to come out and then to find love. However, as Mary Evans (2003) teaches us, the concept of love is culturally coded. Particularly, the idea of romantic love has been strongly encouraged since the age of modernization, when the functions of family and marriage have changed from much economic to mainly emotional, though romantic love was also translated in various economic practices (Illouz 1997). Not surprisingly, therefore, it was the idea of romantic love which both magazines pushed forward most vigorously. And what kind of love is this? There are three main components of it, according to the magazines. First, it is monogamous, always involving only two people. Second, it is faithful: both magazines argued against what *Filo* (1988, 15, p. 11) called *wielopartnerstwo* (multipartnership) and advocated strong will against 'the temptations of an accidently met ephebos' (*Etap* 1986, 3, p. 3), also but not exclusively because of the dangers of HIV/AIDS. Finally, it is long-term, 'till death do us part' and 'for better and for worse', as attested by some personal ads in the magazines. The latter examples clearly drew on dominant ideals of marriage and family. The authors of the magazines too inclined to employ the language of these originally heterosexual and heterosexist institutions, for instance, when they talked about same-sex relationships in terms of a 'marital cohabitation' or simply 'gay marriage' (*Etap* 1986, 3, p. 3), 'homosexual marriage' or 'male marriage' (*Filo* 1988, 15, p. 11).

The ideals about the romantic love extended to the characteristics of the ideal partner. In *Biuletyn/Etap*, the most common word—on the verge of overuse—for describing the partner was *wartościowy* (valuable). Many times Selerowicz used the word casually, without explaining what he meant by it. At times, however, he was more precise about it, as in the following example: 'There are among us snitches, thieves, prostitutes and stirrers—we should stay away from these ones. It's better to put our energies into combating bad manners, malice and gossiping, so we can prove that we're valuable people' (*Etap* 1986, 3, p. 4). At one point, Selerowicz also offered tips for Polish homosexuals getting in touch with Western homosexuals, clearly promoting a model of an educated and respectable middle-class man: 'Be yourself, don't try to impress them at all costs [...] Instead, show your wide interests, knowledge of foreign languages, warmth and modesty' (*Etap* 1987, 4, p. 4). Similar set of values occasionally surfaced in *Filo*, for example in an article by Sławek Starosta, where the author reflected on the state of the Polish homosexual movement. Apart from many postulates regarding the change of attitudes towards homosexuals in society at large, he also emphasized that homosexuals need to change themselves: show each other more respect, accept each other regardless of age, look and behaviour, and stop 'gossiping, backbiting and plotting intrigues' (*Filo* 1990, 19, p. 11).

The ideal partner was additionally subjected to very strict beauty standards. Even though the authors of the two magazines did occasionally criticize some homosexuals' 'too high expectations about age, beauty, intelligence and sexual temperament' (*Etap* 1986, 3, p. 4) and argued that penis size does not matter (*Etap* 1986, 4, p. 3; *Filo* 1990, 20, pp. 22–24), they repeatedly articulated clear beauty ideals across different sections of the magazines. The most dominant ones, apart from many vague statements such as 'so beautiful that it's indecent' (*Filo* 1989, 18, p. 29), required from men to be masculine, muscled, hairy and 'generously endowed by nature'. Especially strong was the ideal of a muscled, but also 'proportionally built', body. Both magazines encouraged their readers to work out in order to 'improve your silhouette' (*Etap* 1986, 4, p. 3) and *Filo* published a two-issue series on body building, where the authors, using the very phrase in English, provided many workout tips (1990, 19, pp. 34–35; 1990, 20, pp. 30–31). The ideal was also conveyed visually, through numerous images of beautiful male bodies. Particularly popular were cartoons from the Tom of Finland's *Kake* series, reproduced multiple times in both magazines. In an article accompanying one of the cartoons, *Filo* (1989, 18, p. 15) explained that 'Tom's gay man is not a traditional spoiled poofter […] effeminate, delicate and absolutely passive […], he is a strong macho man.' As the Tom of Finland's case attests, the beauty standards in the Polish magazines were not far from the ones popular at that time (and largely today as well) in the West. One diversion from these ideals was the model of the already discussed 'Greek love'—also quite prominent in the analysed magazines—which applauded the relationship between an older, experienced and masculine man and a younger, inexperienced and delicate 'ephebos', as exemplified in this quote from a poem in *Filo* (1987, 9–10, p. 7): 'your springy seventeen years moved my forty-years-old block.'

Partially due to the strict beauty standards and partially due to the reality of a homosexual life in late communist Poland (e.g. the already mentioned housing problems), the romantic love described in the magazines seemed largely unattainable, particularly for the authors and readers of *Filo*, who were affected by this reality more than Selerowicz. The near impossibility of the romantic love was most often expressed in the *Filo*'s 'Encounters with love' series, where one could read, for example: 'I desperately look for you every day […] I find you only in my dreams' (1989, 18, p. 28). The series, however, was dominated by romantic-erotic stories, which poetically detailed encounters between two lovers, both men and women, such as: 'Tomek dipped his lips into Adam's thicket of matted chest hair and found with his tongue Adam's hard nipple' (1990, 20, p. 40) or, regarding lesbians: 'Once again expelled from the Garden of Eden/I was looking for the Tree of Knowledge/To once again eat the fruit of shame/And feel the taste of your body' (1990, 19, p. 27). In the context where the homosexual romantic love (and sex) seemed near impossible, and where representations of such love and sex were not to be found in mainstream media or in pornographic magazines, the distribution of which was illegal, the romantic-erotic stories published in *Filo* weaved fantasies, created dreams and hopes to which the readers could cling while living their often insecure, closeted and lonely lives. Therefore, it is unsurprising the readers welcomed the 'Encounters with love' series with great enthusiasm, thanking for the stories' 'beauty, subtlety and warmth, which we miss so much in our everyday lives' (*Filo* 1989, 17, p. 16).

The introduction of personal ads in *Biuletyn/Etap* and *Filo* also functioned as a way of combating loneliness, though at a more practical than symbolic level, compared to the romantic-erotic stories just discussed. Selerowicz started to include free homosexual personal ads only after the mainstream monthly *Relaks* (Relax) had stopped publishing them (Chap. 4). He explained that he found it 'important to help lonely people to meet a friend (a partner?)' (*Biuletyn* 1985, 2, p. 2). Yet, in total, he published only ten ads and dropped the section because his readers did not show enough interest in it. The personal ads section proved to be more successful in *Filo*. Even though the section was introduced rather late, only in the second issue of 1989, altogether the magazine published more than 60 ads, always divided into two categories: 'World' and 'Poland'. Similarly to *Biuletyn/Etap*, *Filo* framed the necessity of such a section in terms of combating loneliness: 'If you're lonely and want to meet people with similar interests, send us your ad, which should be no longer than 30 words. Write what you would like to communicate to your future friend along with your age and height' (1989, 17, p. 21). The section included paid ads by both men and women, written in Polish, English or German, as well as a few activist and commercial advertisements, for example by Lambda Praha or local match-making agencies from Bydgoszcz, Cracow, Gdańsk, Wrocław and Zabrze.

6.4   THE SEXUAL SELF

As briefly mentioned in the previous section, the idea of romantic love directly translated into the notion of romantic sex, that is, a passionate sex based on love and with one long-term partner only. This was very clear in *Biuletyn/Etap*, where Selerowicz vigorously campaigned against promiscuity. In one article under the headline 'Together or separately?', he wrote:

> I must admit, collecting lovers has its own advantages. But for me, it is more like running away from ourselves, trying to forget about our own failures and injuries, and, ultimately, clumsily attempting to accumulate the thrills before we grow old in loneliness and with the bitter feeling of a squandered life. (1986, 3, p. 3)

Accordingly, the information provided in his regular column 'Sex guide for gay men' concerned only coupled sex or masturbation, and only in private, always favouring partner sex. Masturbation was framed as 'good fun' and an 'opportunity to get to know your body' but also as a 'good practice for partner sex' (1987, 1, p. 2) and anal sex was presented as means of creating the 'absolute closeness between partners' (1987, 3, p. 2). Additionally, in other issues of the magazine, Selerowicz complained about the Polish homosexuals having sex in public toilets (1985, 3, p. 2) or interested in the conferences of International Gay Association (IGA, later ILGA) exclusively for sexual reasons (1985, 2, p. 2). Far from being sex-negative, Selerowicz nevertheless consistently promoted in *Biuletyn/Etap* values of love and sex much closer to the homophile movement rather than to gay liberation (Churchill 2008; Jackson 2015; see also Chap. 2).

Filo also strongly advocated romantic sex, especially in the 'Encounters with love' series, and often criticized widespread in communist Poland culture of *pikiety*, that is, public places such as toilets, parks and train stations, used by homosexuals for cruising and having sex (for an excellent literary description of the culture, also available in English, see Witkowski 2010). The authors of the magazine argued against *pikiety* for a number of reasons, especially because of the casual sex happening there, which was also connected to the increased risk of HIV infection, as well as due to the dirty conditions and criminal atmosphere associated with these spaces. *Pikiety* were compared to a 'stock exchange' and dubbed a 'huge stinking gutter' (1989, 18, p. 10) or a 'lousy place', where apart from homosexuals one could find 'drunkards, petty criminals and all the other scum' (1990, 20, p. 26). Yet, at the same time, recognizing the lack of alternatives to *pikiety* and trying to meet the expectations of some readers, *Filo* (1987, 7–8, p. 8) launched a regular guide to homosexual meeting places, where readers 'could make themselves feel better through the way of sexual achievements'. Besides, the authors of the magazine published plenty of sex jokes (as well as HIV/AIDS jokes), particularly popular in the special issue on April Fools' Day (1989, SI), where they humorously introduced themselves as female journalists, referring to the famous Italian journalist Oriana Fallaci: Oralna Fellatio, Onania Fellatio, Onania Fallussi and Oralna Fillussi, and proposed a number of new words, mainly in Polish, such as *naniedomaganian kutasu* (cocktassium deficiency) but also one in French: *jamerde* (a combination of *jamais* [never] and *merde* [shit]).

The somewhat more sexually liberal attitude of *Filo* compared to *Biuletyn/Etap* was additionally manifested in the magazine's more favourable attitude towards pornography. Selerowicz was not against pornography as such and did include in his magazine some pornographic images of Tom of Finland. Yet, the topic was never greeted in *Biuletyn/Etap* with as much enthusiasm as it was in *Filo*. The latter included not only many

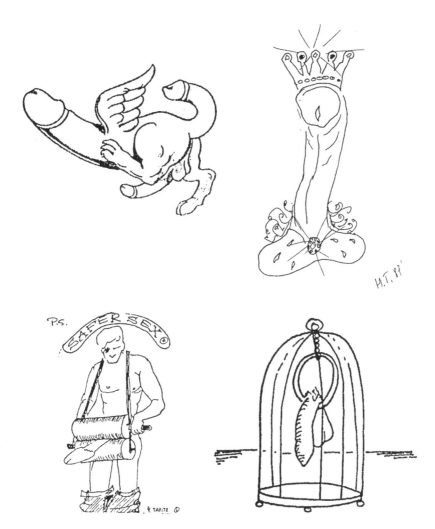

Fig. 6.3   Images of penises in *Filo* (from top-left: 1989, SI, p. 1; 1987, 11–12, p. 5; 1988, 13, p. 3; and 1988, 14, p. 7). Courtesy of Lambda Warszawa

erotic/pornographic stories or images (e.g. see Fig. 6.3) and humorous slogans such as 'We want porn, not **ORMO** [a volunteer police reserve]' (1989, SI, p. 4), but also some serious discussions about the ban on the distribution of pornography in Poland under communism. In one issue,

Filo (1987, 5–6, pp. 2–3) dedicated two full pages to the topic. First, the authors reacted to some complaints from the readers about reproducing explicit images and using vulgar words by explaining that the images were artistic in nature and the words were ironic in intention. Next, they argued that homosexual pornography was prosecuted in Poland more vigorously than heterosexual pornography and made the case for legalizing the former, maintaining that pornography would work as a substitute for sex and, thus, would help to fight against the spreading of HIV. Finally, they reprinted three paragraphs from a book on the Polish Penal Code, where the readers could learn about the legal interpretation of the Polish ban on the distribution of pornography. In one of the last issues, *Filo* (1990, 19, p. 37) also reprinted an interview with a Polish writer, Andrzej Rodos, who wove the vision of liberal changes regarding pornography coming to post-communist Poland: 'Sooner or later, the wave of the porn business will reach us just as jeans, video, Coca-Cola and colourful socks did.'

Besides, *Filo* was fascinated by the sexual liberation characteristic of some Western gay cultures. For example, contrasting Polish pikiety with US darkrooms, the authors of the magazine (1987, 11–12, p. 2) explained that the latter had been created to provide homosexuals with safe sex spaces, that is, the spaces where homosexuals could have casual sex without the fear of being robbed or murdered but also without the chance of being spotted by their neighbours, for example when inviting their sex partners home (see also Fig. 6.1). At the same time, the authors noted that darkrooms, which were supposed to be places of safety, turned into places of death in the age of HIV/AIDS. *Filo* (1989, 18, pp. 7–8) also praised the sexual liberation of West Berlin, which 'for the newcomers from the European East seems to be a colourful and seductive oasis of sex, also homo sex; hence a Sexoase, Homooase...'. The author of the article, a Pole writing from Berlin, applauded the cruising culture of Tierpark, sex trade of Bahnhof Zoo, the city's gay bars, cafés as well as sex and video shops. Writing more about sex video cabins, he emphasized their 'sterile cleanliness' and the diversity of choice they offered: 'The video recorder shows 12 channels at the same time. Choose and change. Insert 5DM [German Mark] and watch to your heart's content. See what madness between men means' (*Filo* 1989, 18, p. 8). Still, as in the previous article, here too the author pointed to the grave dangers of HIV/AIDS inseparable from the Western gay sex cultures.

The HIV/AIDS epidemic, even if it has never reached crisis propor-tions in Poland (see Chap. 4), did play an important role in discourses on sex in both analysed magazines. In *Biuletyn/Etap*, HIV/AIDS was pre-sented as yet another, though not necessarily the main, argument against promiscuity. Many times in the magazine, Selerowicz explained that total abstinence from sex is impossible and could even lead to neurosis. At the same time, he emphasized that HIV poses a real danger and that AIDS leads directly to death within three years, adding that the probability of HIV infection increases when one have sex with a lot of different people: 'A minor, invisible to the eye wound during a casual sex, a one-night stand, is enough to get infected without even realizing it. High promiscu-ity (having sex with many strangers) increases the danger geometrically' (*Biuletyn* 1985, 1, p. 1). Moreover, later on, Selerowicz actually suggested the near inevitability of HIV infection for homosexuals sleeping around:

> Those of us who stay faithful to our friends have still nothing to be afraid of. But those who continue to have sexual adventures with casual partners need to realize that, sooner or later, they will come into contact with an infected person. (1986, 1, p. 1)

Thus, the discourse of the dangers of HIV/AIDS in *Biuletyn/Etap* was used (among other things which I will discuss in the following chapter) to strengthen the idea of romantic love coupled with the notion of romantic sex.

The authors of *Filo* too regularly advised against promiscuity in the context of the HIV/AIDS epidemic, for example: 'Remember that the best guarantee of safety is a steady partner. If you've been absolutely faith-ful to each other for the last 3–4 years, you can be sure that you're free from the HIV virus without a blood test' (1988, 14, p. 6). Still, while for *Biuletyn/Etap* HIV/AIDS functioned chiefly as another argument in sup-port of romantic love and sex, for more sexually liberal *Filo* sexual fidelity was more a necessity in the age of HIV/AIDS rather than a universal value. This is particularly clear at the visual level. In the first issues of the magazine (1986–1987), the authors included frequent reproductions of sexually explicit drawings by Aubrey Beardsley, a lover of Oscar Wilde, with many portraits of men with monstrous penises (*Filo* reproduced the drawings from the Polish book about the artist by Ewa Kuryluk 1976). Many other images too were holding a joyous celebration of the penis: the pages of the magazine abounded in the drawings of phallus-shaped amulets, penises wearing the crown and covered in diamonds, or depicted as independent creatures—possibly humans themselves—with legs and hands but also wings. Yet, as Fig. 6.3 demonstrates, such images were juxtaposed with the images of penises being pressed or caged, with some clear references to the HIV/AIDS epidemic as in the image including the phrase 'safer sex' in English. The epidemic, therefore, changed the meaning of sex for the authors of *Filo*—as much as it did for gay liberation (Piontek 2006, p. 32)—by coupling sex with fear and death, and requiring from homosexuals to curtail their sexual freedom.

6.5   THE COLLECTIVE SELF

The making of the Polish modern homosexual was not limited in *Biuletyn/Etap* and *Filo* to establishing the essence of homosexuality and prescribing the ideals of love and sex but included creating a homosexual community of interest. Probably because both magazines were made by well-educated though not necessarily wealthy people, the community of interest most often centred around what could be qualified as a 'high culture'. The magazines, especially *Filo*, introduced to their readers hundreds of acclaimed books and films but also some paintings, exhibitions and theatre plays which presented homosexuality in a favourable light. Sometimes, they simply listed the works; other times, they ran major features devoted to a specific work or artist, for example the American play *Bent*, UK film *My Beautiful Laundrette* (*Filo* 1989, 16, pp. 12–13), French musical *La Cage aux Folles* (The Cage of Mad Queens) (*Filo* 1989, 17, p. 15), UK painter David Hockney (*Filo* 1988, 15, p. 18) or French writer Jean Cocteau (*Filo* 1989, 17, p. 5). Occasionally, they also strengthened their message by adding that the discussed works or artists are 'pleasing to the homosexual soul' and 'recommended for all homosexuals' or demanding that 'every gay man should know them' (e.g. *Filo* 1987, 9–10, p. 6). Thus, they recognized homosexuality not only as a (natural) sexual practice but also as a cultural practice (Halperin 2012, p. 35), and were creating a gay canon, knowledge of which was intended to connect Polish homosexuals.

As the examples of works and artists just mentioned attest, the gay canon showed a strong Western bias. The lists of recommended works in *Filo* too were dominated by, and in some cases exclusively devoted to, Western works. For example, a three-issue series on 'Gay literature in the world' (1987, issues: 4, 5–6 and 7–8) included only works from the United States, United Kingdom, West Germany and France as well as one title from Italy, Pier Paolo Pasolini's *Amado Mio*; clearly equating the world with the West. At the same time, in different sections, *Filo* listed many Polish works with homoerotic content but only rarely discussed works from other parts of the world, including other Eastern Bloc countries; with the two most popular exceptions being the already mentioned films *Another Way* (Hungary) and *Coming Out* (East Germany). Similar Western bias could be found in *Biuletyn/Etap*. In an issue fully devoted to 'homoerotic literature' (1986, 2), Selerowicz started by introducing French books, which he hailed as 'the earliest and the most valuable homoerotic masterpieces' (p. 1), and continued by discussing books from the United States, United Kingdom and Italy as well as those written in German or Spanish. At the very end, he also mentioned 'Slavic literature' but noted that 'in fact, only in Polish literature we could find the themes we are interested in' (p. 2), pointing to such authors as Witold Gombrowicz, Jerzy Andrzejewski and Jarosław Iwaszkiewicz. Clearly, apart from the Polish homoerotic works, the readers of the analysed magazines were strongly encouraged to familiarize themselves with the Western gay canon, which may be understood as an attempt at realizing the vision of 'queer cosmopolitanism' (Weeks 2011, p. 36).

Over time, both magazines broadened the scope of the gay canon so it also included so-called 'low culture', particularly pop music. Again, the pages of the magazines abounded in Western cultural references, including Bronski Beat, Duran Duran, Boy George, Michael Jackson, Prince and Wham (*Biuletyn* 1985, 4, pp. 2–3), Elton John, George Michael and Rod Steward (*Etap* 1987, 2, p. 1), David Bowie, Freddy Mercury and Fancy (*Filo* 1988, 14, p. 11) as well as—considered as lesbian or at least ambiguous—Dolly Parton and Suzan Vega (*Filo* 1988, 15, p. 19). *Filo* (1988, 13, p. 7) additionally introduced the concept of a 'gay disco', which specifically referred to 'homosexual duos' such as Communards, Erasure and Pet Shop Boys. Non-Western references were even less common here than in the 'high culture' sections of the magazines. Again, Polish artists were more popular than any other non-Western artists. The magazines mentioned, for instance, a male duo Papa Dance (*Filo* 1988, 13, p. 7), Gdańsk-based rock band Marilyn Monroe—'which seems to be the best gang of homosexuals in Poland and possibly in the entire area east of the Elbe' (*Filo* 1988, 15, p. 19)—as well as famous Polish diva Violetta Villas, whose songs had apparently achieved a cult status among Polish homosexuals, especially the lyrics of one of her songs: *Ja jestem Violetta, wrażliwa kobietta* (I am Violetta, a sensitive womanetta) (*Etap* 1987, 2, p. 1). A few Eastern Bloc examples included an openly homosexual band Borghesia from Yugoslavia (*Biuletyn* 1985, 4, p. 3) and effeminate pop star Valery Leontiev from the Soviet Union (*Filo* 1988, 14, p. 11).

Apart from recommending their readers what they should read, watch or listen to, the authors of the magazines also gave them tips about what to wear, expanding the gay canon so it included also fashion. Here too we can find an overwhelming dominance of the West. Selerowicz (*Biuletyn* 1985, 4, p. 3), for example, criticized some Polish homosexuals, so-called *cioty tekstylne* (textile poofters), for blindly following the trends promoted in mainstream magazines. In the West, he explained, people take fashion less seriously and homosexuals still prefer a 'simple, casual and sport look'. *Filo* (1989, 17, p. 20), in turn, complained about the scarcity of men's fashion columns in Polish mainstream media and criticized what we would call today the heterosexim of the few which did exist, complaining that 'they do not discuss such topics as earrings, chains and bracelets for men.' In the rest of the article, entitled 'Style: Our own correspondence from Paris', the authors gave a detailed list of tips about what to wear and how to wear it, especially concerning trousers, shirts, jackets, shoes, socks and, indeed, earrings. 'In this season', one could learn, 'men wear two small gold ring earrings next to each other, either in the left ear or in the right ear, but only in one of them [...] Pearl, silver or gold ball earrings have gone completely out of fashion' (*Filo* 1989, 17, p. 20). *Filo* (1988, 14, p. 10) also reported that already in the 1930s homosexuals in California had developed their own fashion style, characterized by jackets with wide and padded shoulders.

On top of that, *Filo* occasionally introduced to its readers particular aspects of Western gay sex and bar cultures, the function of which was not only to assume/create an interest in the cultures but also to present them as role models, presumably better developed and more interesting than their Polish equivalents. In the previous section, I already gave an example of the magazine praising sex cultures of West Berlin. Similarly, in an interview with a Pole who had immigrated to Munich, *Filo* (1990, 19, p. 26) described the cruising cultures of the city, concentrated around the English Garden, where visitors could allegedly find anything they wanted: 'Youngsters or men with a belly. Of masculine, feminine or neuter gender. Sadists contra masochists. Paedophiles and lesbians. Take your pick. The true Tower of Babel of homo-community.' The same piece provided additional information about Munich's gay bar culture, which, compared to its Polish equivalent, was more affordable and better developed: it included a much greater diversity of bars, some of which—like the Munich's bar 'New York'—'had a dance floor the size of the Warsaw Central train station' (*Filo* 1990, 19, p. 26). Besides, while discussing the demonstrations against Section 28 in the United Kingdom, the magazine also introduced some gay slang terms in English, for example 'queen', translated as *superciota* (superpoofter) and 'queers' (in the slogan 'God save the queers'), translated as *pedały* (faggots) (*Filo* 1988, 15, p. 3).

Finally, *Filo* featured some of the most popular West European gay and lesbian magazines. For example, it informed about the tenth anniversary of *Gai Pied*, adding that the French magazine had been applauded by the president François Mitterrand, who himself sent a congratulatory telegram to the authors of the magazine (*Filo* 1989, 17, p. 6). In the same issue, *Filo* also briefly discussed Dutch *De Gay Krant*, 'the biggest gay magazine in Europe' (1989, 17, p. 22), focusing on its special section with nude photographs of ordinary Dutch homosexuals. Similarly to Western gay sex and bar cultures, the Western magazines were much praised by *Filo*: they were depicted as bigger, more widely recognized and with greater resources than Polish magazines. Additionally, *Filo* (1988, 15, p. 13) admired the number and diversity of advertisements in the Western magazines: 'Everything is advertised there: from video companies to cinemas, saunas, hotels, restaurants, bars as well as shorts and briefs.' The comparisons between *Filo* and its Western counterparts are particularly striking in a reportage detailing the visit of two *Filo*'s authors to the editorial office of the West German magazine *Magnus*, created in 1989 by the merger of *Rosa Flieder* and *Siegessäule*. In the reportage, we read that the visitors 'sighed wistfully when seeing all those wonders of modern technology [e.g. IBM computers] which *Magnus* owned, compared to *Filo*'s equipment (one typewriter and no telephone)' (*Filo* 1990, 20, p. 9). Yet, the authors of the reportage also informed about the planned visit of *Magnus*'s authors to the editorial office of *Filo*, vaguely suggesting that 'Maybe they too will learn something from us...' (*Filo* 1990, 20, p. 9).

6.6   Conclusion

What kind of a homosexual does emerge from the 1980s Polish gay and lesbian magazines? It is a homosexual, more often a man than a woman, who was born this way; as much as homosexuals at different times and in different places were. It is a homosexual who is self-aware, accepts himself or herself the way they are and does not hide their homosexuality from family or friends, or at least plans to or wants to come out to them. This kind of a homosexual also longs for a romantic love, a long-term and monogamous relationship with a 'valuable', faithful and beautiful partner, with whom he or she can have a romantic sex, thus putting the fear of HIV and AIDS behind them. Finally, the homosexual belongs to a community of interest, sharing with its members an enthusiasm for books, films, songs and other cultural products which present homosexuality in a favourable light, following the latest fashion trends from the West and cherishing Western sex and bar cultures as well as gay and lesbian magazines. Such an image of a homosexual was fairly characteristic of both analysed magazines, with the only substantial difference between them being a somewhat more sexually liberal attitude of *Filo*, at least some of its authors, compared to *Biuletyn/Etap*. *Filo*'s homosexual was at times allowed to exercise, or more often to dream about, sexual freedom, nonetheless curtailed by the fear of HIV/AIDS epidemic. Additionally, *Filo*'s homosexual seemed to be a bit less serious than the one of *Biuletyn/Etap*, allowing himself or herself to make occasional jokes about dating, sex as well as HIV and AIDS.

This image of a homosexual from the Polish magazines very much resembles Dennis Altman's concept of the modern global gay, who expresses his or her homosexuality openly, has long-term primary relationships with other homosexuals and mix with other homosexuals (1997, p. 425) but also is, or at least wants to be, 'young, upwardly mobile, sexually adventurous, with an in-your-face attitude toward traditional restrictions and an interest in both activism and fashion' (1996, p. 77; the evidence for the interest in activism will be provided in the following chapter). The image is also not far from Jeffrey Weeks' (2011) idea of a 'queer cosmopolitanism'. Because the readers of *Biuletyn/Etap* and *Filo* were regularly introduced to the Western gay canon, sex and bar cultures as well as lesbian and gay magazines, they could indeed 'potentially feel at home in all parts of the worlds where [one could find] a similar repertoire of cafés, bars, clubs, saunas, cruising areas, local neighbourhoods, styles of dress, modes of behaviour and value systems' (Weeks 2011, p. 36), even though for the majority of the readers the prospect of travelling to 'all parts of the worlds' remained rather limited. An inescapable conclusion of this chapter is that the authors of the Polish magazines did actively draw on Western discourses while constructing and reconstructing the idea of homosexuality, either implicitly—by adopting the ideas of natural homo-sexuality or the ideals of romantic love and sex—or explicitly—by referring to Western cultural products and employing Western terms and concepts of 'gay', 'lesbian', 'coming out', 'darkroom' or 'safer sex'.

That being said, the authors of the magazines realized (and in the case of *Filo* were also themselves subjected to) particular historical and geographical circumstances of Polish homosexuals in the 1980s. These circumstances often required a selective adoption as well as strategic and creative adaptation of Western discourses on homosexuality. While embracing the idea of natural homosexuality did not necessarily pose a great challenge in the Polish context, becoming out and proud could lead to a context-specific problems related to, for example, a highly prejudiced society and limited access to housing. Therefore, in the magazines, next to repeated calls to come out, one could also find tips on how to give a witty riposte to probing questions about one's homosexuality (*Biuletyn* 1985, 3, p. 1). Furthermore, the already mentioned problems, together with the scarcity of safe meeting places for homosexuals in Poland, made it difficult (for some, impossible) to pursue the ideals of romantic love and sex or, alternatively, of sexual liberation. Sometimes, the magazines played the role of alleviating these problems, for instance, by providing their readers with dreams and hopes of such romantic-erotic relationships (e.g. in the 'Encounter with love' series in *Filo*) or by creating new chan-nels of communication for them (e.g. through the 'personal ads' sections in both magazines). Other times, they denied or resisted the problems, for instance, by recommending their male readers to wear earrings—an act equal to coming out in that context—or by challenging the ban on the distribution of pornography. In any case, neither the global gay nor the cosmopolitan queer could ignore the fact that they arrived in, or were carried to, late communist Poland.

BIBLIOGRAPHY

Altman, D. (1996). Rupture or continuity? The internationalization of gay identi-ties. *Social Text, 48*(3), 77–94.

Altman, D. (1997). Global gaze/global gays. *GLQ: A Journal of Lesbian and Gay Studies, 3*(4), 417–436.

Altman, D. (2001). *Global sex.* Chicago: University of Chicago Press.

Boellstorff, T. (2003). I knew it was me: Mass media, "globalization," and lesbian and gay Indonesians. In C. Berry, F. Martin & A. Yue (Eds.), *Mobile cultures: New media in queer Asia* (pp. 21–51). Durham: Duke University Press.

Bravmann, S. (1997). *Queer fictions of the past: History, culture, and difference.* Cambridge: Cambridge University Press.

Churchill, D. S. (2008). Transnationalism and homophile political culture in the postwar decades. *GLQ: A Journal of Lesbian and Gay Studies, 15*(1), 31–66.

Copen, C. E., Chandra, A., & Febo-Vazquez, I. (2016). Sexual behavior, sexual attraction, and sexual orientation among adults aged 18–44 in the United States: Data from the 2011–2013 National Survey of Family Growth. *National Health Statistics Reports, 88*, 1–13.

D'Emilio, J. (1992). *Making trouble: Essays on gay history, politics, and the university.* New York: Routledge.

Enteen, J. B. (2010). *Virtual English: Queer internets and digital creolization.* Routledge: New York.

Evans, M. (2003). *Love: An unromantic discussion.* Cambridge: Polity.

Foucault, M. (1978). *The history of sexuality, volume 1: An introduction.* New York: Pantheon Books.

Frątczak, A. (2012). Polish feminist and LGBT press: Twenty years of emancipation. In K. Pokorna-Ignatowicz (Ed.), *The Polish media system 1989–2011* (pp. 157–179). Kraków: Krakow Society for Education: AFM Publishing House.

GUS. (2013). Ludność. Stan i struktura demograficzno-społeczna. Narodowy Spis Powszechny Ludności i Mieszkań 2011. Retrieved January 24, 2017, from http://stat.gov.pl/cps/rde/xbcr/gus/LUD_ludnosc_stan_str_dem_spo_NSP2011.pdf

Halperin, D. M. (1990). *One hundred years of homosexuality and other essays on Greek love.* New York: Routledge.

Halperin, D. M. (2012). *How to be gay?* Cambridge, MA: Harvard University Press.

Illouz, E. (1997). *Consuming the romantic Utopia: Love and the cultural contradictions of capitalism.* Berkley: University of California Press.

Jackson, J. (2015). The homophile movement. In D. Paternotte & M. Tremblay (Eds.), *The Ashgate research companion to lesbian and gay activism* (pp. 31–44). Farnham: Ashgate.

Kinsey, A. C., Pomeroy, W. B., & Martin, C. E. (1948). *Sexual behavior in the human male.* Philadelphia, PA: W. B. Saunders.

Kornatowska, M. (1986). *Eros i film.* Łódź: Krajowa Agencja Wydawnicza.

Kuryluk, E. (1976). *Salome albo o rozkoszy: O grotesce w twórczości Aubreya Beardsleya.* Kraków: Wydawnictwo Literackie.

Long, S. (1999). Gay and lesbian movements in Eastern Europe: Romania, Hungary, and the Czech Republic. In B. D. Adam, J. W. Duyvendak & A. Krouwel (Eds.), *The global emergence of gay and lesbian politics: National imprints of a worldwide movement* (pp. 242–265). Philadelphia: Temple University Press.

Martin, F. (2009). That global feeling: Sexual subjectivities and imagined geographies in Chinese-language lesbian cyberspaces. In G. Goggin & M. McLelland (Eds.), *Internationalizing internet studies: Beyond anglophone paradigms* (pp. 285–301). New York: Routledge.

Massad, J. A. (2007). *Desiring Arabs.* Chicago: University of Chicago Press.

McIntosh, M. (1968). The homosexual role. *Social Problems, 16*(2), 182–192.

McLellan, J. (2011). *Love in the time of communism: Intimacy and sexuality in the GDR.* Cambridge: Cambridge University Press.

Omolo, J. (2017). *Strangers at the gate: Black Poland.* Warszawa: Moyo International Investments Company.

Özbay, C. (2010). Nocturnal queers: Rent boys' masculinity in Istanbul. *Sexualities, 13*(5), 645–663.

Petchesky, R. (2000). Sexual rights: Inventing a concept, mapping an international practice. In R. Parker, R. Barbosa, & P. Aggleton (Eds.), *Framing the sexual subject: The politics of gender, sexuality and power* (pp. 81–103). Berkeley: University of California Press.

Piontek, T. (2006). *Queering gay and lesbian studies.* Urbana: University of Illinois Press.

Plummer, K. (Ed.). (1981). *The making of the modern homosexual.* London: Hutchinson.

Sokolová, V. (2014). State approaches to homosexuality and non-heterosexual lives in Czechoslovakia during state socialism. In H. Havelková & L. Oates-Indruchová (Eds.), *The politics of gender culture under state socialism: An expropriated voice* (pp. 82–108). London: Routledge.

Ward, J. (2012). Born this way: Congenital heterosexuals and the making of heteroflexibility. In S. Hines & Y. Taylor (Eds.), *Sexualities: Past reflections, future directions* (pp. 91–108). Basingstoke: Palgrave Macmillan.

Weeks, J. (2011). *The languages of sexuality.* London: Routledge.

Weeks, J. (2015). Gay liberation and its legacies. In D. Paternotte & M. Tremblay (Eds.), *The Ashgate research companion to lesbian and gay activism* (pp. 45–57). Farnham: Ashgate.

Witkowski, M. (2010). *Lovetown.* London: Portobello Books.

CHAPTER 7

(Re)building Politics

Homosexual identity is the cornerstone of homosexual politics. While embracing the identity does not need to necessarily result in doing the politics, it is difficult to imagine homosexual activism without anchoring it in homosexual identity (Adam et al. 1999, p. 350). In Chap. 2, I discussed how homosexuality has been translated into a political practice in the West, pointing to the emergence of homosexual activism in the late nineteenth century in Europe and describing the development of the homophile movement, gay liberation, HIV/AIDS activism and queer activism (Paternotte and Tremblay 2015). From its very beginning, homosexual, or more broadly lesbian, gay, bisexual and transgender (LGBT), politics has been much transnational in scope: activists have regularly visited each other and exchanged magazines, letters and e-mails, which often led to developing similar sets of aims, embracing similar notions of identity, using similar modes of activism as well as establishing joint associations to lobby international institutions through the discourse of universal human rights. This cooperation and co-constitution, however, has not been on an equal footing but was dominated first by German and then by US activists. At the same time, the New York's Stonewall Riots have begun to occupy a near mythical place in the history of LGBT organizing, both in the United States and abroad (e.g. Bacchetta 2002; Bravmann 1997; Piontek 2006), while the aims, names and symbols of gay liberation—established in the

© The Author(s) 2018
L. Szulc, *Transnational Homosexuals in Communist Poland*,
Global Queer Politics, DOI 10.1007/978-3-319-58901-5_7

aftermath of the riots—have been universalized and taken up by other LGBT organizations around the world.

LGBT activists in Central and Eastern Europe (CEE) have also been recognized as participants in a transnational network of mutual influences, yet, virtually only after the fall of communism in Europe in 1989 (e.g. Ayoub and Brzezinska 2015; Binnie and Klesse 2011; but see Dimitrijević and Baker 2017, McLellan 2012). As I explained in more detail in Chap. 1, the Eastern Bloc tends to be thought of as 'set in aspic' (McLellan 2011, p. 21), as a nearly totally isolated place of no-time, including the absence of any adoption of LGBT rights and any development of LGBT activism. The popular narrative of the region's 'transition' from communism to capitalism and democracy (Kubik 2013) has also been applied to the realm of LGBT politics, establishing the year 1989 as the beginning point of the LGBT movement in CEE (Mizielińska and Kulpa 2011). Occasionally, authors do recognize activist initiatives in the Eastern Bloc but they tend to mention them only briefly or disregard them as not serious, systematic or professional enough to be fully considered as 'activism' (e.g. Pearce and Cooper 2016; Torra 1998). In Chaps. 3 and 4, I challenged the idea by detailing more systematic attempts at homosexual self-organizing in CEE and Poland respectively, pointing at the same time to strong transnational ties of the activists in the Eastern and Western Blocs in the 1980s.

In this chapter, I will look more closely into activism models emerging during the last decade of the Cold War in Poland. I will again draw on my qualitative content analysis of *Biuletyn/Etap* and *Filo*, this time to analyse how the authors of the magazines conceptualized activism: What reasons did they give for self-organizing? Around which issues and drawing on which histories did they build their politics? And to what extent were they rebuilding the politics of Western homosexual movements? First, I will demonstrate that both magazines used the narrative of 'shared discrimination' in order to encourage their readers to get involved in activism. Second, I will examine the magazines' practices of writing homosexual histories, identifying the beginning point of homosexual activism and defining its 'catalytic events' (Darsey 1991). Third, I will focus on the vision for the movement which the activists developed in the magazines, interrogating their formulations of aims and modes of activism. Fourth, I will point to the commonly expressed criticism in the magazines about the nonrepresentation and misrepresentation of homosexuals in the mainstream media, and discuss the solutions they proposed in order to change the image of homosexuals in society at large. Finally, I will move on from the level of discourse to the level of practice and demonstrate how the magazines were providing homosexuals with useful knowledge and advice, and I will suggest that we should call this practice an 'information activism'.

7.1   MAKING AN ACTIVIST

Homosexuals are a diverse group of people: 'There are among us [communist] party members and priests, artists and workers, juveniles and old folks', the authors of *Filo* (1988, 15, p. 8) explained. They hastened to add, however, that what unites all Polish homosexuals is the shared experience of discrimination, pointing specifically to the 1985 undercover operation of the Polish police forces against homosexuals, named in the very title of the quoted piece, 'No More "Hyacinth".' The authors continued to explain that 'the sense of danger unites us, it makes us feel like we belong to a community after all' (*Filo* 1988, 15, p. 8). Hence, it can be argued that by regularly reporting on Operation Hyacinth—informing of its course, speculating about its reasons, giving voice to its victims— *Filo* evoked a sense of belonging among its readers. At the same time, the magazine did not make any calls for actions in this regard, did not ask its readers to publicly protest against the operation. Though, it did actively encourage them to stand for themselves, explaining to them their rights in case they were stopped, detained or interrogated by the police. *Biuletyn/Etap* too, explicitly or implicitly, referred to Operation Hyacinth couple of times, more extensively exploiting its activist potential: at one point, Andrzej Selerowicz encouraged people affected by the operation to inform journalists, homosexual groups or the national AIDS Committee about their persecution so they 'could protest in their name to the authorities' (*Etap* 1987, 4, p. 2). At another point, he informed that if the police did not stop harassing homosexuals in Poland, the International Lesbian and Gay Association (ILGA) would organize a protest against it, stating firmly that 'The times when homosexuals faced discrimination without a word of objection are long gone' (*Etap* 1987, 2, p. 3).

Apart from state persecution, both magazines identified a number of other forms of shared discrimination, especially criminal acts such as robberies, beatings or even murders committed against homosexuals who searched for sexual partners in public places, the so-called *pikiety*. *Filo* regularly (much more often than *Biuletyn/Etap*) reported on such cases, usually drawing on sensational articles in mainstream newspapers. For example, in one issue, in the section 'Press Review', *Filo* (1988, 14, p. 4) informed about two murders and one beating of homosexuals, the stories which had been covered in *Głos Wybrzeża* (Coast Voice), *Sprawy i Ludzie* (Affairs and People) and *Życie Krakowa* (Cracow's Life). In fact, there were so many such and similar cases discussed in the magazine that at one point *Filo* (1988, 15, pp. 7–8) gathered all of them under the title 'Kryminałki dyrdymałki' (Offences nonsenses). The playful title should not be viewed as a dismissal or ignorance of the criminal acts but can be regarded as a coping strategy, which helped to deal with their great abundance and close proximity. After all, among those murdered were also two friends of *Filo*'s editorial team (see 1989, 17, p. 28; 1990, 19, p. 16). Both *Biuletyn/Etap* and *Filo* additionally identified the discourse of blaming homosexuals for the HIV/ AIDS epidemic as yet another form of shared discrimination, which should unite homosexuals and provoke them to organize themselves. Reporting on a debate in the West about mandatory HIV testing, for instance, Selerowicz concluded that 'it requires from gay organizations to launch a strong counter-attack if we want to avoid "witch burnings"' (*Biuletyn* 1986, 1, p. 2).

The examples of different forms of discrimination against homosexuals were often anchored in but not limited to the Polish context. Both magazines gave plenty of similar examples from around the world. They pointed out, for instance, the terribly tragic situation of homosexuals in Chile under Augusto Pinochet (*Filo* 1989, 18, p. 6) and in Iran under the Supreme Leaders of the Islamic Revolution (*Filo* 1990, 20, p. 8), the murders of homosexuals in Brazil (*Filo* 1990, 20, p. 6) and Czechoslovakia (*Filo* 1989, 17, p. 28) as well as the state surveillance of homosexuals 'both in Poland and in Austria and West Germany' (*Biuletyn* 1985, 3, p. 2). Thus, the shared experience of discrimination was universalized: it was presented as characteristic of all homosexuals around the world, including those in the West, in a similar fashion to the shared experience of women's oppression in second-wave feminism (e.g. Morgan 1984), even though the authors of the magazines never explicitly compared homosexual movement to feminist movement. *Filo* did, however, compare homosexuals to the Jews presenting the latter as a role model group in terms of political action. In the already mentioned article 'No More "Hyacinth",' the authors explained: 'Our community can be compared to the Jews: even though they form a very diverse group, if there is any persecution against them, all Jews around the world respond with a counter-attack; protests, demonstrations, boycotts, etc. in different countries' (*Filo* 1988, 15, p. 8). Setting aside the generalizing view of the Jews such framing offered, the comparison can be considered strategically driven. Yet, despite such comparisons between the two groups, the authors also argued that Jews are in a better position than homosexuals because the former can change their faith while the latter cannot change their sexuality (ignoring the fact that Jewishness also works as an ethnicity and can be inscribed in the body) (*Filo* 1987, 5–6, p. 8).

At the same time when pointing to the shared, indeed universal, experience of homosexual discrimination, the magazines stimulated the emergence of homosexual political self. As Selerowicz explained, 'Homosexuality is not just about two men going to bed, it has also a socio-political aspect if it is related to discrimination' (*Biuletyn* 1985, 1, p. 2). In the following issue of *Biuletyn* (1985, 2, p. 1), he added that the discrimination of homosexuals is rooted in centuries-long prejudices, which will not change all of a sudden, but 'you won't fix the problem by burying your head in the sand.' The authors of *Filo* too emphasized the necessity for self-organizing: 'Who will help us, if we don't help ourselves?' (1989, 17, p. 1), they asserted, ignoring the fact that all positive legal changes regarding homosexuality had been introduced in Poland up to that time by the state itself, without any demands from organized homosexuals (see Chap. 4). Both magazines supported their calls for self-organizing by telling success stories from abroad, especially from the West. *Biuletyn/Etap* focused mainly on the successes of Homosexual Initiative Vienna (HOSI) and ILGA but also wrote about, for example, gay activists in Canada who had pushed through the Parliament a bill prohibiting the discrimination of homosexuals (1987, 1, p. 3). The bill, Selerowicz explained, would prevent firing homosexuals from work or throwing them out of their apartments because of their homosexuality, pointing to some practical advantages of homosexual activism for individuals. *Filo*, in turn, told many success stories of such groups as ILGA (1988, 15, p. 2), Dignity (1989, 18, p. 24) as well as the Hungarian Homeros Lambda, informing about its official registration in 1988 and concluding that 'instead of envying them [Homeros' activists], we would better work harder to organize ourselves' (1989, 16, p. 3).

Furthermore, both magazines invested in creating what we could call an activist ethos. *Biuletyn/Etap* mainly advocated the respect for activists from other homosexuals, who were apparently inclined to dismiss the former as 'crazy poofters' (1984, 4, p. 1), but also emphasized that thanks to the engagement in the movement, homosexuals get the opportunity to meet 'valuable' people (1985, 2, p. 1). *Filo* employed somewhat more creative—and arguably more aggressive—strategies to make activism desirable. On the one hand, it presented activism as a way out of cruising for sex in *pikiety*, here considered as dirty, dangerous and devaluing practice. In a short story published in the magazine, the main character was devastated to learn that the public toilet where he came to cruise for sex had been closed for renovation. At that very moment, an angel appeared to him and said: 'You stupid faggot! You will wander around pikiety no more. Go to your friends and start organizing yourselves: establish an association, open clubs, bars and discos. Stop mixing with shit and urine' (*Filo* 1989, 17, p. 24). On the other hand, *Filo* presented activists as sexually appealing and those despising activists as sexually repulsive. One of the magazine's authors shared his true story about bringing home a man he had just met but then losing interest in him and throwing him out after the man expressed his contempt for homosexual activists (*Filo* 1989, 18, p. 23). Another author discussed research results from Norway which had shown that openly gay men tend to have safer sex than closeted gay men and that the former are more common among activists, humorously concluding that 'If you were to make love, it should only be to an activist' (*Filo* 1990, 19, p. 9).

Finally, the analysed magazines also suggested a number of small practical steps their readers could take to become involved in activism. In one of the earliest issues of *Biuletyn/Etap* (1984, 1, p. 1), Selerowicz listed three such activities: (1) collecting and sending him press cuttings from Polish articles on homosexuality; (2) searching for homosexuality-related information in Polish libraries, particularly regarding law and literature; and (3) forming a group of trusted friends to distribute a hand or xerox copy of *Biuletyn/Etap* and to read together an 'awareness-raising literature', both fiction and non-fiction. *Filo*, in turn, encouraged their readers to join their editorial team: 'We hope that new people will join *Filo* so it could become more interesting and more diverse, and so it could help people to figure out their homosexual identity' (1989, 18, p. 2). Besides, both magazines urged the readers to get in touch with already existing homosexual groups. *Biuletyn/Etap*, for example, provided addresses of six subgroups of ILGA, such as Action Secretariat, Women's Secretariat or Christian Churches (1986, 4, p. 1) as well as the *Etap* group in Wrocław, mentioning at the same time that other groups had been formed in Gdańsk, Łódź and Warsaw (1987, 2, p. 1). *Filo* too regularly reported on the development of Polish groups in different cities and provided their addresses. In the late issues, the magazine devoted much space to present the newly established Association of Lambda Groups, again giving its address and encouraging their readers to join it.

7.2 WRITING HISTORIES

One of the key aspects of establishing a movement is to make and celebrate its history: identifying its beginning point and defining its 'catalytic events' (Darsey 1991). Still, as Bravmann (1997, p. ix) points out, there are 'multiple, complex, and inconsistent ways that historical arguments motivate gay and lesbian identities, communities, and politics'. One way *Biuletyn/Etap* and *Filo* were involved in the practice of history making was to write the history of the Polish homosexual movement as it happened. Both magazines ran stories about newly established homosexual groups in Poland, their first and subsequent meetings, their activities, plans and aims. This practice of writing history as it happens did not, however, possess much symbolic power: the developments of Polish homosexual groups and magazines were not explicitly recognized as of historical significance. Neither was Operation Hyacinth discussed in strong symbolic terms. Even though, as shown in the previous section, the magazines informed about the operation regularly, they did not mythologize it as the key moment in the history of the Polish movement; probably, because the history of the operation was still a very recent one and there were more speculations than facts about it at that time. Though, in one issue, *Filo* (1988, 15) did take some first tentative steps towards mythologizing Operation Hyacinth by arguing that Polish homosexuals started to integrate themselves because of the operation (p. 5) and by marking its 'third anniversary' (p. 8).

More regional than only national in scope was the history of the Nazi persecution of homosexuals, which too played a fairly prominent role in both analysed magazines. *Biuletyn* reported on many initiatives of commemorating homosexuals as victims of Nazism, undertaken by activists in German-speaking countries, particularly in Austria (1987, 1, p. 2), East Germany (1983, 4, p. 1) and West Germany (1987, 4, p. 2). *Filo* more often simply described the history of the Nazi persecution, for example in the article entitled 'Homosexuals in concentration camps' (1989, 18, pp. 9–10), or briefly explained the history when discussing relevant cultural products, for example in a piece reviewing Martin Sherman's play *Bent* (1989, 16, p. 12). *Filo* also encouraged its readers to commemorate homosexuals murdered in concentration camps in Poland by bringing to the places of former camps pink flowers, possibly with the words 'For homosexual victims of Nazism' on the ribbon (1987, 7–8, p. 6). Besides, the magazine drew much on the symbolism of the history, mainly by telling the story or adopting the symbol of the pink triangle, first used by the

Nazis to mark homosexuals in concentration camps and then reclaimed by gay liberation organizations in the West (Gianoulis 2004; Kajda and Michalik 2016). Similarly to Operation Hyacinth, the Nazi persecution of homosexuals did not provide Polish activists with a founding myth. It did, however, offer an evidence of terrible discrimination shared by homosexuals on the continent regardless of differences between them. Moreover, it offered an evidence of a present-day discrimination since, as both magazines pointed out, homosexuals had still not been officially recognized as victims of Nazism.

It was the Stonewall Riots that were granted the strongest symbolic power in the analysed magazines, confirming a near mythical status of the event in homosexual, or LGBT, activism as such (Bravmann 1997; Piontek 2006). Both magazines not only informed about the riots but also explicitly marked them as a 'turning point', a 'symbol for a whole host of self-aware homosexuals' (*Biuletyn* 1984, 1, p. 1) and a 'new impetus to fight for gay rights in the United States, and probably elsewhere' (*Filo* 1989, 17, p. 8). For *Filo*, Stonewall—as well as gay liberation established in its aftermath—additionally provided a fertile source of inspiration. In one of the early issues of the magazine, its authors hailed 29 June as the International Gay Day (written both in Polish and in English) and encouraged their readers to mark it by bringing pink flowers to the places of former concentration camps (1987, 7–8, pp. 1 and 6). In the following issue, facing the confusion on the part of some readers about the choice of this particular date, the authors explained that 'many gay organizations honour this day because it was that day twenty years ago, in 1967, when the police forces raided a New York bar "Stonewall" and homosexuals did not stay silent as usual but fought back,' incorrectly dating the riots at 29 June 1967 instead of 28 June 1969 (1987, 9–10, p. 4). Besides, *Biuletyn/Etap* and *Filo* drew on gay liberation more implicitly, for example by embracing its symbols such as lambda sign and pink triangle, though not the rainbow flag, the latter mentioned only once in *Filo* (1990, 19, p. 7) as a 'multicoloured flag' spotted in West Berlin.

Other histories of homosexual activism which were told in *Biuletyn/ Etap* and *Filo* functioned more as news pieces or inspirational stories rather than key points in the history of homosexual self-organizing. Among the most popular ones in this respect were the histories of HIV/AIDS activism, coming in the vast majority from the United States. For example, both magazines (*Etap* 1987, 4, p. 2; *Filo* 1988, 13, p. 3) mentioned the 1987 National March on Washington for Lesbian and Gay Rights during which the AIDS Memorial Quilt was displayed (Blair and Michel 2007; Capozzola 2002). *Filo* additionally ran many stories about the US group AIDS Coalition to Unleash Power (ACT UP), for example, about its protests organized during the 1989 International AIDS Conference in Montreal (in cooperation with Canadian AIDS Action Now! and Réaction-SIDA) (1989, 18, p. 31); its weekly *Outweek* established in New York in June 1989 (1990, 19, p. 8); and its boycott of Phillip Morris launched against the company's financial support for a homophobic senator Jesse Helms (1990, 20, p. 7). Occasionally, the magazine also presented the work of other Western HIV/AIDS organizations, for example of ACT UP London (1990, 20, p. 47) and Deutsche AIDS-Hilfe (1990, 19, p. 7). Besides, *Filo* celebrated World AIDS Day, established by the World Health Organization in 1988 (e.g. 1989, 18, p. 21), and got inspired by the candle marches, organized by the International AIDS Candlelight Memorial since 1983, explaining that the marches had become popular around the world and proposing that 'Maybe next year we could organize it in Poland too?' (1989, 17, p. 25), which indicates that some Western activist initiatives became direct inspirations for Polish activists.

Information about Western European organizations was also prominent in the analysed magazines. Both *Biuletyn/Etap* and *Filo* abounded in articles on ILGA, presenting its history, profile and goals, praising its close connections with major international organizations, and reporting on the outcomes of its annual conferences. In a three-and-a-half-page-long piece about the 1989 ILGA's conference in Vienna, the author explained the importance of the conference, emphasizing its cosmopolitan aspect: the aim of the conference, he argued, was

> to establish new contacts and re-establish the old ones with gays from around the world, to cross swords and bury the hatchet, to create a strong feeling of community among 'our' people who came from different parts of the globe to join their hands and hearts. (*Filo* 1989, 18, p. 3)

Not surprisingly, *Biuletyn/Etap* published many articles about HOSI, the group with which it was associated. Already in the first issue (1983, 1, p. 2), one could read that HOSI had about 300 members, included many different subgroups such as religion, theatre or press groups, and published *Lambda Nachrichten* (Lambda News). *Filo*, in turn, presented (though, rather sporadically) stories of other Western European movements and their achievements such as the Dutch project of Homomonument (1987,

9–10, p. 7) or a UK 'festival of gay art' (1987, 11–12, p. 1). The histories of homosexual self-organizing before gay liberation were mentioned only twice and only in *Filo*, which described the World League for Sexual Reform founded in Europe in 1928 (1987, 7–8, p. 4) and introduced the key person behind it, Magnus Hirschfeld (1990, 20, p. 43).

Finally, both magazines published many articles about homosexual self-organizing in the Eastern Bloc. The dominant narrative in this respect was that the entire region was undergoing a kind of homosexual awakening. Selerowicz, for example, pointed out that more and more organizations from different continents were joining ILGA, anticipating that the time had come for Poland (*Biuletyn* 1985, p. 2). *Filo* regularly informed about new (often first) homosexual initiatives undertaken in different Eastern Bloc countries such as Hungarian Homeros Lambda, 'the first officially registered organization in socialist countries' (1988, 13, p. 3), East German church groups (e.g. 1989, 16, p. 2), Slovenian student groups (e.g. 1989, 17, p. 4), Czechoslovakian Lambda Praha (e.g. 1990, 20, p. 11) as well as Leningrad-based Gay Laboratory (1988, 13, p. 2) and the Moscow Association of Lesbians and Homosexuals (1990, 19, p. 16). The majority of this information came from the Eastern Europe Information Pool (EEIP) programme and its annual conferences, the latter being nearly as meticulously described as ILGA's annual conferences. Furthermore, *Filo* pointed to a number of intra-bloc exchanges of ideas and offers of support, for example when Homeros decided to publish its own magazine modelled on *Filo* (1988, 15, p. 9) and when more experienced groups in the region, Etap and Homeros, committed to assist homosexual activists in the Soviet Union and Romania respectively (1989, 18, p. 6). Clearly, apart from writing the history of the Polish homosexual movement as it happened, the two magazines largely, if selectively, relied on the history of movements elsewhere, particularly in the West, in order to promote activism, find inspiration for their work but also to create a common homosexual history.

7.3   Vision for the Movement

In the beginning, *Filo* did not spend much time discussing activism but focused mainly on listing homoerotic or homosexual cultural products. Still, it was already in the mid-1987 when Ryszard Kisiel published the first short note on activism, informing his readers about the inaugural meeting of homosexual activists from across Poland in Warsaw on 1 March 1987.

Through this and similar news pieces, *Filo* started to gradually develop and, more or less explicitly, promote its vision for the Polish homosexual movement. The magazine reported that one of the key issues discussed during the inaugural meeting of Polish activists was 'the legal problems with the registration of our groups' (*Filo* 1987, 5–6, p. 1). The theme of registration was regularly brought up in subsequent issues of the magazine, which shows the importance of the official recognition by the state for the early homosexual groups in Poland. Though, *Filo* (1987, 9–10, p. 1) also informed that some activists preferred to remain in the underground, unfortunately without explaining their reasons. As already noted in Chap. 4, the groups saw the chance and framed their demands for official registration primarily within the discourses of HIV and AIDS. For example, while listing different Polish HIV/AIDS-related organizations, *Filo* (1987, 5–6, p. 5) pointed out that 'All that's missing is a homosexual organization. Therefore, we believe that our request for registration will not be rejected. Let's not lose this opportunity like we lost it in the liberal 1970s.' Or, as a reader stated in a letter to the editor: 'Now we get a chance, we have to ride the crest of AIDS' (1988, 14, p. 8). Later on, *Filo* informed its readers about Etap and the Warsaw Homosexual Movement (WRH) filing registration requests and reported on recent developments in this respect (e.g. 1988, 14, p. 2; 1989, 16, p. 16).

In order to succeed in registering their groups, the activists defined main obstacles and made strategic decisions, trying to adapt their demands and the ways they framed them to their assessment of the existing sociopolitical context. The communist state, even though regularly criticized for its systematic persecution of homosexuals, was not seen as a problem at the ideological level: 'the government raises no objections against the registration of our organization but there are objections on the part of the Catholic Church, which has enormous influence in Poland' (*Filo* 1988, 15, p. 3). In fact, *Filo* twice reported on the support of the Ministry of Health and Social Care which the Warsaw activists received to fight the spreading of HIV but also to officially register their organization (1987, 5–6, p. 4; 1987, 9–10, p. 1). Accordingly, pointing to the successful registration of Homeros Lambda, the authors of the magazine emphasized that 'Gay activism in socialist countries cannot be apolitical. The work of Homeros Lambda requires a great responsibility, including the recognition of the existing social, political and economic order in Hungary' (*Filo* 1988, 15, p. 9). In the same article, one activist suggested that Polish groups should not join ILGA before being recognized in Poland so not to be accused of 'being controlled by emigration in the West' (*Filo* 1988, 15, p. 10). Countering other prejudices against homosexuals in Poland at that time, *Filo* also argued to stress in registration requests that 'our groups do not promote homosexuality but work only to serve the already existing community' (1989, 17, p. 3).

The accusation that the emerging Polish homosexual movement was steered by 'emigration in the West' was apparently made by a spokesperson of the Polish Police Headquarters in an article in the *Polityka* weekly (*Filo* 1988, 15, p. 10). *Filo*'s authors were probably correct to relate this accusation to the cooperation of Polish activists with ILGA and HOSI. As I showed in Chap. 4, some Polish mainstream media at that time did mention the connection between, for example, the WRH, Etap and ILGA (Tumiłowicz 1987, p. 6) and the Polish Police Headquarters did know about the contacts of Polish activists with HOSI (IPN documents) . Interestingly, an activist from Bydgoszcz made a similar accusation, directed specifically at Selerowicz. As Selerowicz explained in *Biuletyn/ Etap* (1987, 3, p. 3), he had received a letter from the activist accusing him of 'insincere intentions' and 'despicable methods', concluding that 'We do not want Polish homosexuals to be steered carelessly and irresponsibly from abroad.' In response, Selerowicz described how he saw his role in the Polish movement: 'I have never laid claim to being the leader of homosexuals in Poland. Taking the patronage over the gay movement, I have only sought to support it, discussing the form of this support with the representatives of different groups' (*Etap* 1987, 3, p. 3). In general, however, the cooperation between Selerowicz and key activists in Poland was working rather well. In fact, after closing down *Biuletyn/Etap* because of the emergence of relatively strong homosexual groups in Poland (*Etap* 1987, 4, p. 4), Selerowicz continued to work with them as well as published some articles in *Filo*.

Lesbian-related issues in the Polish homosexual movement were discussed only in *Filo*, mainly in its last issues, after Paulina Pilch joined the editorial team in June 1989. The first note on this topic, however, appeared already in the mid-1987, when *Filo* (1987, 9–10, p. 1) informed that the group in Warsaw has a lesbian section named after the famous Polish writer Maria Dąbrowska. In other articles, the authors introduced some lesbian organizations abroad, particularly the International Lesbian Information Service (e.g. 1989, 18, p. 6; 1990, 20, p. 7). Yet, the most often discussed issue was the number of lesbians in the movement. On the one hand, *Filo* pointed to the low engagement of lesbians in Polish groups. Responding to a letter from a female reader, who asked for 'more space for women' in *Filo*, the magazine's authors wrote: 'Space is not an issue; if only women sent us more articles...' (1989, 18, p. 2). Similarly, Pilch complained: 'At the third national meeting of Polish homosexuals in Warsaw (01.04.1989), there were only four women among several dozen men. Three women from Warsaw (including myself) and one from Wrocław. To be honest, this is a bit depressing' (1989, 17, p. 25). On the other hand, the low number of lesbians in Polish movement was contrasted with the greater engagement of women in organizations abroad, mainly in Homeros Lambda, with 30 per cent of female members and a woman holding the position of a vice-president (1989, 17, p. 3), but also in Austrian HOSI and Italian Arcigay (1990, 20, pp. 5 and 9). Occasionally, *Filo* also pointed to the separation of lesbian activists from gay activists, for example in ILGA (1989, 18, p. 6) and East German Homosexuelle Arbeitskreis Gruppe Binokel (1988, 15, p. 10).

The most detailed vision for the movement was presented in one of the last issues of *Filo* (1990, 19, pp. 11–12), in a two-page article entitled 'Homosexual movement in Poland: Why? How? For whom?' The author of the article, Sławek Starosta, first explained that his propositions are based on his three-year experience of working in the WRH as well as his 'fairly good knowledge of the more advanced homosexual movements in the West', again illustrating the importance of the West as an inspirational resource for Polish activists. Starosta continued by arguing that the main aim of the Polish movement should be to change the attitudes towards homosexuals in both homosexuals and heterosexuals so as to bring 'full normality' to the former. 'This normality', he added, 'entails not only rights (to equality, dignity, respect) but also obligations (the same that heterosexuals have, without privileges or special treatment)' (1990, 19, pp. 11–12). Next, Starosta listed more specific aims of the movement targeted at homosexuals and heterosexuals respectively. Regarding the former, he suggested to promote self-acceptance and coming out to family and friends as well as to build homosexual infrastructure (bars, clubs, discos) and movement. Regarding the latter, he proposed to focus on 'informative-persuasive activities', so to counter the stereotypical representations of homosexuals as 'queens, perverts or child molesters' in society at large. Finally, he briefly pointed to the importance of HIV/AIDS activism and finished the article by suggesting to create a nationwide homosexual association, which would work as a loose federation of largely autonomous groups, possibly also special-interest groups focused on, for example, psychological support or political lobbying, or directed at specific groups of homosexuals such as lesbians or people living with HIV.

Starosta's idea about a nationwide federation of largely autonomous homosexual groups materialized when the three most active groups— Etap, Filo and the WRH—set up the Association of Lambda Groups. In last three issues, *Filo* informed in detail about developments in this regard. For example, the magazine reported on the inaugural meeting of the association in Warsaw on 28 October 1989, in which, apart from homosexual activists, participated also a medical doctor Maria Malewska and psychologist Marek Kotański, both actively involved in the fight against the spreading of HIV (1989, 18, p. 30). Besides, *Filo* announced the official registration of the association on 23 February 1990 and listed all names of its leaders, starting with the Wrocław activist Ryszard Ziobro, who had been chosen as the president of Lambda (1990, 19, p. 3). In the very last issue, *Filo* (1990, 20) additionally reprinted (as an appendix) the full declaration of aims of the new association, which basically overlapped with the aims set by Starosta. In the declaration, the activists also asserted that 'more or less visible gays and lesbians are everywhere' (5 per cent of the population), encouraged homosexuals to accept themselves and come out as well as ensured, in a rather defensive tone, that they did not want to promote homosexuality and that they disapproved of pornography, paedophilia and prostitution. Starting as a one-page magazine not particularly interested in the idea of homosexual movement, *Filo* gradually included more activism-related information and soon morphed into the main space for the discussions of the vision for the Polish homosexual movement.

7.4   Visibility Politics

The 'informative-persuasive activities' which Starosta proposed in order to promote an image of homosexuals as 'normal' (*Filo* 1990, 19, pp. 11–12) point to the most common activist theme in *Biuletyn/Etap* and *Filo*, which was the theme of visibility (equally popular in the Western activism, see e.g. Doyle 2016; Gross 2001). Specifically, the analysed magazines assumed the great power of the mainstream media over creating a particular image of homosexuals and, thus, over shaping particular attitudes towards them in society at large. As the authors of *Filo* (1989, 18, p. 17) explained at one point: 'Art often becomes the tool of social and political struggle, sometimes bringing about unexpected yet highly desirable changes. Especially film, with its plentiful means of expressions and mass reach, shows enormous potential in this regard.' The authors continued by giving two examples of such powerful films: the UK-US *Midnight Express* (1978), which was argued to provoke changes in the Turkish penal code so to allow foreign prisoners to serve their sentences in their home countries, and West German *Jagdszenen aus Niederbayern* (Haunting Scenes from Bavaria, 1968), which together with the 1965 play by Martin Sperr under the same title, was credited in *Filo* with paving the way to the decriminalization of same-sex acts in West Germany in 1969. This theme of visibility got boiled down in the analysed magazines to two main issues: nonrepresentation and misrepresentation of homosexuals.

Regarding nonrepresentation, both magazines regularly pointed out the invisibility of homosexuality in Polish mainstream media as well as literature and social sciences. For example, when Selerowicz (1986, 2, p. 2) was presenting his overview of (mainly Western) 'homoerotic literature', he complained that 'Polish literary critics have so far devoted absolutely no attention to this topic [homoeroticism/homosexuality], even though they scrutinized the works of homosexual authors from all possible angles.' Similarly, as I already mentioned in the previous chapter, *Filo* (1989, 18, p. 11) criticized the lack of information in Polish history books about same-sex practices of Polish kings, emphasizing at the same time that French and English historians had readily addressed the issue. *Filo*, more firmly embedded in Polish context than *Biuletyn/Etap*, additionally lamented the censoring of some Western films broadcasted in Poland, where homoerotic or homosexual scenes were simply cut off. The examples included such films as *Bilitis* (1977), *Lulu* (1980) and *Hécate* (1982), the last one shown without 'the scenes about the physical love of the main character to juvenile Arab boys, which made the film completely incomprehensible' (*Filo* 1988, 15, p. 17). Besides, *Filo* pointed to two cases where homoerotic or homosexual references in Western originals were replaced by other references in their Polish translations or adaptations: the book *Queer* by William Burroughs translated into Polish with the title *Ćpun* (Junkie) (1987, 5–6, p. 7) and the play *Separate Tables* by Terence Rattigan, which, when staged in Poland, no longer dealt with homosexuality but heterosexual prostitution instead (1987, 11–12, p. 4).

Regarding misrepresentation, the magazines often simply criticized negative representations of homosexuality in particular cultural products—for example, 'primitive stereotypes and clichés' reproduced in the Polish book *Gorące Uczynki* (Red-handed) by Witold Jabłoński (*Filo* 1989, 17, p. 25)—without explaining what makes a representation negative. In a similar vague way, both magazines condemned the representation of homosexuality in an atmosphere of 'scandal', advocating more 'subtle' depictions of homosexuals (e.g. *Biuletyn* 1984, 4, p. 2; *Filo* 1987, 7–8, p. 2). There were, however, some occasions when the magazines became more precise about what they considered as a negative representation. Applauding the French film *La Cage aux Folles* (The Cage of Mad Queens, 1978) by Édouard Molinaro, *Filo* (1987, 7–8, p. 7) emphasized its 'joyful' take on homosexuality: 'not making fun of it, nor predatory, nor tragic'. *Filo* also criticized Polish TV and press for presenting homosexuals as more prone to commit criminal acts, including paedophilia. In one issue, the magazine compared a police officer who in an article about same-sex prostitution of juveniles had equated homosexuals with criminals, to 'a shoemaker, who gets only broken shoes for repair and hence concludes that all shoes are of low quality' (*Filo* 1987, 11–12, p. 3). Another time, *Filo* (1988, 13, p. 5) disapproved of the depictions of homosexuals as effeminate, though it stressed that such depictions are a problem only when they become dominant, thus, encouraging a diversity in the representations of homosexuality. Pilch, in turn, criticized the representation of lesbians as 'whores, thieves, junkies, drag dealers, gangsters, etc.' (*Filo* 1989, 18, p. 31) in the book *Elles se rendent pas compte* (They Do Not Realize, 1950) by Boris Vian, reprinted in parts in the Polish mainstream magazine *Fikcje i Fakty* (Fictions and Facts).

One reaction of the analysed magazines to this overwhelming (sometimes ignorant, sometimes deliberate) nonrepresentation and misrepresentation of homosexuals in Polish mainstream media, culture and science was to point their readers to counter-examples, which from time to time too managed to find their way to the Polish mainstream, such as the films *La Course à l'échalote* (The Shallot Race, France, 1975), *The Dresser* (UK, 1983) and *Baryton* (Baritone, Poland, 1984) (*Filo* 1987, 11–12, p. 5). *Filo* (1990, 19, p. 24) also discussed at length a Polish documentary on transsexualism, entitled *Transsex* (1988) by Marek Drążewski, praising it for showing the difference between homosexuality and transsexualism, and for promoting tolerance towards transsexuals. Another reaction to the nonrepresentation or misrepresentation of homosexuals in the mainstream was to organize home screenings of (considered as good) films with homoerotic or homosexual themes. Together with the Łódź-based group Amiko, Filo organized a 'Gay club video' in March 1987, where they showed the West German film *Zum Beispiel San Francisco* (*For Example San Francisco* 1985) by Loretta Walz, which the activists had received with

Polish subtitles from HOSI (1987, 5–6, p. 8). In one of the last issues, *Filo* (1989, 18, p. 18) even proposed to hold a 'public festival of gay and lesbian films' in Poland, asking its readers for video cassettes with the films listed in the article. Occasionally, *Filo* also made calls for actions in order to secure the positive representation of homosexuals in the mainstream media. In one call, for example, it encouraged its readers to write letters to the newly established *Playboy*-like magazine *Pan* (Gentleman) in support of one of its readers' request to launch a regular column for homosexuals (*Filo* 1988, 14, p. 4).

The issue of visibility of homosexuality additionally included the visibility of emerging homosexual movement in Polish mainstream media, particularly important for the members of the WRH, who actively sought the attention of journalists. *Filo* reported on a number of successful cases in this respect, mainly interviews with WRH activists, for example in a radio programme (1987, 7–8, p. 2) or in the *Radar* magazine (1987, 9–10, p. 4) but also an article in the *Argumenty* magazine on homosexuality, which mentioned the existence of Etap, Filo and the WRH (1987, 11–12, p. 4). In one of the last issues, *Filo* (1990, 19, p. 38) proudly announced that 'There have been so many programmes and publications about our homosexual movement that it is impossible to track it all.' Nevertheless, in the interviews, the activists most often used pseudonyms and were placed with their backs to the camera, which was criticized by a reader in a letter to the editor:

> I think that if the activists decided to participate in a TV programme, they should not sit there with hidden faces. It's just humiliating! Sitting like criminals before the jury [...] No! This is not fair! Let's fight for our dignity too. Why would we hide our faces? (*Filo* 1988, 14, p. 8)

This gradually changed, especially when activists decided to register the Association of Lambda Groups and, for that reason, 15 of them had to provide their real names (*Filo* 1989, 18, p. 30). Around the same time, since the mid-1989, some authors of *Filo*, including Kisiel and Pilch, started to use their full real names in the magazine, which illustrates how the visibility politics, at first only talked about in *Filo*, became increasingly embraced by the magazine's authors as an everyday practice.

Filo also affirmed its belief that the important aspect of changing the image of homosexuals in Poland lies in the hands of homosexuals themselves. Therefore, it encouraged its readers to break up the stereotypes about homosexuals in their everyday lives, by coming out and demonstrating to their friends and families that homosexuals are worthy of respect. Not surprisingly, such calls for a kind of 'everyday activism' went hand in hand with strong normative prescriptions and usually took a form of condemning what was considered as an undesirable behaviour. The prescription for romantic love—the importance of which I discussed in Chap. 6—was the most common one in this respect. As the author of one piece argued: 'We [homosexual men] have a lot of friends—not friends really, just men—with whom we go to bed. Of course nobody will accept that because such relationships are deprived of affection' (*Filo* 1990, 20, p. 27). In the same issue, *Filo* also revealed that the 80 per cent of the letters that the magazine had received complained about homosexuals cruising for sex in *pikiety*: 'They bring shame on us. They wander around train stations and harass passers-by, or get drunk and quarrel with police officers. And based on that the society forms its opinion about all of us.' Another prescription was related to exhibiting effeminacy, as exemplified in this letter to the editor: 'Those odious limp-wristed poofters [...], they get drunk, go to the train station and start raving [...] Of course, people see it all! No wonder they don't show much tolerance towards homosexuals' (1989, 17, p. 17). The visibility politics in *Filo*, therefore, included what we could call 'visibility policing': it was not limited to the critique of nonrepresentation and misrepresentation of homosexuality in society as such but included the critique of homosexuals themselves, specifically those who did not meet the expectations of 'respectability' and who were required to change their everyday behaviour to promote a more positive image of homosexuals at large.

7.5   INFORMATION ACTIVISM

While activism tends to be associated with such activities as serving community, campaigning or protesting, in this section I suggest to recognize the magazines' practice of providing homosexuals with useful knowledge and advice as an 'information activism', particularly in the context of late-communist Poland, where access to information relevant to homosexuals was much restricted. I already pointed out in Chap. 6 that *Biuletyn/ Etap* and *Filo* listed hundreds of cultural products which had depicted homosexuality in a favourable light, or at least subtly referred to it in a more homoerotic rather than homosexual fashion, and thus provided its readers with resources for self-awareness, self-acceptance, love, sex and for creating a homosexual community of interest. At the same time, *Filo* compiled many lists of homosexual meeting places in Poland, thus, informing its readers not only about where they could find information on homosexuality but also about where they could meet other homosexuals. The lists included gay nude beaches (1987, 7–8, p. 8), bars and cafés (1987, 11–12, p. 8) as well as public baths and *pikiety* (1988, 14, p. 12) in different cities across Poland. The authors of *Filo* had an access to the *Spartacus International Gay Guide* at that time but complained that its information about Eastern Bloc countries was notoriously out-of-date. The issue must have been of major importance because the activists raised it at the EEIP conference in Warsaw (1988, 15, p. 10) and, in the last issue of *Filo* (1990, 20, p. 43), announced their plans to create their own guide to the region.

Filo additionally facilitated contacts within and between specific homosexual subgroups. Most remarkably, it included interviews with Polish homosexuals diagnosed with HIV or AIDS, encouraging its readers to visit the patients in hospitals (1989, 17, p. 11) or to support them by doing a volunteer work or donating money (1990, 20, p. 6). The magazine also informed about the Third International Conference for People Living with HIV to be hosted in Denmark in 1989, and provided the address of the Danish organization Positivgruppen, which Polish people living with HIV could contact to receive an invitation for the conference (1988, 15, p. 13). Provoked by other international events directed at specific segments of homosexuals, *Filo* encouraged different Polish homosexual subgroups to get in touch with their Western counterparts. For example, it communicated that during the World Congress of Esperanto in Warsaw in 1987, a group of about 20 gay men from around the world would like to meet Polish homosexuals speaking the language and provided contact details to one of the group's members (1987, 5–6, p. 1). Other examples include the announcements of the gay and lesbian bodybuilding contest 'Physique 89', organized in San Francisco in 1989 by the Arcadia Body Building Society (1989, 16, p. 15), as well as the workshop for stuttering homosexuals at the Third World Congress for People Who Stutter, held in Cologne in 1989 (1989, 18, p. 9). As mentioned before, *Filo* was also connecting people more directly through personal ads as well as by organizing film nights, new year parties or *gejwczasy* (gaycation) (1988, 15, p. 11).

The practice of giving tips, common in both analysed magazines, is yet another, and probably the strongest, manifestation of information activism. The most popular tips were about HIV prevention and legal provisions. I will discuss these particular tips in more detail in the following paragraphs. Both magazines, however, abounded in many other kinds of tips. As already mentioned in Chap. 6, *Biuletyn/Etap* included a step-by-step guide to coming out to family (1984, 4, pp. 1–2) and a four-part 'Sexual guide for gay men' series, zooming in on such topics as getting to know your body, masturbating, cuddling and having an anal sex (issues from 1986, 4 to 1987, 3). *Filo*, in turn, introduced a special section entitled 'Medical guide', ran through the last four issues, where the readers could familiarize themselves with the anatomy of male reproductive system, get to know how to examine themselves as well as learn about various genital and rectal infections. Besides, *Filo* provided detailed tips on fashion and working out, along with some very short but practical advice, for example on 'How to remove sperm stains from clothes?' (1987, 7–8, p. 8). Regarding the latter, *Filo* recommended first to wait until the stains dry, so they become more visible, and then brush them off or rub them with hands.

Importantly, both magazines regularly gave HIV prevention tips. The information was somewhat more accurate in *Biuletyn/Etap* than in *Filo*, probably because Selerowicz had easier access to more reliable sources available in the West. Nevertheless, even though *Filo* was sometimes mixing 'HIV virus' with 'AIDS virus' and at one point claimed that it was possible to get infected by saliva (1988, 14, p. 6), both magazines generally provided a high quality information directed specifically at homosexual men. They both also explicitly referred to the idea of 'safer sex'. Clearly drawing on Western discourses on this topic, they explained what the phrase in English stands for: 'sexual intercourse during which your mucus, sperm or blood does not meet the blood of your partner' (*Etap* 1986, 3, p. 1) or simply 'safer sex [literally translated into Polish], cause there is no such thing as a 100 percent safe sex [...], there is always a risk but you can choose how high it would be' (*Filo* 1990, 19, p. 9). The most common tip in *Biuletyn/Etap* and *Filo* was to avoid casual sex with many partners, which is illustrated by the drawings regularly published in *Filo* (see Fig. 7.1). Occasionally, *Filo* also presented more liberal views, mainly by reproducing safer sex information from the West. In the last issue (1990, 20), the magazine included an appendix on 'Homosex and AIDS'—a translation of the Dutch leaflet published under the same title by the Dutch Health Promotion and Education Office in 1988—where the conclusion read: 'It does not matter how many times you do it but how you do it.'

Fig. 7.1 Images of safer sex in *Filo* (1988, 14, p. 6). Courtesy of Lambda Warszawa. Translation: *uważaj* (be careful), *bezpieczny seks* (safer sex), *tak* (yes) and *nie* (no)

Other popular HIV prevention tips included to kiss, cuddle and masturbate instead of having oral or anal sex as well as to use condoms during anal sex. However, an access to good quality condoms in late communist (but also early democratic) Poland remained heavily restricted. *Filo* regularly lamented the quality of Polish condoms 'Eros', produced by Cracow-based company Stomil, pointing out that they could be better used as balloons since they were very thick and full of talcum powder (1990, 20, p. 3) and informing its readers when and where they could buy condoms produced in the West (1987, 9–10, p. 8). Additionally, *Filo* (1988, 14, p. 7) warned its readers that the Polish condoms break easily after getting in touch with fat-based lubricants such as petroleum jelly, which was particularly popular as a lubricant among homosexuals in Poland at that time (see also Fig. 7.2). Here too the magazine complained about the lack of good quality lubricants in Poland: 'Far, far away, over five hills and rivers, someone invented water-based lubricants, we are left with water and saliva' (1990, 19, p. 9). In another issue, *Filo* recommended a range of other substances to be used with condoms to smoothen anal sex, including glycerine or baby shampoo, both diluted with water, as well as egg whites (1989, 17, p. 11).

Furthermore, both magazines regularly published legal tips. Sometimes, they simply reminded their readers that according to the Polish law homosexuality was not illegal and, therefore, it could not be the only reason for

Fig. 7.2 Images of condoms in *Filo* (from left: 1988, 15, p. 8, 1990, 20, p. 25). Courtesy of Lambda Warszawa. Translation (from left): 'The only possible use of "Eros"' and 'Quality check'

any action taken against them by the police forces (e.g. *Biuletyn* 1984, 4, p. 1; *Filo* 1987, 3, p. 2). As Operation Hyacinth attested, however, the police did stop, interrogate and detain homosexuals based solely on their (assumed) homosexuality or same-sex acts (Chap. 4) and the authors of the magazines realized that. *Filo* introduced a special legal section entitled 'Your rights', later 'Under the article', where it detailed information about the rights of anyone stopped by the police on the street. The magazine pointed out that police officers were obliged to introduce themselves, show their police cards as well as explain why and in what capacity they were stopping a person: as a witness, suspect or defendant. In case you were stopped as a witness, the magazine continued, you could refuse to give your fingerprints or be photographed (1988, 13, p. 6; 1988, 15, p. 5). In another issue, *Filo* additionally reported on a homosexual who challenged the police's illegal detention of him and won the case in the Supreme Court, proving to its readers that the Polish law at that time, when obeyed, was on the side of homosexuals (1987, 11–12, p. 3). Some other legal tips provided by the magazine explained the intricacies of the ban on the distribution of pornography (1987, 5–6, p. 3) and discussed legal consequences of putting AIDS on the official list of infectious diseases (1987, 4, p. 1).

7.6   CONCLUSION

Polish gay and lesbian magazines of the 1980s were much preoccupied with talking activism since the very beginning of their existence (*Biuletyn/ Etap*) or at least soon after they were created (*Filo*). 'Intended for internal use only for homosexuals and lesbians', as *Filo* (1987, 9–10, p. 2) once declared, the magazines worked towards creating a homosexual solidarity and aimed to turn it into political identity. They pointed to the common experience of discrimination by state and society, which homosexuals in Poland and elsewhere shared regardless of differences between them and used that argument to encourage homosexuals to come together, integrate and, ultimately, self-organize. Drawing on versatile histories of homosexual activism in both the Western and Eastern Blocs, the magazines started to outline their own vision for the Polish homosexual movement, which soon became dominated by the issue of creating a nationwide association of homosexuals that would be officially recognized by the state. The main aim of such an association was defined as to increase self-acceptance among homosexuals themselves as well as to win the acceptance of society towards homosexuals, the latter mainly through 'informative-persuasive activities' (*Filo* 1990, 19, p. 11–12), focused on promoting a positive image of homosexuals in the public sphere. At the same time, *Biuletyn/ Etap* and *Filo* were involved in what I suggested we should call an information activism: they pointed their readers to countless resources relevant to homosexuals and provided them with plentiful tips ranging from such crucial topics as HIV prevention and legal provisions to the issues of coming out, sexual health and sex life.

While building Polish homosexual politics, the authors of the magazines routinely drew on foreign examples. This was possible because of their recognition of the shared experience of discrimination as the lowest common denominator of all homosexuals around the world, even if the form and intensity of the discrimination were different in different contexts. The magazines recognized the Stonewall Riots as the key 'turning point', if not simply the beginning point, of homosexual movement worldwide, contributing to a wider phenomenon of mythologizing the event in LGBT politics (Bravmann 1997; Piontek 2006). Moreover, they often employed the symbolism of the Stonewall Riots and gay liberation by celebrating the day of the riots and adopting lambda sign and pink triangle. The histories of other homosexual organizations in the Western and Eastern Blocs too were often discussed in *Biuletyn/Etap* and *Filo*, providing Polish activists with inspiration and encouragement but never reaching the symbolic status of Stonewall. For example, following many groups in German-speaking countries, *Filo* began to commemorate homosexual victims of Nazism and, inspired by the International AIDS Candlelight Memorial, proposed to organize in Poland a candle march in solidarity with people living with HIV. *Filo* also looked up to Homeros Lambda, congratulating it for being the first officially registered organization in the Eastern Bloc, and applauding the active involvement of lesbians in the organization. Homeros Lambda, in turn, got inspired by *Filo* and decided to start publishing a similar magazine of its own (*Filo* 1988, 15, p. 9). The intra-bloc connections were greatly facilitated by ILGA, particularly by its EEIP programme, pointing to the important role of the international association not only as a direct point of contact, providing resources and inspirations, but also as an intermediary in the transnational construction of LGBT identities and politics in CEE.

Nevertheless, unlike its Western counterparts at that time, Polish homosexual activists were largely focused on internal activism. They did want to get recognized by the state and were gradually embracing a broader visibility politics but the core of their activism was directed at homosexuals themselves. Also, the activists did not adopt the confrontational politics of gay liberation. Just like the Stonewall Riots, so too Operation Hyacinth provoked much anger among homosexuals and motivated some of them to fight for their rights. Yet, Polish activists did not bring their fight to the streets. Also, as the analysed magazines attest, they did not challenge the communist state at the ideological level. After all, the Polish law was not discriminatory against homosexuals and some segments of the state, especially the Ministry of Health and Social Care, showed their sympathy towards homosexual activists and offered them their support. The key problem was not state ideology but state practice. Therefore, *Filo* favoured changing the system to overthrowing it: the magazine provided their readers with legal tips so to help making the law being obeyed and it published some voices arguing for cooperation with the police forces in order to change their attitudes towards homosexuals (1988, 14, p. 8). Both magazines also did not promote the kind of in-your-face activism within society characteristic of gay liberation and some other homosexual movements. Instead, they aimed at gaining respect from society by informing and persuading it as well as by requiring from homosexuals themselves to earn people's respect in their everyday life. Certainly, while drawing on many aims, names, symbols and histories of the Western homosexual politics, Polish activists of the 1980s made their own strategic decisions and informed choices about how to do activism.

BIBLIOGRAPHY

Adam, B. D., Duyvendak, J. W., & Krouwel, A. (1999). Gay and lesbian movements beyond borders? National imprints of a worldwide movement. In B. D. Adam, J. W. Duyvendak & A. Krouwel (Eds.), *The global emergence of gay and lesbian politics* (pp. 344–371). Philadelphia: Temple University Press.

Ayoub, P. M., & Brzezinska, O. (2015). Caught in a web?: The Internet and the deterritorialization of LGBT activism. In D. Paternotte & M. Tremblay (Eds.), *The Ashgate research companion to lesbian and gay activism* (pp. 225–243). Ashgate: Farnham.

Bacchetta, P. (2002). Rescaling transnational "queerdom": Lesbian and "lesbian" identitary-positionalities in Delhi in the 1980s. *Antipode, 34*(5), 947–973.

Binnie, J., & Klesse, C. (2011). Researching transnational activism around LGBTQ politics in Central and Eastern Europe: Activist solidarities and spatial imaginings. In R. Kulpa & J. Mizielińska (Eds.), *De-centring western sexualities: Central and eastern European perspectives* (pp. 107–129). Farnham: Ashgate.

Blair, C., & Michel, N. (2007). The AIDS Memorial Quilt and the contemporary culture of public commemoration. *Rhetoric & Public Affairs, 10*(4), 595–626.

Bravmann, S. (1997). *Queer fictions of the past: History, culture, and difference.* Cambridge: Cambridge University Press.

Capozzola, C. (2002). A very American epidemic: Memory politics and identity politics in the AIDS Memorial Quilt, 1985–1993. *Radical History Review, 82*(1), 91–109.

Darsey, J. (1991). From "Gay is Good" to the scourge of AIDS: The evolution of gay liberation rhetoric, 1977–1990. *Communication Studies, 42*(1), 43–66.

Dimitrijević, O., & Baker, C. (2017). British-Yugoslav lesbian networks during and after the Great War. In C. Baker (Ed.), *Gender in twentieth-century Eastern Europe and the USSR* (pp. 49–63). London: Palgrave Macmillan.

Doyle, V. (2016). *Making out in the mainstream: GLAAD and the politics of respectability.* Montreal: McGill-Queen's University Press.

Gianoulis, T. (2004). Pink triangle. *GLBTQ Encyclopedia.* Retrieved February 13, 2017, from http://www.glbtqarchive.com/ssh/pink_triangle_S.pdf

Gross, L. (2001). *Up from invisibility: Lesbians, gay men, and the media in America.* New York: Columbia University Press.

Kajda, K., & Michalik, T. (2016). Made in Sachsenhausen. Rekontekstualizacja i reapropriacja odwróconego różowego trójkąta wśród grup gejowsko-lesbijskich w Ameryce Północnej jako przykład kradzieży symbolicznej'. *InterAlia: A Journal of Queer Studies, 11b*, 170–183.

Kubik, J. (2013). From transitology to contextual holism: A theoretical trajectory of postcommunist studies. In J. Kubik & A. Linch (Eds.), *Postcommunism from within: Social justice, mobilization, and hegemony* (pp. 27–94). New York: NYU Press.

McLellan, J. (2011). *Love in the time of communism: Intimacy and sexuality in the GDR.* Cambridge: Cambridge University Press.

McLellan, J. (2012). Glad to be gay behind the wall: Gay and lesbian activism in 1970s East Germany. *History Workshop Journal, 74*(1), 105–130.

Mizielińska, J., & Kulpa, R. (2011). "Contemporary peripheries": Queer studies, circulation of knowledge and East/West divide. In R. Kulpa & J. Mizielińska (Eds.), *De-centring Western sexualities: Central and eastern European perspectives* (pp. 11–26). Farnham: Ashgate.

Morgan, R. (Ed.). (1984). *Sisterhood is global.* Garden City: Anchor Press/Doubleday.

Paternotte, D., & Tremblay, M. (Eds.). (2015). *The Ashgate research companion to lesbian and gay activism.* Farnham: Ashgate.

Pearce, S. C., & Cooper, A. (2016). LGBT activism in Eastern and Central Europe. In N. Naples (Ed.), *The Wiley Blackwell encyclopedia of gender and*

sexuality studies. Retrieved September 8, 2016, from   http://onlinelibrary.
   wiley.com/doi/10.1002/9781118663219.wbegss707/abstract.

Piontek, T. (2006). *Queering gay and lesbian studies.* Urbana: University of Illinois
   Press.

Torra, M. J. (1998). Gay rights after the iron curtain. *The Fletcher Forum of World
   Affairs, 22*(2), 73–87.

Tumiłowicz, B. (1987). Inny homo. *Argumenty, 42*, 6.

CHAPTER 8

Conclusion

One aim of this book was to debunk the myths of the homogeneity and essence of Central and Eastern Europe (CEE) with respect to lesbian, gay, bisexual and transgender (LGBT) issues, specifically homosexuality. Another was to challenge the teleological narrative of the region's alleged 'transition' from no LGBT rights and activism under communism to a sudden emergence of such rights and activism after 1989.

Drawing on different historical sources, in particular the Eastern Europe Information Pool (EEIP) reports, and also the works of other scholars who have investigated homosexuality in Eastern Bloc countries, I have shown the complexity of the region in relation to homosexuality before 1989. This complexity is probably best illustrated by the different legal status of homosexuality in Eastern Bloc countries. The Soviet Union's harsh 'sodomy law' (Healey 1993, 2002; Kon 1993) too often stands for how the entire region dealt with homosexuality. In Russia, same-sex acts were decriminalized already in 1922, then recriminalized in 1933–1934 and again decriminalized in 1993, after the fall of the Soviet Union in 1991. The countries which belonged to the Soviet Union also decriminalized same-sex acts only after the 1991 breakthrough or have not yet done so: Ukraine in 1991, Estonia and Latvia in 1992, Lithuania in 1993, Belarus in 1994, Moldova in 1995, Kyrgyzstan, Kazakhstan and Tajikistan in 1998, Azerbaijan and Georgia in 2000, Armenia in 2003, while at the beginning of 2017 male same-sex acts are still illegal in Turkmenistan (up to two years

© The Author(s) 2018
L. Szulc, *Transnational Homosexuals in Communist Poland*,
Global Queer Politics, DOI 10.1007/978-3-319-58901-5_8

of imprisonment) and Uzbekistan (up to three years of imprisonment) (Baker 2017b, p. 230). Yet, the Soviet Union did not require uniformity in this respect from its satellite countries, most of which decriminalized same-sex acts before 1989: Poland in 1932, Czechoslovakia and Hungary in 1962, Bulgaria and East Germany in 1968, the only exception being Romania, which did so only in 1996 (Hildebrandt 2014; Torra 1998). As I showed in Chap. 3, this diversity of legal provisions on homosexuality often reflected a diversity of state practices and media representations of homosexuality in the Eastern Bloc.

Similarly, the history of the first more systematically organized homosexual groups in the region is not uniform. It was clearly more difficult for homosexuals to organize themselves in those countries which criminalized homosexuality and where homosexuals were severely persecuted, such as the Soviet Union and Romania, though even in the Soviet Union activists undertook an initiative to form the Gay Laboratory group in Leningrad in 1984 (Essig 1999, p. 58; Kon 1993, p. 103). Most likely, the earliest and strongest homosexual groups in the Eastern Bloc were formed in East Germany, starting with the Homosexual Interest Group Berlin (HIB) in the 1970s (Kleres 2001, p. 135; McLellan 2012) and continuing with about 20 Homosexual Working Groups associated with the Evangelical Church in the 1980s (Chap. 3; Hillhouse 1990; McLellan 2011). Homosexuals in some other communist countries too started to organize themselves in the 1980s, mainly in the second half of the decade, especially in Czechoslovakia (working closely with sexologists), Slovenia (based at the University of Ljubljana), Hungary and Poland (Chaps. 3 and 4). One of the key triggers for creating these groups came from the West, in the form of Western mainstream and alternative cultural products (including gay and lesbian magazines), travel experiences and migrations between the Eastern and Western Blocs as well as, most importantly, more formalized attempts by Western activists at stimulating Eastern homosexuals to self-organize, especially the EEIP programme established by the International Gay Association (IGA, later ILGA) in 1981. Another important trigger was the emergence of discourses about HIV and AIDS, which helped to increase visibility of homosexuality in public spheres in most of the Eastern Bloc countries and provided activists in some countries, for sure in Poland (Chap. 4) and Hungary (Kurimay and Takács 2016), with a powerful framework within which they could formulate their demands for the official recognition of their groups. In Poland, an additional effective trigger was the intensified harassment of homosexuals in the form of Operation Hyacinth.

Despite the common conflation of communism and homophobia in Western perceptions or history-writing, some Eastern Bloc states in fact displayed an ambivalent attitude towards homosexuality. Often, the ruling communist parties did not take a clear stance on homosexuality and reacted to it differently, sometimes contradictorily, in different situations. While it was common among communist states during the Cold War to consider homosexuals as a 'criminogenic' group and to conduct close surveillance of them as well as to compile 'homosexual inventories' (Chap. 3, McLellan 2011; Stella 2015; Szulc 2011, 2016; Takács 2017), in some countries the state also supported the first homosexual groups. The best example is the Hungarian state, which allowed for the official registration of Homeros Lambda in March 1988, hoping to reach more homosexuals in the fight against the spreading of HIV but also to have more direct control over them (Kurimay and Takács 2016, p. 11). Also, while not officially recognizing homosexual organizations, the authorities in East Germany and Slovenia did not actively oppose them and even occasionally endorsed them. In Poland too, the first homosexual groups received some, if limited, support from the state, especially from the Ministry of Health and Social Care (Chap. 7). Agnès Chetaille (2017, p. 5) additionally points out that

> In Warsaw regular meetings [of homosexual activists] were held in the premises of the youth club of PRON (Patriotyczny Ruch Odrodzenia Narodowego) [Patriotic Movement for National Rebirth], an organization created by the Party-state in 1982 to try and counter-weight the influence of Solidarność [Solidarity]. In 1988, the ILGA international conference for Eastern and Central Europe even took place in the premises of the Party's Committee for the Mokotów district in Warsaw. Later on, the Warsaw initiative developed in close relationship with the official students' union at the University of Warsaw. (Chetaille 2017)

In that context, it is not surprising that some homosexual groups in the Eastern Bloc imagined it was possible to organize themselves within the confines rather than in opposition to the communist state and ideology, at least in East Germany (EEIP 1985), Hungary (Kurimay and Takács 2016) and Poland (Chap. 7).

The evidence gathered in this book, as well as in the works of scholars quoted here, clearly demonstrates that homosexuals in CEE did organize themselves more systematically already towards the end of the Cold War. This fact undercuts the reductive idea of a wholesale rupture in 1989, as if systematic homosexual self-organizing in the region could emerge only after the fall of communism in Europe. The year 1989 did bring about important changes for homosexuals in the region, especially greater freedom of expression and association, which in Poland translated into the first official registration of a homosexual organization, the Association of Lambda Groups, in 1990 (Adamska 1998; Gruszczyńska 2009). Yet, as I explained in Chap. 4, the association was created by three homosexual groups which had been established already in the 1980s. Therefore, it is crucial to recognize not only the changes but also the continuities between pre-1989 and post-1989 homosexual activism in CEE (for a similar argument in relation to gender politics see Baker 2017a; Gal and Kligman 2000). Tellingly, at one point when I interviewed Paulina Pilch, specifically asking about her experience and involvement in the Polish homosexual movement *before* 1989, she commented:

> You have this very strict boundary of 1989 and this is a bit problematic. It is difficult for me to remember, for example, when I read Erica Jong for the first time. I'm sure it was during my high school but that encompasses the time before as well as after 1989.

As the quote demonstrates, the year 1989 is one of many other points in time which become significant to a different extent for different individuals and in relation to different aspects of homosexual activism in CEE.

At the same time, it is also problematic to consider the changes in CEE after 1989 in terms of a teleological transition, allegedly always towards more liberalism in issues related to gender and sexuality as well as towards Western norms, values and rights that would allow 'backward' countries to catch up with the supposedly more 'progressive' West. First, the year 1989 brought about not only progressive but also regressive changes in gender and sexuality issues in CEE, most infamously the tendency towards 'retraditionalization' (Kligman 1992) and 'repatriarchalization' (Velikonja 2009), in Poland exemplified by the introduction of a stricter abortion law in 1993 (Kulczycki 1995; Zielińska 1993, 2000). At the same time, public opinion polls show that social acceptance towards homosexuality did not dramatically increase in Poland during about ten years after the fall of communism in the country (Perdzyńska 2009; Selinger 2008). Second, CEE underwent some changes in state attitudes towards gender and sexuality already before 1989, both progressive ones (e.g. the decriminalization of same-sex prostitution in Poland in 1970) and regressive ones (e.g. the increased prison time for same-sex acts in Romania in 1957). Third, as I showed in Chap. 3, during the Cold War some Eastern Bloc countries had in fact a more progressive legislation towards homosexuality than some Western Bloc countries. This, I suggested, together with the lack of a sexual revolution around 1968 in CEE, could be among the main reasons why homosexuals in Poland did not organize themselves more systematically before the 1980s: instead of being more harshly persecuted or less innovative than their Western counterparts, they might not have felt an urgent need for this. Finally, the twentieth century saw a number of significant larger socio-economic changes—such as industrialization, urbanization and secularization—which greatly affected the conceptualization and organization of gender and sexuality and which were characteristic not only of the Western but also of the Eastern Bloc (Adam 2001; McLellan 2011).

Taking seriously into account some similarities between the blocs as well as differences within them we may wonder if it makes sense at all to talk about homosexuality, or gender- and sexuality-related issues, in terms of 'Western Europe' versus 'Eastern Europe'. And what does 'Eastern Europe' stand for anyway, especially after the fall of communism in Europe, when stronger political, economic and military ties between countries in the region have no longer been forced upon them? In the editorial to the special issue of *DIK Fagazine* on 'Communist Homosexuality 1945–1989', accompanying the conference held under the same title in Paris in February 2017 (https://eastqueerconference.wordpress.com/), Karol Radziszewski (2017, p. 2) expresses similar confusion about the definitions of CEE by listing a number of popular names for the region: 'Eastern Europe? Central-Eastern Europe? Central and Eastern Europe? East Central and South-East Europe? Eastern Europe, Northern and Central Asia? The Baltics? The Balkans? Europe? Oh, so many questions!' Catherine Baker (2017a, p. 7) likewise questions the idea of CEE in the introduction to her recent collection *Gender in Twentieth-Century Eastern Europe and the USSR*, where she proposes that we consider the importance of geopolitical entities other than communist or post-communist space, for example the post-Habsburg space and the post-Ottoman space. Nevertheless, I agree with her when she points out some commonalities in the Eastern Bloc countries regarding, for example, the instrumentalization of the so-called woman question (or, I could add, the state surveillance and registration of male homosexuals), suggesting that it is still useful to think about CEE as of a 'region', 'as long as one is transparent about how concepts of "region" order knowledge' (Baker 2017a, p. 7; see also Binnie 2016).

8.1   RUSTED PINK CURTAIN

A further aim of this book was to counter the myth of the near total isolation of the Eastern Bloc by tracing cross-border flows of cultural products, identity paradigms and activism models related to homosexuality in order to argue for the recognition of the transnational construction of homosexuality, or LGBT identities and politics, in CEE already before 1989.

In the course of the book, I listed countless Western cultural products dealing with homosexuality, or at least homoeroticism, which found their way to the Eastern Bloc, especially to Poland. Some of them circulated in the mainstream media, for example in specialized magazines, such as the play *The Normal Heart* published in the theatre magazine *Dialog* (*Filo* 1987, 7–8, p. 7); at film festivals, such as the film *Caravaggio*, which was shown during a Warsaw festival of British films (*Filo* 1987, 3, p. 5); and on TV, such as the film *The Dresser*, shown on the first channel of the Polish Public TV (*Filo* 1987, 11–12, p. 5); even though in some cases Polish censorship simply cut off homosexual or homoerotic scenes. Additionally, because there was not much research on HIV and AIDS in the Eastern Bloc in the early 1980s, the first reports on the topic in the mainstream media in CEE simply reprinted articles from the Western media—particularly *Newsweek, Time* and *Der Spiegel* (EEIP 1986, p. 2)—and, thus, introduced to CEE audiences Western homosexual movements and subcultures. Some Eastern Bloc cultural products depicting homosexuality or homoeroticism also reached Western audiences, most notably the Hungarian film *Another Way*, which was applauded at the 1982 Cannes Film Festival. Besides, migration and travelling between the blocs, while surely more difficult before 1989 than afterwards, were not impossible. After all, Andrzej Selerowicz started publishing his magazine after immigrating to Austria and Ryszard Kisiel set up *Filo* after receiving Western gay magazines from homosexual sailors. *Filo* also published stories from Poles living in or travelling to Munich (*Filo* 1990, 19, p. 26), West Berlin (*Filo* 1989, 18, pp. 7–8) or the Soviet Union (*Filo* 1989, 16, p. 4).

Western activists also supported and in many cases stimulated the first more systematic attempts at homosexual self-organizing in the Eastern Bloc. Josie McLellan (2011) emphasizes the important role of Peter Tatchell from the UK Gay Liberation Front in the formation of HIB in East Germany in the 1970s. ILGA's EEIP programme, in turn, energized most homosexual activists in CEE in the 1980s by providing them with resources and inspirations, by connecting activists from different Eastern Bloc countries (mainly through the organization of the EEIP conferences) as well as by twinning Eastern groups with Western counterparts, for example the Warsaw Homosexual Movement (WRH) with the Swiss HACH, and *Filo* with the Norwegian Tupilak and the Swedish RFSL Stockholm (Chap. 3). ILGA and Homosexual Initiative Vienna (HOSI), to which the EEIP programme had been delegated, did not penetrate all CEE countries to the same degree. The strongest connections were established with homosexuals in Czechoslovakia, East Germany, Hungary, Poland and Slovenia, though Laurie Essig (1999, p. 58) also reports that the foundation of the Gay Laboratory in the Soviet Union was directly inspired by ILGA. Arguably, the EEIP programme had the strongest influence on the development of the Polish homosexual movement, mainly because of (1) the key role of the Polish representative (Selerowicz) in the programme and his special focus on Poland (publishing *Biuletyn/Etap*), and (2) the relative independence of the Polish movement from any segment of society or the state and, hence, its greater need for international support.

As I showed in Chap. 5, gay and lesbian magazines played a central role in building and sustaining transnational connections between activists on opposite sides of the Iron Curtain, at least in the case of Poland. It was the magazines, *Biuletyn/Etap* and *Filo*, around which the first more systematic homosexual groups were formed in the country. I argue to recognize the magazines as transnational, by which I do not mean that they targeted an international audience (they were chiefly aimed at Polish homosexuals) but that they were products of a unique combination and imbrication of multiple geographical scales, including city, country, bloc, continent and the world. *Biuletyn/Etap* was produced in Austria by a Pole embedded in a Western activist network and distributed in Poland with the help of the Wroclaw-based group Etap. *Filo* was produced in Gdańsk, a big Polish city at the coast, which enabled regular contacts with homosexual sailors, and within the confines of Polish censorship, state surveillance and social homophobia. Both magazines were much inspired by their Western counterparts: they used similar wording, discussed similar topics or simply translated Western texts and reproduced Western images; but they also juxtaposed them with regional, national and local stories. They participated in a transnational network of gay and lesbian magazines, the authors of which exchanged their publications by mail, featured each other's magazines and visited each other's editorial offices. In that sense, the magazines should be considered as key agents in the transnational construction of homosexuality during the twilight years of the Cold War, even though they most likely did not reach far beyond urban intellectual circles.

In *Telling Sexual Stories*, Ken Plummer (1995, p. 87) writes that 'Communities and identities produce stories, stories produce identities and communities.' In accordance with this insight, I argued that *Biuletyn/Etap* and *Filo* became important actors in constructing and reconstructing homosexual identities as well as building and rebuilding homosexual politics in Poland in the 1980s. Regarding identities, I showed in Chap. 6 how the magazines pushed forward the idea of homosexuality as natural, transhistorical and transcultural, and promoted an 'out and proud' model of homosexuality, romantic love and sex, as well as, in the case of *Filo*, of sexual liberation. They also aimed to create a homosexual community of interest, proposing a number of commonalities (usually related to culture and lifestyle) which connect, or could connect, homosexuals regardless of differences between them. In doing so, the magazines often explicitly drew on Western terms and concepts—such as 'gay', 'lesbian', 'coming out', 'darkroom' and 'safer sex'—by either casually using them in articles and images or carefully reflecting on their meaning. Still, while some Western concepts of homosexual identities clearly travelled to Poland, not always were they—or, in some cases, could they—be implemented in this particular cultural and historical context, for example due to the housing shortage or the lack of gay and lesbian cultural infrastructure (cafés, bars, discos). As a result, the magazines were forging more ambivalent homosexual identities: *Biuletyn/Etap*, for example, while strongly advocating coming out, also gave tips about how to wittily respond to probing questions about one's homosexuality, and *Filo*, while repeatedly shaming casual sex in public places, the so-called *pikiety*, at the same time provided a guide to homosexual cruising spots.

Regarding politics, I pointed out in Chap. 7 that the analysed magazines drew on the idea of a universal experience of discrimination against homosexuals and presented many success stories of mainly Western but also some Eastern homosexual organizations to encourage their readers to get involved in activism. Drawing on many histories of homosexual self-organizing, especially the Stonewall Riots and gay liberation, they presented their own vision for the Polish homosexual movement, which focused on the registration of a nationwide association which would work mainly towards greater acceptance of homosexuals by homosexuals themselves and by society at large. While in practice they were doing what I suggested we should call an information activism (that is, providing homosexuals with useful knowledge and advice), discursively they were most interested in the nonrepresentation and misrepresentation of homosexuals in the mainstream public sphere, recognizing the importance of visibility politics. While it is not clear if this preoccupation with visibility politics in the Polish magazines was directly inspired by Western homosexual movements, themselves much concerned with visibility, it could be argued that it was anchored in the very idea of an 'out and proud' homosexuality, which did find its way to the magazines through Western discourses of coming out (Chap. 6). Again, however, the Western influences were not entirely formative of Polish homosexual politics at that time. Minding local specificities and having their own preferences as to how to organize themselves, Polish homosexual activists decided not to challenge the communist state at the ideological level or to embrace an in-your-face activism within society. They chose assimilation over provocation, even if that required conforming to particular ideas of respectability.

Taken together, the research results presented in this book indicate that the transnational construction of homosexuality, or LGBT identities and politics, did occur in CEE already before 1989, even if it arguably accelerated after that landmark year. In fact, this globalization process could be traced much further back in time, even before the rise of communism in Europe. In Poland, for example, it could be located at the very beginning of the twentieth century, fuelled by the establishment of more progressive sexology and the emergence of a feminist movement (Gawin 2008; Górnicka-Boratyńska 1999; Janicki 2015). My focus, however, has been on the Poland of the 1980s, when the first gay and lesbian magazines were published and the first more systematic activist groups emerged in the country. The analysed magazines attest that the Western influence on shaping Polish homosexual identities and politics at that time was paramount. In this respect, my research confirms a major part of the argument of Dennis Altman (1996, 1997, 2001) and Joseph Massad (2002, 2007) about the hegemony of the West in the globalization of LGBT identities and politics, at least in the second half of the twentieth century. At the same time, my research also shows that the Western influence should not be understood simply in terms of a 'homogenization', more specifically a 'Westernization' or 'Americanization', of the non-West. Adopting Western aims, names, symbols and histories does not necessarily mean simply copying Western ways of being, living or acting. What was happening in the analysed magazines was rather a selective adoption as well as a sometimes necessary, sometimes strategic and creative adaptation of Western ideas so as to make them meaningful in a specific cultural and historical context and for specific individuals. Therefore, geopolitical structures in the globalization of LGBT identities and politics would be better understood as 'conditions of possibility', in the words of Inderpal Grewal and Caren Kaplan (2001, p. 671): they enable, instruct and inspire but do not fully determine particular identities and politics.

8.2   Networked Sexual Globalization

How could the insights from my research help to refine the theoretical framework about the globalization of homosexuality or, more broadly, sexuality? In Chap. 2, I explained I find it most useful to think about the globalized world as a network (Crane 2008; Radhakrishnan 2010). The main components of a network are nodes—understood as geographical locations or, more accurately, geopolitical entities—and connections between the nodes. I find the network metaphor useful because, in my understanding of it, it allows us to recognize (1) geopolitical structures: some nodes are more influential than others (centres and peripheries), which requires from us that we remain 'critical of the ways in which the center occupies the peripheries' (Oswin 2006, p. 788); and (2) the multiplicity of connections between nodes, which helps us to go beyond the thesis of 'homogenization' and broaden our focus to consider the actual diversity of influences. Also, even though the model of the globalized world as a network is primarily spatial in nature (it describes the connections between different geographical locations), it allows us to add a temporal aspect to it: the network is not fixed but changes over time. It is crucial that we recognize this dynamic nature of the network to acknowledge that nodes can become more or less central and connections can become more or less strong, existing connections can be broken and new connections can be established (e.g. after the fall of the Soviet Union in 1991 or during the decline of the US political and economic hegemony in the 2000s, see Mennell 2010; Nederveen Pieterse 2010). Besides, only by adding the temporal aspect to the model can we recognize the third main component of the network, which are flows, since flows can exist only in a period but not in a moment of time.

Applying such a model, this book aimed to trace particular flows (of homosexual identity paradigms and activism models) during a particular period of time (the last decade of the Cold War) and from the perspective of a particular peripheral node (communist Poland). Drawing on my analysis of two Polish gay and lesbian magazines, *Biuletyn/Etap* and *Filo*, I would like now to formulate a number of key properties of peripheral nodes. First, the nodes can be of different scales: for example continents, regions, countries, provinces, cities, neighbourhoods or even street corners. In my project, I primarily worked at the level of a country (Poland), although my focus on activist magazines and groups forced me to stay mostly at the level of cities (particularly Gdańsk, Wrocław and Warsaw), while at times trying to broaden my research scope to include the entire region (CEE). Second, nodes are not monolithic: they are characterized by internal diversity. I pointed to a number of contradictory discourses within the two analysed magazines as well as between them (especially about romantic love versus sexual liberation), not to mention that the magazines constitute only a tiny, if prominent, part of discourses on homosexuality in late communist Poland. At the same time, however, it is important to recognize what is assumed or prevalent across the entire node: in my research, for example, the idea of homosexuality as natural, transhistorical and transcultural was clearly endorsed in both analysed magazines. Third, nodes are not static: they change over time. One example from my research is the emergence of systematic lesbian content in *Filo* after Pilch joined the magazine's editorial team in June 1989.

Even though my own project did not focus much on studying centres, I argue that they show the same properties as peripheries because they are also nodes. Therefore, like peripheries, centres can be of different scales: for example the West, the United States, New York City or Wall Street. Centres are also not monolithic. The West, for example, usually considered as *the* centre of the globalized world, in my research was broken down into such disparate elements as different organizations (e.g. ILGA, US GLF and ACT UP, Austrian HOSI, West German AIDS-Hilfe, Danish Positivgruppen, Norwegian Tupilak and Swedish RFSL Stockholm), magazines (e.g. US *Advocate*, UK *Capital Gay*, French *Gai Pied*, West German *Rosa Flieder*, Dutch *De Gay Krant*, Swiss *Anderschume Kontiki*, Finish *Seta* and Swedish *Kom Ut!*) as well as people (e.g. Aubrey Beardsley, Dolly

Parton, Boy George, Jean Cocteau, Ralf König and Tom of Finland, but also Poles living in or travelling to the West such as Selerowicz). Finally, centres are not static but change over time. In Chap. 2, I showed how Western homosexual activism went through different phases from the homophile movement to gay liberation to HIV/AIDS activism to queer activism (Paternotte and Tremblay 2015). Besides, I explained how the centre of Western homosexual activism shifted from Western Europe, especially Germany, in the late nineteenth and early twentieth centuries to the United States in the late 1960s and early 1970s.

Arguably, flows between nodes are the most interesting part of globalization processes. Before I move on to describe their characteristics, however, I would like to briefly discuss what it is that flows. This, of course, depends on one's research focus. Studies in economic globalization are mostly preoccupied with flows of capital (and people), while those in cultural globalization with flows of ideas (and people). My project was devoted to cultural globalization and traced the flows of homosexual identity paradigms and activism models. What is crucial to understand in this respect is that the flowing ideas are in themselves multiscalar, that is, they are products of a unique combination and imbrication of multiple geographical scales. By this I mean that they are not pure constructs of any 'original' culture but, in a globalized world, have been shaped and reshaped by encounters with other cultures, be it through immigrants, travellers or the exposure to other cultures' cultural products (see also Binnie 2016). For example, studies demonstrate that LGBT identities and politics in the United States have been co-constituted by immigrants from Cuba (Peña 2004), the Philippines (Manalansan 2000, 2003), Puerto Rico (Negrón-Muntaner 1999) and Europe (Povinelli and Chauncey 1999, p. 440). Similarly, Andrew Shield (2017) points to the participation of post-war Muslim immigrants to North-Western Europe in the 1968 sexual revolution. In my research, in turn, I analysed the EEIP reports, which had been commissioned by a Western organization (IGA) but produced by an Austrian group (HOSI) with a key contribution by a Polish citizen living in Vienna (Selerowicz). Such a combination of influences in the production process of the reports provokes us to question their 'Westernness' or, alternatively, to recognize their combined Western and non-Western character.

Building on that thought, I suggest that we think about the flows of ideas as of travels with departure and arrival places. Such a conceptualization of flows, I argue, is useful because it does recognize more or less prevalent movements of ideas from one place to another—thus, acknowledging geopolitical structures—but, thanks to the metaphor of a departure place, it does not push us into making claims about any 'true' geographical, or cultural, origin of ideas. There are two key characteristics of such flows of ideas which I would like to highlight. First, the flows are multiple and at times overlapping. On the one hand, this means that each node is exposed to the influence of flows coming from multiple nodes. The magazines I analysed, for example, were largely influenced by the flows coming from the West—or from many different Western locations, to be precise—but also by the flows coming from non-Western locations, particularly from other Eastern Bloc countries (e.g. the EEIP conferences, Kisiel's travels to Bulgaria or screenings of the Hungarian film *Another Way* in Poland). On the other hand, it means that there are multiple flows between every two nodes, which take place through multiple channels such as different mainstream or alternative cultural products (e.g. songs, films, theatre plays, academic and non-academic books, gay and lesbian magazines) as well as different people (e.g. migrants, travellers, sailors). One implication is that the flows of some ideas from centres to peripheries could be stronger than the flows of other ideas. For example, because of the ban on the distribution of pornography in communist Poland, it was harder (though not impossible) for pornographic magazines than for non-pornographic magazines to travel to Poland in the 1980s.

Second, the flows are multidirectional. This means that they do not run only from centres to margins but also from margins to centres as well as between centres and between margins, even if they are not all of the same strength. Again, while the analysed magazines were greatly influenced by Western cultural products, they also found their way to the West: for example they were featured in some Western gay and lesbian magazines, such as the UK *Capital Gay* and *Gay Times* as well as Canadian *X-tra* (*Filo* 1990, 19, p. 38). In addition, they became an inspiration for some other Eastern Bloc homosexual groups, at least for Homeros Lambda, which decided to publish a magazine modelled on *Filo* (1988, 15, p. 9). My research also shows that the flows between nodes can be indirect, that is, they can be established, facilitated and controlled by intermediaries. One example would be the film *Zum Beispiel San Francisco* (For Example San Francisco, 1985), which focused on HIV/AIDS activism in the United States but was produced in West Germany, translated into Polish in Austria and then sent to Poland to be shown at the 'Gay club video', organized by activists from Gdańsk and Łódź (*Filo* 1987, 5–6, p. 8). In this respect, it is crucial to recognize the role of key intermediaries in the cross-border flows of ideas. For Polish homosexual activists in the 1980s, such a key intermediary was the EEIP programme, more specifically HOSI or even Selerowicz himself. It was the EEIP programme that (1) established new connections between homosexual activists within the Eastern Bloc (e.g. by organizing the EEIP conferences), (2) provided them with resources, inspiration and information (e.g. by publishing *Biuletyn/Etap*) as well as (3) connected them with Western activists (e.g. by inviting Eastern activists to ILGA annual conferences, twinning their groups with Western groups and informing Western activists about their situation through the publication of the EEIP reports, the *Rosa Liebe unterm roten Stern* book and the 'Ostreport' column in *Lambda Nachrichten*).

8.3   Hoax Queer Wars

Finally, what do the insights from my research tell us about the idea of 'queer wars' proposed by Dennis Altman and Jonathan Symons (2016), with which I started this book? Or, more broadly, about the general tendency to instrumentally use gender- and sexuality-related issues, particularly LGBT rights, in world politics in recent decades (e.g. Engeli et al. 2012; Picq and Thiel 2015; Weber 2016)? My conclusion is that the queer wars are a hoax. By this I mean they are first and foremost discursive wars very poorly grounded in 'essential'—'natural' or 'traditional'—differences between particular regions. Instead, they draw on regional othering, the practice which constructs a fundamental difference between, in our case, the West and CEE, allegedly dating back to the times of the Cold War or maybe even earlier. Yet, just because the wars are discursive does not mean they do not have any material consequences: they are discourses employed by particular actors for reaching particular goals in national and international politics. Most evidently, the West wages queer wars—in the form of homonationalism (Puar 2007, 2013)—to discredit and discriminate against immigrants of colour, mostly Arabs and Muslims; Vladimir Putin wages queer wars to re-establish Russia as the leader of an alternative value system to the dominant Western model (Makarychev and Medvedev 2015; Romanets 2017); and Jarosław Kaczyński and Viktor Orbán, Polish and Hungarian leaders respectively, wage queer wars—by calling for a 'cultural counter-revolution' (Foy and Buckley 2016)—to re-define current power structures within the European Union as well as to appeal to their respective national constituencies.

Because queer wars are hoax wars, they have forced some awkward alliances (more imaginary than actual) between countries within the West or within CEE which did not necessarily have, and often still do not have, much in common in terms of laws, practices or attitudes towards LGBTs. For example, during the Cold War, Poland was politically associated with the Soviet Union but it could hardly have been further away from it in terms of the legal status of homosexuality. In the latter respect, Poland was much closer to, for instance, Denmark, both countries having decriminalized same-sex acts in the 1930s (1932 and 1933 respectively). The Soviet Union, in turn, was much closer to, for instance, Ireland, both countries decriminalizing same-sex acts only after the Cold War, in 1993, and a bit less but still closer to the United States, which fully decriminalized same-sex acts only in 2003 (Hildebrandt 2014; Torra 1998). One may also wonder what the recently proclaimed Hungarian-Polish 'cultural counter-revolution' would mean for LGBTs since, again to limit myself just to legal issues, Hungary allows for same-sex registered partnership and punishes hate crime and hate speech based on sexual orientation while Poland does not. The actual transnational alliances around issues related to gender and sexuality have been formed based on a common ideology rather than shared geography: just as international LGBT organizations such as ILGA or Transgender Europe unite activists from across Europe, so too the recent anti-gender campaigns on the continent are to be found not only in Croatia, Hungary, Poland, Russia and Slovenia but also in Austria, Belgium, France, Germany, Ireland, Italy and Spain (Kuhar and Paternotte 2017; see also Campoy 2016; Korolczuk 2014).

Furthermore, what my research results point to is not only that the West and CEE are complex regions, encompassing different countries with different approaches towards LGBTs at different times, but also that the two regions have been long interconnected with each other, including during the Cold War, when they were supposed to be effectively separated by the Iron Curtain and the Berlin Wall. As I discussed more theoretically in the previous section, homosexual identity paradigms and activism models travelling from the West to the East, but also (to a lesser extent) the other way round, were already products of multiple cultural influences and as such they informed, without therefore determining, the understandings of homosexuality at their places of arrival. In other words, it is vital to recognize the mutual co-constitution of different geopolitical entities. As Larry Knopp and Michael Brown (2003, pp. 421–422) conclude in their paper on 'Queer diffusions', 'The different subjectivities and resistances that we have associated with different places have clearly shaped each other in a complex, multilateral, and diffuse process of mutual constitution.' In the same spirit, I would like to finish this book by making a rather dull yet heartfelt plea to put more effort in recognizing our similarities than presuming, exaggerating or fabricating our differences, to focus more on what unites us than on what divides us, to refuse fighting those hoax queer wars.

BIBLIOGRAPHY

Adam, B. D. (2001). Globalization and the mobilization of gay and lesbian communities. In P. Hamel, H. Lustiger-Thaler, J. Nederveen Pieterse & S. Roseneil (Eds.), *Globalization and social movements* (pp. 166–179). Basingstoke: Palgrave.

Adamska, K. (1998). *Ludzie obok: Lesbijki i geje w Polsce*. Toruń: Pracownia Duszycki.

Altman, D. (1996). Rupture or continuity? The internationalization of gay identities. *Social Text, 48*(3), 77–94.

Altman, D. (1997). Global gaze/global gays. *GLQ: A Journal of Lesbian and Gay Studies, 3*(4), 417–436.

Altman, D. (2001). *Global sex*. Chicago: University of Chicago Press.

Altman, D., & Symons, J. (2016). *Queer wars*. Cambridge: Polity.

Baker, C. (2017a). Introduction: Gender in twentieth-century Eastern Europe and the USSR. In C. Baker (Ed.), *Gender in twentieth-century Eastern Europe and the USSR* (pp. 1–22). London: Palgrave Macmillan.

Baker, C. (2017b). Transnational "LGBT" politics after the Cold War and implications for gender history. In C. Baker (Ed.), *Gender in twentieth-century Eastern Europe and the USSR* (pp. 228–251). London: Palgrave Macmillan.

Binnie, J. (2016). Critical queer regionality and LGBTQ politics in Europe. *Gender, Place & Culture: A Journal of Feminist Geography, 23*(11), 1631–1642.

Campoy, A. (2016). A conspiracy theory about sex and gender is being peddled around the world by the far right. *Quartz*. Retrieved January 6, 2017, from https://qz.com/807743/conservatives-have-created-a-fake-ideology-to-combat-the-global-movement-for-lgbti-rights/

Chetaille, A. (2017, February 2–3). *Between repression and incitement: State control and emergence of homosexual groups in Poland in the 1980s*. Paper presented at the Communist Homosexuality conference, Paris.

Crane, D. (2008). Globalization and cultural flows/networks. In T. Bennett & J. Frow (Eds.), *The SAGE handbook of cultural analysis* (pp. 359–381). London: Sage.

Engeli, I., Green-Pedersen, C., & Larsen, L. T. (Eds.). (2012). *Morality politics in Western Europe: Parties, agendas and policy choices.* Basingstoke: Palgrave Macmillan.

Essig, L. (1999). *Queer in Russia: A story of sex, self, and the other.* Durham, NC: Duke University Press.

Foy, H., & Buckley, N. (2016). Orban and Kaczynski vow "cultural counter-revolution" to reform EU. *Financial Times.* Retrieved March 8, 2017, from https://www.ft.com/content/e825f7f4-74a3-11e6-bf48-b372cdb1043a

Gal, S., & Kligman, G. (2000). *The politics of gender after socialism: A comparative-historical essay.* Princeton, NJ: Princeton University Press.

Gawin, M. (2008). The sex reform movement and eugenics in interwar Poland. *Studies in History and Philosophy of Biological and Biomedical Sciences, 39,* 181–186.

Górnicka-Boratyńska, A. (Ed.). (1999). *Chcemy całego życia. Antologia polskich tekstów feministycznych z lat 1870–1939.* Warszawa: Res Publika.

Grewal, I., & Kaplan, C. (2001). Global identities: Theorizing transnational studies of sexuality. *GLQ: A Journal of Lesbian and Gay Studies, 7*(4), 663–679.

Gruszczyńska, A. (2009). Sowing the seeds of Solidarity in public space: Case study of the Poznan March of Equality. *Sexualities, 12*(3), 312–333.

Healey, D. (1993). The Russian revolution and the decriminalisation of homosexuality. *Revolutionary Russia, 6*(1), 26–54.

Healey, D. (2002). Homosexual existence and existing socialism. New light on the repression of male homosexuality in Stalin's Russia. *GLQ: A Journal of Lesbian and Gay Studies, 8*(3), 349–378.

Hildebrandt, A. (2014). Routes to decriminalization: A comparative analysis of the legalization of same-sex sexual acts. *Sexualities, 17*(1/2), 230–253.

Hillhouse, R. J. (1990). Out of the closet behind the Wall: Sexual politics and social change in the GDR. *Slavic Review, 49*(4), 585–596.

Janicki, K. (2015). *Epoka hipokryzji: Seks i erotyka w przedwojennej Polsce.* Kraków: Znak.

Kleres, J. (2001). Cherries blossoming in East(ern) Germany? In H. Flam (Ed.), *Pink, purple, green: women's, religious, environmental and Gay/Lesbian movements in Central Europe today* (pp. 120–131). New York: Columbia University Press.

Kligman, G. (1992). The politics of reproduction in Ceauşescu's Romania: A case study in political culture. *East European Politics and Societies, 6*(3), 364–418.

Knopp, L., & Brown, M. (2003). Queer diffusions. *Environment and Planning D: Society and Space, 21*(4), 409–424.

Kon, I. (1993). Sexual minorities. In I. Kon & J. Riordan (Eds.), *Sex and Russian society* (pp. 89–115). London: Pluto.

Korolczuk, E. (2014). "The War on Gender" from a transnational perspective – Lessons for feminist strategising. In Heinrich Böll Foundation (Ed.), *Anti-gender movements on the rise? Strategising for gender equality in Central and Eastern Europe* (pp. 43–53). Berlin: Heinrich Böll Foundation.

Kuhar, R., & Paternotte, D. (2017). *Anti-gender campaigns in Europe: Mobilizing against equality*. Lanham, MD: Rowman & Littlefield.

Kulczycki, A. (1995). Abortion policy in postcommunist Europe: The conflict in Poland. *Population and Development Review, 21*(3), 471–505.

Kurimay, A., & Takács, J. (2016). Emergence of the Hungarian homosexual movement in late refrigerator socialism. *Sexualities.* Published online before print. Retrieved February 26, 2017, from http://journals.sagepub.com/doi/abs/10.1177/1363460716665786?journalCode=sexa

Makarychev, A., & Medvedev, S. (2015). Biopolitics and power in Putin's Russia. *Problems of post-communism, 62*(1), 45–54.

Manalansan, M. F., IV. (2000). Diasporic deviants/divas: How Filipino gay transmigrants "play with the world". In C. Patton & B. Sánchez-Eppler (Eds.), *Queer diasporas* (pp. 183–203). Durham, NC: Duke University Press.

Manalansan, M. F., IV. (2003). *Global divas: Filipino gay men in the diaspora*. Durham, NC: Duke University Press.

Massad, J. A. (2002). Re-orienting desire: The Gay International and the Arab World. *Public Culture, 14*(2), 361–385.

Massad, J. A. (2007). *Desiring Arabs*. Chicago: University of Chicago Press.

McLellan, J. (2011). *Love in the time of communism: Intimacy and sexuality in the GDR*. Cambridge: Cambridge University Press.

McLellan, J. (2012). Glad to be gay behind the wall: Gay and lesbian activism in 1970s East Germany. *History Workshop Journal, 74*(1), 105–130.

Mennell, S. (2010). Globalization and Americanization. In B. S. Turner (Ed.), *The Routledge international handbook of globalization studies* (pp. 554–567). London: Routledge.

Nederveen Pieterse, J. (2010). History and hegemony: The United States and twenty-first century globalization. In B. S. Turner (Ed.), *The Routledge international handbook of globalization studies* (pp. 96–113). London: Routledge.

Negrón-Muntaner, F. (1999). When I was a Puerto Rican lesbian: Meditations on *Brincando el charco: Portrait of a Puerto Rican. GLQ: A Journal of Lesbian and Gay Studies, 5*(4), 511–526.

Oswin, N. (2006). 'Decentering queer globalization: Diffusion and the "global gay". *Environment and Planning D: Society and Space, 24*(5), 777–790.

Paternotte, D., & Tremblay, M. (Eds.). (2015). *The Ashgate research companion to lesbian and gay activism*. Farnham: Ashgate.

Peña, S. (2004). *Pájaration* and transculturation: Language and meaning in Miami's Cuban American gay worlds. In W. Leap & T. Boellstorff (Eds.), *Speaking in queer tongues: Globalization and gay languages* (pp. 231–250). Urbana: University of Illinois Press.

Perdzyńska, K. (2009). Stosunek do osób homoseksualnych w świetle badań opinii społecznej w Polsce w latach 1988-2007. In I. Krzemiński (Ed.), *Naznaczeni:*

Mniejszości seksualne w Polsce raport 2008 (pp. 14–32). Warszawa: Instytut Socjologii UW.

Picq, M. L., & Thiel, M. (Eds.). (2015). *Sexualities in world politics: How LGBTQ claims shape international relations.* Abingdon: Routledge.

Plummer, K. (1995). *Telling sexual stories: Power, change and social worlds.* London: Routledge.

Povinelli, E. A., & Chauncey, G. (1999). Thinking sexuality transnationally: An introduction. *GLQ: A Journal of Lesbian and Gay Studies, 5*(4), 439–450.

Puar, J. (2007). *Terrorist assemblages: Homonationalism in queer times.* Durham, NC: Duke University Press.

Puar, J. (2013). Rethinking homonationalism. *International Journal of Middle East Studies, 45*(2), 336–339.

Radhakrishnan, S. (2010). Limiting theory: Rethinking approaches to cultures of globalization. In B. S. Turner (Ed.), *The Routledge international handbook of globalization studies* (pp. 23–41). London: Routledge.

Radziszewski, K. (2017, January). Homosexualité Communiste? *DIK Fagazine, 11,* 2–3.

Romanets, M. (2017). Virtual warfare: Masculinity, sexuality, and propaganda in the Russo-Ukrainian war. *East/West: Journal of Ukrainian Studies, IV*(1), 159–177.

Selinger, M. (2008). Intolerance toward gays and lesbians in Poland. *Human Rights Review, 9*(1), 15–27.

Shield, A. D. J. (2017). *Immigrants in the sexual revolution: Perceptions and participation in Northwest Europe.* London: Palgrave Macmillan.

Stella, F. (2015). *Lesbian lives in Soviet and Post-Soviet Russia: Post/socialism and gendered sexualities.* Basingstoke: Palgrave Macmillan.

Szulc, L. (2011). Queer in Poland: Under construction. In L. Downing & R. Gillett (Eds.), *Queer in Europe: Contemporary case studies* (pp. 159–172). Farnham: Ashgate.

Szulc, L. (2016). Operation Hyacinth and Poland's pink files. *Notches: (Re)marks on the History of Sexuality.* Retrieved March 17, 2016, from http://notches-blog.com/2016/02/02/operation-hyacinth-and-polands-pink-files/

Takács, J. (2017). Listing homosexuals since the 1920s and under state socialism in Hungary. In C. Baker (Ed.), *Gender in twentieth-century Eastern Europe and the USSR* (pp. 157–170). London: Palgrave Macmillan.

Torra, M. J. (1998). Gay rights after the Iron Curtain. *The Fletcher Forum of World Affairs, 22*(2), 73–87.

Velikonja, M. (2009). Lost in transition: Nostalgia for socialism in post-socialist countries. *East European Politics and Societies, 23*(4), 535–551.

Weber, C. (2016). *Queer international relations: Sovereignty, sexuality and the will to knowledge.* Oxford: Oxford University Press.

Zielińska, E. (1993). Recent trends in abortion legislation in Eastern Europe, with particular reference to Poland. *Criminal Law Forum, 4*(1), 47–93.

Zielińska, E. (2000). Between ideology, politics and common sense: The discourse of reproductive rights in Poland. In S. Gal & G. Kligman (Eds.), *Reproducing gender: Politics, publics, and everyday life after socialism* (pp. 23–57). Princeton, NJ: Princeton University Press.

TIMELINE

01.09.1932	Implementation of the new Polish Penal Code which decriminalized consensual same-sex acts, set the age of consent at 15 for both same-sex and opposite-sex acts, but criminalized same-sex prostitution with the punishment of up to three years of incarceration.
01.01.1970	Implementation of the new Polish Penal Code which decriminalized same-sex prostitution.
28.04 & 05.05.1974	Publication of the first socio-political article in the Polish mainstream press which treated homosexuality seriously and sympathetically: 'Homoseksualizm a opinia' (Homosexuality and opinion) by Tadeusz Gorgol in *Życie Literackie* (Literary Life).
08.08.1978	Establishment of the International Gay Association (IGA, later ILGA) by homosexual activists from ten Western countries gathered in Coventry in the United Kingdom.
1980	Establishment of the first known Polish homosexual group, Męskie Ochotnicze Pogotowie Seksualne (Male Volunteer Sexual Service, MOPS), in Piotrków Trybunalski, focused pri-

© The Author(s) 2018
L. Szulc, *Transnational Homosexuals in Communist Poland*,
Global Queer Politics, DOI 10.1007/978-3-319-58901-5

marily on facilitating contacts between homosexual men.

19–21.04.1981   Emergence of the idea of the Eastern Europe Information Pool (EEIP) at the annual IGA conference in Turin.

21.02.1981   Publication of a sympathetic article on homosexuality in the most popular Polish weekly at that time, *Polityka* (Politics): 'Gorzki fiolet' (Bitter violet) by Barbara Pietkiewicz.

06.1982   Publication of the first EEIP report, compiled by Homosexual Initiative Vienna (HOSI) for IGA.

07.10.1982   Release of the first mainstream film in the Eastern Bloc which openly featured homosexuality (lesbianism): Hungarian *Egymásra Nézve* (Another Way), directed by Károly Makk, with two leading roles played by Polish actresses, Jadwiga Jankowska-Cieślak and Grażyna Szapołowska.

03.1983   Publication of the first issue of the first known Polish gay magazine *Biuletyn* (renamed *Etap* in mid-1986), created by Andrzej Selerowicz in Vienna and published until December 1987.

Summer 1983   First meeting of Polish homosexual activists with Andrzej Selerowicz in Warsaw.

24.09.1983   Publication of the first known article on HIV/AIDS in the Polish mainstream media: an interview with a professor from the Medical School of Warsaw entitled 'AIDS znaczy strach' (AIDS means fear) in the *Polityka* weekly.

Late 1983   Warsaw mainstream monthly *Relaks* (Relax) started to publish explicitly homosexual personal ads until July 1984, re-introduced later on (for sure published in mid-1987).

10. 1984   Publication of the book *Rosa Liebe unterm roten Stern: Zur Lage der Lesben und Schwulen in Osteuropa* (Pink Love under the Red Star: The Situation of Lesbians and Gay Men in Eastern Europe) by HOSI, authored by Gudrun Hauer, Kurt Krickler, Marek (Andrzej Selerowicz) and Dieter Schmutzer.

15–16.11.1985	First wave of Operation Hyacinth conducted by the Polish police forces in cooperation with the secret service in order to create a kind of state 'homosexual inventory', repeated at least twice in 1986 and 1987 (see below).
23.11.1985	Publication of the first article in the Polish mainstream media authored by an openly homosexual person: 'Jesteśmy inni' (We are different) by Dariusz Prorok (under the pseudonym of Krzysztof T. Darski) in the *Polityka* weekly.
26–27.09.1986	Second wave of Operation Hyacinth.
09.1986	Establishment of the Polish homosexual group Etap in Wrocław, led first by Leszek Truchliński and then by Ryszard Ziobro.
03.11.1986	Publication of the first issue of Polish gay and lesbian magazine *Filo*, created by Ryszard Kisiel in Gdańsk and published in its underground form until May 1990.
23.12.1986	Publication of a piece on homosexuality entitled 'Rozgrzeszenie' (The Shrift) by Ewa Żychlinska and Mariusz Szczygieł in the Polish mainstream scout magazine *Na Przełaj* (Cut Across).
1986	Publication of the book *AIDS: Nowa Choroba* (AIDS: A New Disease) by Zofia Kuratowska (Warszawa: Wiedza Powszechna).
24.01.1987	First meeting of the Polish homosexual group Warsaw Homosexual Movement (WRH), including Waldemar Zboralski, Sławek Starosta and Krzysztof Garwatowski.
01.03.1987	First meeting of homosexual activists from across Poland in Warsaw.
08.06.1987	Publication of the first (and possibly the only) issue of Polish gay and lesbian magazine *Efebos* by the WRH. Some sources indicated that the second issue of the magazine was published in 1988.
20.06.1987	Second meeting of homosexual activists from across Poland in Warsaw in the premises of the Patriotic Movement for National Rebirth (PRON).

29.06–05.07.1987	Polish homosexual groups Etap and the WRH became members of ILGA at its annual conference in Cologne.
06–08.11.1987	First EEIP conference organized in Budapest by ILGA and HOSI for homosexual activists from Eastern Bloc countries.
16–17.11.1987	Third wave of Operation Hyacinth.
03.1988	First official registration of a homosexual group in Eastern Bloc countries, Homeros Lambda in Hungary.
24.03.1988	The WRH submitted an application to the Warsaw City Council in order to register their group but have never received an official reply from authorities.
16–17.04.1988	Second EEIP conference organized in Warsaw and hosted by the WRH.
11.1988	Publication of the first known Polish public opinion survey on homosexuality: 'Opinie o homoseksualizmie: Tolerancja czy potępienie?' (Opinions about homosexuality: Tolerance or condemnation?) by the Public Opinion Research Centre (CBOS).
1.04.1989	Third meeting of homosexual activists from across Poland in Warsaw.
21–23.04.1989	Third EEIP conference organized in Budapest and hosted by Homeros Lambda.
16–22.07.1989	Polish homosexual group Filo became a member of ILGA at its annual conference in Vienna.
28.10.1989	Inaugural meeting of the Association of Lambda Groups organized at Sigma Club at the University of Warsaw by activists from Etap, Filo and the WRH.
23.02.1990	First official registration of a homosexual group in Poland, the Association of Lambda Groups.

INDEX

© The Author(s) 2018
L. Szulc, *Transnational Homosexuals in Communist Poland*,
Global Queer Politics, DOI 10.1007/978-3-319-58901-5

CPSIA information can be obtained
at www.ICGtesting.com
Printed in the USA
LVHW081352240419
615391LV00005B/48/P